LOYAL WHIGS AND REVOLUTIONARIES

LOYAL WHIGS
AND REVOLUTIONARIES/
THE MAKING OF THE REVOLUTION
IN NEW YORK, 1765-1776

Leopold S. Launitz-Schürer, Jr.
Senior Lecturer in History
Department of External Studies
University of Queensland
Brisbane, Australia

New York University Press · New York *and* London

THE PENNSYLVANIA STATE UNIVERSITY
COMMONWEALTH CAMPUS LIBRARIES
DELAWARE COUNTY

Copyright © 1980 by New York University

Library of Congress Cataloging in Publication Data

Launitz-Schürer, Leopold S   1942-
  Loyal Whigs and revolutionaries.

  Bibliography: p.
  Includes index.
  1. New York (State)—Politics and government—
Revolution, 1775-1783.   2. New York (State)—Politics
and government—Colonial period, ca. 1600-1775.
I. Title.
E263.N6L38   974.7'02   79-53579
ISBN 0-8147-4994-1

Manufactured in the United States of America

FOR MY MOTHER AND FATHER

Contents

Preface

This book undertakes a reevaluation of two separate but related developments that were crucial to the making of the American Revolution in New York: first, the rivalry of the Livingston and De Lancey families, and the ways this rivalry shaped politics and the growth of a revolutionary ideology in New York in the decade before independence; second, the struggle for power between the elite as a whole and what may best be termed a middle class—wealthy, articulate, and politically sophisticated—that felt itself excluded from New York's political decision-making process. Conflicts within elites and between discontented social classes were, of course, characteristic of the internal revolutions of other of the Thirteen Colonies. What made the New York experience unique was the extraordinary degree to which the colony's internal conflicts were determined by the personalities, interests, and ambitions of one or two family groups.

Contemporaries recognized the centrality of the Livingston-De Lancey feud in the public life of New York. "There are in this province," observed the *New York Journal* in April 1770, "two ancient and respectable families, viz., the De L-n-y and the L-n who are the only competitors in it for power."[1] John Adams made the same point. Adams wrote that "the two great Families in this Province, upon whose Motions all their Politicks turn, are the De Lanceys and Livingstons."[2] It was the Revolution which finally resolved the rivalry. The Livingstons embraced independence and so won for themselves an honored place among the patriot heroes of the new republic. The De Lanceys enlisted in the ranks of the loyalists, and so met defeat and disgrace, made worse by enforced exile and the loss of their family estates.

The predominance of the Livingstons and De Lanceys dated from the 1740s and 1750s. These two families were not New York's only wealthy or powerful families, but they undoubtedly were the wealthiest, most able, and most ambitious members of the colony's ruling elite. Though historians have long recognized the importance of their rivalry, interpretations of its significance in the politics of the late colonial era have varied considerably. An older view tended to regard the rivalry as a struggle between a "court" or De Lancey faction, representing commercial and landed interests in and near New York City, and a "country" or Livingston party, representing large landed interests of the Hudson Valley. More recent interpretations have rejected the court-country paradigm, emphasizing instead the unstructured character of New York politics. In this view, family banners appear to be of less importance. It is argued that family or factional alliances were not permanent and constantly shifting, representing neither fixed interests nor fixed principles or ideas.

There is a good deal of truth in all these interpretations, but they are more applicable to the period before 1765. With the commencement of the imperial crisis that began with the Stamp Act crisis, the Livingston-De Lancey rivalry assumed a critical role in New York politics, the significance of which historians have not recognized. No detailed study of this rivalry and its effects upon the coming of independence has been written. Such a study is needed because it can help explain New York's apparent reluctance to join the revolutionary movement. The ambiguity of New York's position was not so much the result of widespread loyalist or other conflicting sentiments, as it was the result of the ambiguous behavior of the colony's two leading families. The problem may be briefly summarized: From 1765 to 1776 the Livingstons wrote like radicals, thus providing New York's revolutionaries with a local ideological base, but behaved like moderates; the De Lanceys wrote little, but certainly acted like radicals. Each appeared to act in a manner which obscured their real beliefs and the positions each was to adopt finally toward the issue of independence. The confusion arising from the apparent contradiction in roles was to have profound effects upon politics in New York. It destroyed the political credibility and relevance of the old colonial elite. As neither the Livingstons nor the De Lanceys were capable of responding imaginatively and forcefully to the revolutionary crisis, the way was opened in the political affairs of New York for new leadership composed of men who were able and eager to set New York in new directions that were independent, republican, and in the long run more egalitarian and democratic.

It is the rise of these "new men" from the ranks of the discontented middle classes to places of leadership—a process which one historian has imaginatively described as the growth of a "radical consciousness"—and the relationship between this process and the Livingston-De Lancey rivalry that is more difficult for the historian to explain. In recent years it has become the fashion, as evidenced in the work of such scholars as Bernard Friedman, Jesse Lemisch, Joseph Ernst, and Marc Egnal, to attribute popular radicalism in the revolutionary era to economic issues and economically based class antagonism, a point of view which revives in modern form, so far as New York is concerned, the thesis of Carl Becker's classic, *History of Political Parties in the Province of New York*. Yet while the evidence for a revised economic interpretation is not lacking, such an interpretation is far from convincing. In contrast, evidence for an interpretation based upon contemporary perceptions of the primacy in human affairs of politics and political ideas—themes well emphasized in the studies of Bernard Bailyn, Gordon Wood, Pauline Maier, and R. R. Palmer—is strong and credible. A case in point was the publication in late 1769 of Alexander McDougall's broadside, *To the Betrayed Inhabitants of the City and Colony of New York*, which, it will be argued, was at once the most radical, revolutionary, and influential piece of writing produced in New York in the prerevolutionary decade. Though the document is susceptible of a limited economic or class-based interpretation—there were, for example, scattered references to the colony's unemployment problem and its effects—it was above all else a political statement, an analysis of New York's political ills, and a call for political action and political change. Most importantly, McDougall focused his attention on the Livingston-De Lancey rivalry, thereby directly linking that rivalry to the broader political, social, and economic concerns of New York's middle and lower classes.

Politics, more than class or economic interests, determined the political, economic, and social fate of the Livingstons and De Lanceys. It held the key to the patriotism of the former, the loyalism of the latter. One consequence of the importance of politics was the apparently accidental or even irrational quality in the Livingstons' final committment to "whig revolution" and the De Lanceys' adherence to "whig-loyalism." So far as ideology, economic, or class interests were concerned, surely their final roles in the unfolding revolutionary drama could have been easily reversed. Politics and political fortune—perhaps, J.G.A. Pocock might suggest, fortune in the classical Machiavellian sense—made the difference. The William Livingston who wrote *A Review of Military Operations in North America* in 1757 was an advocate among other things of a strong imperial tie and even of an enhanced British presence in the colony. His cousin Judge Robert R. Livingston was indifferent to the burgeoning revolutionary movement and hostile toward the idea of independence. The De Lanceys supported radical protest against English policy until the political crisis triggered by the McDougall broadside moved them unwillingly and unwittingly into a political isolation that led directly to loyalism.

Research into the revolutionary movement in New York is far from an easy task. The difficulty arises mainly from the striking paucity of De Lancey family papers, which is remarkable considering that the family was undoubtedly one of the most important in colonial America. In contrast a large and revealing body of Livingston family papers is extant, a circumstance that has proved to be a blessing and a curse. The benefits are obvious, but because historians have had to concentrate their attention on the Livingstons, distortion has inevitably resulted. The history of New York in the American Revolution has remained largely the Livingston version of that history. The De Lanceys, not surprisingly, fared poorly at the hands of their old enemies, and they have often received little better treatment from scholars. The De Lanceys will necessarily continue to suffer from the fact that they cannot speak clearly for themselves. Nevertheless, from a careful reading of the records of the Livingstons and their friends, especially of the writings of William Smith, Jr., we can sharpen our understanding of the ideas and behavior of the De Lanceys, and gain fresh perspective on New York's response to the revolutionary crisis. Smith's importance as a commentator can scarcely be exaggerated. As a Livingston confidant and a member of the governor's council, Smith was in a unique position to observe closely New York's public men. In his political career and in the development of his political ideas, Smith progressed from youthful radicalism in the early 1750s, to loyalism in 1776, and finally to the advocacy of conservative, aristocratic government in the last years of his life. He thus embodied conflicting tendencies that were central not only to the development of the Livingston-De Lancey rivalry, but were also central to the history of the American Revolution. Fortunately for historians, Smith was on the whole an astute observer, if not always an unbiased or accurate one, and his carefully recorded memoirs provided a wealth of inside detail on New York politics and personalities that is unmatched by any other single source.

Before I began this study I developed and clarified my views in four published articles: "Whig-Loyalists: The DeLanceys of New York," *New York Historical Society Quarterly,* LVI (July 1972); "A Loyalist Clergyman's Response to the Imperial Crisis in the American Colonies: A Note on Samuel Seabury's Letters of a Westchester Farmer," *Historical Magazine of the Protestant Episcopal Church,* XLIV (June 1975); "The Loyalist Response to the American Revolution: Whig-Loyalism in Colonial New York," *Pacific Circle 3: American Studies Down Under, Proceedings of the Fourth and Fifth Biennial Conferences of the Australian and New*

Zealand American Studies Association, Norman Harper, ed. (Brisbane, 1976); "The Livingston-De Lancey Rivalry and the Coming of the Revolution in New York, 1763-75," *Studies on the American Revolution,* Neville K. Meaney, ed. (Melbourne, 1976).

It is a pleasure to acknowledge the help and support of many teachers and friends. I am indebted to the University of Queensland for financial assistance toward the publication of this book. I owe much to my teachers at McGill University, especially to Alvin R. Riggs and Hereward Senior. In Australia I have received helpful criticism during various stages of my work from Neville K. Meaney of the University of Sydney and Hector G. Kinloch of the Australian National University. For advice and encouragement my father-in-law, L.C.F. Turner of the Australian Royal Military College, Duntroon, and my friend and colleague at the University of Queensland, Joseph M. Siracusa, deserve special mention. Lastly, I am happy to acknowledge the friendly assistance of the librarians at the New York Historical Society, the New York Public Library, the New York State Library, the Museum of the City of New York, the Butler Library of Columbia University, and the Stirling Memorial Library of Yale University. They welcomed me first as a graduate student and have in more recent years continued to extend a helping hand to a visitor from Australia.

My most important support has come from my wife, Caroline, a sympathetic but stern critic, and my best friend.

Notes

1. Quoted in Alfred F. Young, *The Democratic Republicans of New York: The Origins, 1763-1797* (Chapel Hill, N.C., 1967), p. 10.
2. *The Adams Papers: Diary and Autobiography of John Adams,* 4 vols., L.H. Butterfield, ed. (paperback edition, New York, 1964), II, p. 103.

CHAPTER ONE

Introduction: The Livingston-De Lancey Rivalry in New York Politics

During the middle years of the eighteenth century, politics in New York revolved around the rivalry of two great and powerful families, the Livingstons and the De Lanceys. The remarks of contemporaries as well as subsequent events have tended to magnify the differences and divisions between them; in fact, the Livingstons and De Lanceys had much in common. In wealth, in power, in influence and prestige, they were equals. Their political beliefs, or what might be better termed their world view, and their lifestyles were alike. They were in many ways ideal natural allies, and so they might have been had not their ambitions—which were also equal—divided them.

The histories of the rise of these two families were also similar. The American founders, Robert Livingston and Stephen De Lancey, settled in New York in the late seventeenth century. Both men shared a heritage of religious dissent. Livingston's father, the Calvinist preacher, John Livingstone, left his native Scotland in re-

1

sponse to a fear that the restoration of Charles II would result in "an overturning of the whole work of reformation" to serve as pastor to a Presbyterian congregation living in Rotterdam, Holland. Etienne De Lancey, a French Huguenot, abandoned France following Louis XIV's revocation of the Edict of Nantes in 1685 and changed his name to a form more suited to his new Anglo-American environment. By the time of their deaths in 1728 and 1741 respectively, both Livingston and De Lancey had successfully amassed considerable fortunes and high political and social status by shrewd investments in land and trade. Both men had married well, establishing patterns their children and their children's children would continue to emulate. There were, of course, some differences between the families. The Livingstons remained staunch Presbyterians, the De Lanceys embraced the Church of England. The sons of Livingstons were sent to Yale College; De Lancey boys were sent to Cambridge University.

Impressive though the success of the Livingstons and De Lanceys was, it was by no means unique in the history of colonial New York. They were only two among a small group of rich and powerful families who formed the colony's governing elite and whose histories closely paralleled the histories of the Livingstons and De Lanceys. At the forefront of this group were the Van Rensselaers, Van Cortlandts, Heathcotes, Philipses, Schuylers, Morrises, and Johnsons. The extent to which these leading families controlled the affairs of the colony is a matter of dispute. It is clear, however, that New York possessed, in the words of Alfred Young, "a unique landlord aristocracy which no amount of revisionism is likely to erase from the Hudson Valley." [1] It was not, to be sure, a formal or hereditary aristocracy whose position and power were secured by the dignity of its birth, but it is difficult to deny the aristocratic pretensions of men who called their estates "manors" and styled themselves "manor lords."

Land was only one of the principal pillars of New York's aristocracy. Trade and the legal profession were equally important sources of power, influence, and wealth. While it is possible in some cases to distinguish within the elite between landed, mercantile or legal interests, such distinctions carry little weight as the interests of the leading families were thoroughly entwined in all three pursuits. The Livingston family offers an example that was typical. The family's power base was Livingston Manor, south of Albany. From this princely holding, which was second in New York only to the giant Van Rensselaer estate, Rensselaerswyck, the Livingstons' interests in land, trade, and commerce spread through the entire colony. The Livingstons were also prominent members of the New York bar. As the servants and advisors of the great landlords and merchant princes, the lawyers enjoyed unrivaled prestige and influence. In a well-known report to the Board of Trade written in 1765, New York's lieutenant governor, Cadwallader Colden, declared that the attorneys held "the most distinguished Rank in the Policy of the Province." He added that "the power of the Lawyers is such that every man is afraid of offending them and is deterred from making any public opposition to their power, and the dayley increase of it."

Yet New York's aristocracy cannot be understood merely in terms of wealth. Of equal, and perhaps more significance was the aristocratic ideal of the gentleman to which the great families aspired. The notion assumed a spirit of noblesse oblige, and took for granted a deference which was not always forthcoming. The essence of the concept was well expressed in Judge Robert R. Livingston's charge to a grand jury. Grand juries, the judge thought, "should be of the better sort because they are less lyable to temptations want, less fearful of the frowns of power, and may reasonably be supposed of more improved capacities than those of inferior station." The mark of the gentleman was moderation: He was moderate in politics, language, drink, and comportment, avoiding those excesses which turned "a rational Creature" into a "Brute." The goal of a gentleman, Robert Livingston of Clermont told his son, the judge, was "to keep an Estate not to get one." [2] The aristocratic ideal was ably portrayed in William Smith's description of Colonel Lewis Morris, Sr.:

> Colonel Morris had the greatest influence on our publick affairs. He was a man of letters, and, though a little whimsical in his temper, was grave in his manners and of penetrating parts. Being excessively fond of the society of men of sense and reading, he was never wearied at a sitting, till the spirits

of the whole company were dissipated. From his infancy, he had lived in a manner best adopted to teach him the nature of man, and to fortify his mind for the vicissitudes of life . . . [he married] a daughter of Mr. [James] Graham, a fine lady, with whom he lived about fifty years, in the possession of every enjoyment, which good sense and polite manners in a woman could afford.[3]

While most of the great families easily acquired the outward trappings of gentleness (silver plate and "portraits of their ancestors executed in a superior style"), on the whole maintaining the aristocratic ideal was far from easy. The problem was aptly summarized by William Smith: "Our schools are in the lowest order; the instructors want instruction, and through a long, schameful neglect of all the arts and sciences, our common speech is extremely corrupt; and the evidences of bad taste, both as to thought and language, are visible in all our proceedings, publick and private." Despite these deficiencies, the women of New York were much admired for their appearance and dress. They avoided "the practice of extravagant gaming, common to the fashionable part of the fair sex," but it was also said "there is nothing they so generally neglect as reading, and, indeed, all the arts of improvement of the mind," in which the men apparently set the example.[4]

A more fundamental problem confronting the elite was the egalitarian character of New York life. Cheap land was of the utmost significance in shaping society. Every man, William Livingston maintained, was his own "farmer and landlord." Men, he wrote, were "separate independent individuals under no general influence." In the city, the situation was similar. William Smith noted:

The City of New York consists principally of merchants shop-keepers, and tradesmen, who sustain the reputation of honest, punctual and fair dealers. With respect to riches, there is not so great an inequality among us, as is common in Boston, and some other places. Every man of industry and integrity has it in his power to live well, and many are the instances of persons, who come here distressed by their poverty, who now enjoy easy and plentiful fortune.

Cadwallader Colden also noted that many of New York's richest merchants "have suddenly rose from the lowest rank of the People to considerable fortune. . . ." [5]

Political life reflected these circumstances. The pretensions of the elite notwithstanding, it is clear that its leadership rested firmly upon the support of the common people, to whose views the leaders were obliged to refer. The common people, who numbered in 1756 about 100,000, including nearly 14,000 blacks, were characterized as "farmers and mechanics." The majority of farmers were tenants on the large estates, and many, as indicated by recent research, were prosperous. They grew the wheat and the lumber which were New York's principal exports. Wheat was usually turned into flour, and the bolting of flour was a carefully guarded monopoly of New York City, and a source of tension between town and country, the latter of which tended to dominate the legislature.

New York City was the economic center of the colony and widely regarded as an ideal trading center. It was compact, comprising in 1753 about 2,500 buildings crowded together in lower Manhattan. The city was about one mile in length, and half a mile wide, and perceptive merchants boasted that distances within town seldom exceeded a quarter mile, a fact which kept down freight charges. Commenting on this fact, a visitor observed: "The prodigious Advantage of which to a trading City is more easily conceived than expressed. It facilitates and expedites the lading and unlading of Ships and Boats, saves Time and Labour, and is attended with Innumerable Conveniences to its Inhabitants."

The organization of labor and commerce was paternalistic. According to law no one could "keep shop, or sell or Expose to Sale any Goods or Wares by Retail, or Exercise any Handy Craft Trade or Occupation, but such as are Freemen." To become a freeman a merchant paid £3, an artisan 20 shillings. All freemen could vote.[6]

The extent of the franchise is a controversial subject, about which precision is difficult. It appears that the letter of the law was enforced with indifference, with the result that in both town and country, where the freehold qualification was property or a lease worth £40, most adult white males could vote. Moreover, custom and tradition in various localities guaranteed various rights and privileges to the people, and where these provided inadequate protection or opportunity for the advancement of popular rights, demonstrations and rioting offered important alternative avenues for the expression of grievances and opinion. In short, New York was not a democracy. However, its political system—comprised of a governor and council chosen by the king, and an assembly elected by the freeholders, freemen, and tenants in possession of long-term leases—was sufficiently representative and flexible to give the majority of men, freeholders and freemen, farmers and tenants, artisans and mechanics, a significant voice in the affairs of the colony. And New York's social and economic system provided sufficient scope for enterprising individuals, regardless of their station, to rise to the ranks of the elite.[7]

If the power of the great families over the common people was limited, the influence of the Livingstons and De Lanceys over other members of the elite was even more restricted. Everywhere in New York could be found families who enjoyed a considerable measure of local prominence and power. In Suffolk County, Long Island, for example, the Nicholls and Floyds predominated. These families had some influence in neighboring Queens County where elections traditionally tested the strength and influence of the Hicks and Jones families. In Kings County power was divided between the Lotts, Garretsons, De Beavoises, and Lafferts, while the men of consequence in Richmond County, Staten Island, were John Lecount, Paul Micheau, William T. Walton, Walter Dongan, Jacob Reseau, Joseph Bedell, Richard Morrill, and the Cosens family. New York City was the political heart of the colony. It was De Lancey family headquarters and the base for many of the leading commercial and landed magnates, among them the Livingstons, Beekmans, Waltons, Philipses, Jaunceys, Wattses, and Crugers. North of the city lay the Hudson River Valley and the great manors, legacies of the Dutch period, which gave New York its unique character. The Livingstons, Van Cortlandts, Heathcotes, and Philipses owned extensive property in Westchester County. Westchester, immediately to the north of the city, contained six manorial estates: Scarsdale, Cortlandt Manor, and Philipsburgh, which together comprised an area of four hundred square miles, and Morrisania, Fordham, and Pelham. Livingstons, Beekmans, and Philipses held large tracts in Dutchess County. Livingston Manor and the Manor of Rensselaerswyck, the largest property in the colony, lay within Albany County, as did the estates of the Schuylers and Johnsons.[8]

Between the great families there existed a state of perpetual political warfare. The rivalry between the De Lanceys and the Livingstons eventually came to symbolize the rivalries within the colony's elite, but in fact it did not develop until the 1740s at the earliest. Prior to this time, no simple formula can be applied to explain the intricacies of the colony's politics. The confusion and instability owed much to Leisler's Rebellion of 1689-1691. The rebellion was triggered by news that James II had abandoned his throne to William and Mary. In Boston Sir Edmond Andros, "who was perfectly devoted to the arbitrary measures of King James," and who was also governor of the Dominion of New England of which New York was a part, was arrested.[9] In June 1689 Andros' New York lieutenant, Francis Nicholson, fled New York. A militia captain, Jacob Leisler, took charge of the colony. Leisler "was a man in tolerable esteem among the People, and of a moderate fortune, but destitute of every qualification necessary for the enterprise." [10] Still, had Leisler stuck to his original intention merely to secure the colony to protestantism and the new monarchy, his career might have ended in success. As it was, he split the colony between the older, more established elite, represented most strongly by the large commercial and landed interests of Albany and the Hudson Valley, and a newer, emerging merchant class based in New York City. Leisler came to a bad end. When Leisler refused voluntarily to surrender his control of the government upon the arrival of Governor Henry Sloughter in March 1691, he was arrested, convicted of high treason, and hanged May 16, 1691.

The ramifications of the Leislerian controversy shaped the conduct of New York politics for years after Leisler's demise. The split between the anti-Leislerians, representatives of a country, though not exclusively landed, interest, and the Leislerians, men more narrowly tied to the immediate needs of New York City, continued and grew in significance as the related problems of imperial policy and defense increasingly came to dominate political debate within the colony. By the administration of Governor William Burnet (1720-1728) distinctive imperial and antiimperial interests had emerged. At issue was the fur trade, the cornerstone of many a New

York fortune, and its future in imperial policy. The imperialists, many of whom were erstwhile anti-Leislerians, were led by Lewis Morris and his son, Lewis, Jr., Robert and later Philip Livingston, Cadwallader Colden, William Smith, Sr., and after 1737 William Johnson. The imperialists argued for an aggressive military posture aimed at excluding the French from the fur trade and at breaking the military and economic ties between the French and their Indian allies. They were opposed by the antiimperialists, led by Adolph Philipse, Stephen De Lancey, and later James De Lancey. The antiimperialists favored a more neutral course toward the French. Unlike the imperialists, their interest in the fur trade was indirect. As suppliers of the hardwood and cloth the Indians demanded, they were only too happy to maintain their profitable and quasi-legal French connections. But in fact, as Thomas Elliot Norton has recently demonstrated, the antiimperialists were by Burnet's time losing interest in furs altogether. More and more their first concern was the pursuit of economical government, a policy at odds with the expansionist dreams of the imperialists.[11]

Under Burnet, whom an admiring William Smith, Jr. described as "a man of sense and polite breeding," the imperialists received a sympathetic hearing in official circles, but under Burnet's successors, John Montgomerie, and upon Montgomerie's death in July 1731, Colonel William Cosby, it was a different story.[12] Cosby, supported by Philipse and the De Lanceys, attempted to drive the Morrises out of politics. The governor removed Lewis Morris from his position of chief justice, replacing him with James De Lancey in 1733. The Morrises, father and son, retaliated. Both stood for and won election to the House of Assembly as representatives for Westchester County. More importantly, they founded the colony's first "opposition" newspaper, the *New York Weekly Journal*, edited by James Alexander and printed by John Peter Zenger. For its criticisms of the governor, the paper's printer, Zenger, was arrested on a charge of libel. The attack on Zenger failed ignominiously; despite the concerted efforts of the administration, Zenger's lawyer, Andrew Hamilton, won his client's acquittal.

The Zenger case brought into prominence for the first time James De Lancey, the most gifted and remarkable politician of New York's colonial period, and a man whose influence was to determine much of the course of the colony's history to the coming of independence. As Cosby's closest advisor, the decision to charge Zenger with libel had apparently been largely De Lancey's; "sometimes," De Lancey reportedly said of some "low ballads" published in the *Journal*, "heavy halfwitted men get a knack of rhyming, but it is time to break them of it, when they grow abusive, insolent, and mischievous within it." [13] In his zeal to prosecute Zenger, De Lancey went so far as to have his defense counsel disbarred, a move that backfired when Zenger's supporters brought in Hamilton from Philadelphia. The Zenger trial brought no credit to either Cosby or De Lancey. William Smith, Jr., whose father was one of the attornies disbarred by De Lancey, assessed the actions of both men this way: "It is some extenuation of his [Cosby's] faults, that he was the dupe of others; and an apology for Mr. De Lancey, his chief minister, that he was then a young man, ill read in a profession, which he took up without aid and by his education abroad, was little acquainted with the affairs of the colony." [14]

If De Lancey's judgment in the Zenger case was faulty, it was one of the few mistakes he was to make in an otherwise brilliant political career. [15] The eldest son of possibly the richest man in New York, James De Lancey was born November 27, 1703. While it could be predicted that Stephen De Lancey's standing in the colony would go a long way to guaranteeing his son's success, little was left to chance in the boy's upbringing. At age eighteen De Lancey was dispatched to Corpus Christi College, Cambridge, thence to Lincoln's Inn to read law. He returned to New York in 1725 and with his father's assistance set up a law practice. Stephen De Lancey had married the most eligible girl in the New York of his day, Anne Van Cortlandt; James equalled his father in his marriage to Anne Heathcote, daughter of Caleb Heathcote and the heiress to Scarsdale Manor.

What was really remarkable about De Lancey's career were his superb English connections. In the passage quoted above, William Smith implied that young De Lancey's years abroad had been something of a disadvantage. In fact, quite the reverse was true. Modern studies of the eighteenth-century empire reveal clearly that no aspiring colonial politician could afford to be without important English friends. De Lancey's friends were first class. His father's business interests put him in touch with some of London's most important merchants and businessmen. His connections through the Heathcotes were even more significant. His father-in-law's brother, Sir Gilbert Heathcote, was head of the Bank of England, and a man of great wealth and influence. John Heathcote, Sir Gilbert's son, was very close to De Lancey, and an intimate of Sir Robert Walpole and the Duke of Newcastle. Luck too seemed to be with De Lancey. For example, his Cambridge tutor, Thomas Herring, became Archbishop of Canterbury in 1747. His sister, Susannah, caught the eye of Captain Peter Warren, later Admiral Sir Peter, the hero of the capture of Louisbourg, who married her in 1731. Warren counted among his friends such luminaries as Admiral Lord Anson, the Duke of Bedford, and the Earl of Sandwich.[16]

Cosby's death in March 1736 inaugurated the seven-year administration of Lieutenant Governor George Clarke. Clarke was regarded as an ally of the Philipse-De Lancey faction, though once in power relations between them cooled. Meanwhile, De Lancey, "discerning the advantages of popularity . . . studied to recommend himself to the House." The result was that when the new governor, George Clinton, arrived in September 1743, the chief justice effectively controlled the governor's Council and the House of Assembly.

Clinton was a navy man, who preferred "ease and good cheer to the restless activity of ambition." Not happy with his appointment to New York, the governor hoped, William Smith reported, for a posting "to some indolent and more lucrative station." [17] The appointment was ideal from De Lancey's point of view, however. Ingratiating himself with Clinton, De Lancey quickly became the governor's senior advisor and confidant. He was soon rewarded with a new commission as chief justice tenable during good behavior. The terms of the commission were directly contrary to Clinton's instructions, which specified that judges should hold office during the pleasure of the Crown, but the governor defended De Lancey's commission on the grounds that De Lancey's political support and advice were indispensable. The two men worked well together for several years, but in 1746 the politics of King George's War led to a rupture in their relations. Clinton was angered first by the part De Lancey played in engineering the defeat of a bill proposed by himself to stiffen penalties against army deserters, and second by De Lancey's obsession with economy and his insistence that the cost of the war effort be borne by the Mother Country. Too late an angry Clinton began to see that his confidence in De Lancey had been "too great," but he was powerless to prevent De Lancey's continued advance.[18] De Lancey's connections at home were considerably better than the governor's and in 1747 De Lancey received, with Warren's help, a commission as lieutenant governor.

De Lancey's campaign for economical government appealed to the colony's merchants and farmers, who shared the chief justice's distaste for the ever-growing costs of the war against France, and during the next few wars De Lancey consolidated his position. His success was evidenced by the returns for the Assembly elections of 1752. Of 27 representatives who gathered for the opening of the Twenty-Seventh Assembly on October 24, 1752, 12 were De Lancey's relatives or close friends who "held his character and sentiments in the highest esteem." William Smith reported that: "Of the remaining 15 he only wanted one to gain a majority under his influence, than which nothing was more certain; for except Mr. Livingston, who represented his own manor, there was not among the rest a man of education or abilities qualified for the station. They were, in general, farmers, and directed by one or more of the twelve members. . . . Of the whole House, the only wealthy able member, neither connected with Mr. De Lancey nor in the sphere of his influence, was Mr. Livingston." [19]

To his enemies, De Lancey's grasp of the organs of power, whether on the bench, in the Council, or in the Assembly seemed "amazing." [20] His mastery of the colony almost seemed to defy explanation. It was with awe and more than a touch of envy that De Lancey's two most brilliant critics undertook an assessment of his abilities and character. William Livingston wrote in his well known anti-De Lancey tract, *A Review of Military Operations in North America:*

Of all provincial affairs he is the uncontrouled director. As Chief Justice, great is his interest in the counties: with his sway in elections he rules the assembly: and with his sov-

ereignty over the house controuls a governor. His influence
with the members of the assembly being the main source of
his exorbitant power, never will he serve the Crown at the
risque of a dissention with the house. He will only stand by a
governor while at his devotion, and standing fair with the
people; but in case of a rupture, instantly sacrifice prerogative
on the alter of popularity. His own interest is his idol, and
everything else made subservient to procure it veneration and
esteem. The men who are his greatest tools, are generally by
himself the most despised; and sometimes treated with despite
and insult. If they discover the least freedom of resentment
(which few of them dare discover), he can with a smile, or a
joke, or a promise, or a bottle, at once dissipate the struggling
resolution, and reduce them to their primitive obsequiousness.
By hints—by threats and blandishments—by emissaries—by
dark insinuations and private cabals, he is able to render any
measure hateful or popular—to put down, or raise up, whom,
when, and what he pleases.[21]

In his *History of the Province of New York*, William Smith
recalled:

Mr. De Lancey's genius exceeded his erudition. His knowledge of the law, history and husbandry excepted, the rest of
his learning consisted only of that small share of classical
scholarship which he had acquired at Cambridge, and by a
good memory retained. He was lively in conversation without
ornament, subtle and watchful with an appearance of joviality
and negligence. He was all his days addicted to company and
knew mankind well from the highest to the lowest orders. He
read an hour or two every morning with a view to retail something of it in the evening and being generally at the head of
his company, he found it easy to introduce all such subjects as
tended to the lustre of his own character. He was too indolent
and volatile for profound researches in the law; but what he
had read he could produce in an instant, for with a tenacious
memory he had an uncommon vivacity: his first thought was
the best; he seemed to draw no advantages from meditation,

and it was to this promptness that he owed his reputation . . .
Upon the whole, his accomplishments rendered him an ornament to the country which gave him birth. None of his predecessors possessed natural talents superior, if equal to his and
could this ambition have found sufficient scope for their improvement within the lords of his profession, he might have
acquired the degrees requisite to adorn the first seat at West-
minister Hall . . . He was cheerful, facetious and instructive:
. . . Caesar was his idol, Richard Cromwell his contempt, and I
have often heard him say in his cups that he had rather be the
head of a dog than the tail of a lion. He verified this principle
in early youth, shunning the society of his superiors for a dominion over his inferiors and equals. Nothing but the richness
of his past could have saved such a false ambition from ruin.[22]

It was in response to De Lancey's hold on New York, which
lasted to his death in July 1760, that the Livingstons, relegated to a
permanent secondary position in public affairs by De Lancey's long
shadow, emerged as leaders of the opposition, developing in the
process their own style "opposition" whig ideology. The rise of the
Livingstons was made easier by the passing of Lewis Morris, Sr. in
1746 and by the results of the 1752 elections, but as well the family
was ably served by a small group of young politicians, organizers,
and political writers. The key men responsible for mounting the
challenge to De Lancey were the sons of Philip Livingston, second
lord of the manor: Robert, third lord of the manor, Peter Van
Brugh, Philip, and William. Robert Livingston managed the family
estate and also represented the manor in the Assembly. His three
brothers attended Yale. Peter Van Brugh and Philip Livingston
were successful merchants operating from bases in New York City.
William Livingston, intellectually the most gifted of the brothers,
embarked on a law career, though increasingly his attention turned
to politics. Associated with the brothers in the faction's inner circle
were their cousin, Judge Robert R. Livingston, and two friends of
William Livingston from his Yale days, the lawyers John Morin
Scott and William Smith, Jr., the husband of Livingston's cousin,
Janet Livingston. William Livingston was the leader of the trio, but
Smith, New York's leading historian and the son of one of the col-

ony's preeminent attorneys, also possessed formidable intellectual powers and connections, and he emerged briefly in the late 1760s and early 1770s as a key Livingston political organizer and advisor. Only as the Revolution approached did his influence decline. As an observer and commentator, however, he remained close to the inside of New York politics well into the Revolutionary War.

William Livingston, Smith, and Scott together formed the intellectual heart of the Livingston faction, giving it purpose and direction. Collectively, they were known to friend and foe alike as the "Triumvirate." The roots of this brain trust went back at least as far as the Zenger case, during which the trio's legal mentors, James Alexander and William Smith, Sr., father of the younger Smith, had acted for the defense. In the 1740s the Triumvirate and some of their friends formed the Society of the Promotion of Useful Knowledge, and in 1752 they set up the Whig Club. The Triumvirate were also very active in Presbyterian circles, whose numbers, a contemporary observer reported, "in general consisted of people of the middle rank." [23] From these various associations came the idea in late 1752 for the *Independent Reflector,* a series of essays written chiefly by Livingston, defending the idea of balanced government and attacking the De Lancey-Anglican faction. The immediate occasion for writing the *Reflector* essays was to attack a scheme to found a college in New York City under the patronage of the Church of England, a project opposed by the Livingstons and other militant dissenters. The dissenters, who comprised a majority of the colony's 96,000 citizens, had nothing against the setting up of a college; indeed, the idea for a college had originated with them. But dissenters "took the alarm," when Anglicans offered to put up money and land to insure the scheme's success.[24] Given the Laudian inclinations of many American churchmen, and the recurring fear among dissenters that the college or similar institution might become part of a larger plan to bolster the Church establishment in the colonies, dissenters advocated the establishment of a nonsectarian school. The De Lancey-Anglican faction carried the day. King's College (later Columbia University) was founded in 1754 under Church auspices, shortly after James De Lancey assumed charge of New York on the death by suicide of Governor Sir Danvers Osborn. But for De Lancey there was a price to pay. As Smith explained: "His incaution respecting the institution of the college . . . and the oil of religious zeal being poured upon the coals, kindled a flame, neglected at the beginning, but in its consequences destructive of his popularity, and unfriendly to his repose all the rest of his life." [25] The immediate upshot of the college controversy was that the De Lanceys and their friends suffered setbacks at the polls in 1758 and 1761, losing control of the House of Assembly to the Livingstons.

Given the attitude of the Triumvirate toward the De Lancey administration and, more importantly, the political repercussions of the college issue, it is hardly surprising that De Lancey supporters viewed the Triumvirate and their work with distrust and suspicion. Thomas Jones, the grandson of a onetime privateer, the son of David Jones, a long-serving assembly representative for Queens County, and the husband of Anne De Lancey, daughter of the chief justice, reported that the Whig Club was nothing less than a hotbed of sedition. "In this club," Jones wrote, "matters were settled, plans laid, schemes devised, and resolutions formed, for carrying the grand project into execution, of pulling down the Church, ruining the constitution, or heaving the whole province into confusion." In line with this opinion was Jones' assessment of the characters of the Triumvirate:

Of this young triumvirate, then first verging upon the stage of life, William Livingston bore the character of a sensible, cunning, shrewd fellow; well versed in the law, though a very indifferent speaker; of an ill-natured, morose, sullen disposition; satirical and abusive in his writings; violent in his conversation; a bigot in religion; wanton, cruel, and unfeeling in his temper; ungenerous in his sentiments; uncouth in his manners; impatient of contradiction; and of a savage persecuting spirit. Smith was considered as an artful, close, designing man, with a good share of understanding, and well read in the law; a fluent, easy speaker, with an unbounded deal of ambition, hypocrisy, and craft; a most profound dissembler; enjoyed a smooth, glib, oily tongue, with a steady, demure, puritanical countenance; a noted flatterer, a great sycophant, and a person who could without the least compunction abandon his word, his honor, his religion, or his friendship, to carry a favorite point, to serve a particular purpose, or to gratify his pride, his avarice, or his ambition. John Morin Scott was (at first) of a very different case; he was honest, open and generous, a good lawyer, a fluent speaker, was candid in his profession, just and fair in his dealings, and honor and integrity, was caressed and esteemed by his acquaintances, possessed a jovial, hearty, free and engaging disposition, loved company and was a boon companion. Had he followed his own good sense, instead of becoming the dupe of the two former, or had he continued in his native religion instead of changing it for that of his two presbyterian friends and companions, he might have been a very useful member of society, and gone through life with the estimation, good will and friendship of his fellow citizens; but being extremely warm in his disposition, and foolishly engaging himself in all the politics of the republican faction with the violence and acrimony of a madman, he rendered himself despicable in the estimation of all moderate men, and to every friend to order and good Government.[26]

As for the political writings of the Triumvirate, Jones wrote that they scribbled:

... with a rancor, a malevolence, and an acrimony, not to be equalled but by the descendants of those presbyterian and republican fanatics, whose ancestors had in the preceding century brought their Sovereign to the block, subverted the best constitution in the world, and upon its ruins erected presbyterianism, republicanism, and hypocrisy ... the established Church was abused, Monarchy derided, Episcopacy reprobated, and republicanism held up, as the best existing form of government in the known world.[27]

In fact, the ideology of the Livingstons was unexceptionable and moderate and perfectly in accord with the mainstream of conventional Whig thinking. This ideology took for granted that English and American liberty rested on the succession of the British crown in the House of Hanover, the supremacy of Protestantism, and the maintenance of the English system of government, the particular glory of which was its nice balance of monarchy, aristocracy, and democracy. William Livingston himself put it this way:

> The political creed of an American colonist was short but substantial. He believed that God made all mankind originally equal—that he endowed them with the rights of life property and as much liberty as was compatible with the rights of others—that he bestowed on his vast family of the human race the earth for their support, and that all Government was a political institution between man naturally equal not for the aggrandisement of one or a few but for the general happiness of the whole community.[28]

Though liberal and optimistic in outlook, Livingston's whiggism was tempered by the conviction that human nature was essentially evil. It was the task of government to check the passions of men. "Government, at best, is a Burden, tho' a necessary one," Livingston wrote. He continued: "Had Man been wise from his Creation, he would always have been free. We might have enjoyed the Gifts of liberal Nature, unmolested, unrestrained. It is the Depravity of Mankind, that has necessarily introduced Government; and so great is this Depravity, that without it, we could scarcely subsist." The English constitution, with its balance of monarchy, aristocracy, and democracy, was, Livingston thought, the best. But even the best form of government was very fragile, and the dangers were many. Thus Livingston warned: "But as the most robust and durable Frame of animal Nature is incapable of withstanding the incessant Shocks of Debauchery and Intemperance, so the best devised civil Constitution, is subject to Corruption and Decay, thro' the Pride, Ambition and Avarice of those in whose Care it is lodged." The lesson was surely obvious. A people who were not attentive to the preservation of their liberties soon found themselves the victims of "Oppression, Poverty, and Ruin." [29]

By themselves Livingston's political ideas were scarcely unique. His were the conventional beliefs of the day with which no one in New York or in any of the other Thirteen Colonies would have disagreed. What made Livingston's ideology novel was his belief that in fact the De Lancey administration had brought about the ruin of the constitution so much apprehended by all good whigs. So strong was this conviction that it led Livingston, in manner reminiscent of the tory Bolingbroke, to abandon momentarily his customary iconoclasm and antiauthoritarian posture. In *A Review of Military Operations in North America* Livingston advocated the assertion of the royal prerogative in New York as a necessary counterweight to De Lancey's influence. Having ridiculed the lieutenant governor's public devotion to the rights of the Crown (could the great Shakespearean actor, David Garrick, Livingston asked, have "personated Richard the Third in a livelier manner, than this gentleman the *real* advocate for the royal instruction?"), Livingston advised:

> For a law indefinite, making provision for the salary allowed by the King to his Governors; and competent salaries to all judges, justices, and other necessary officers and ministers of government—such a law, I say, would effectually render a Governor independent of the assembly, and consequently of any undue influence in it. Nor without such independence, or an abridgement of Mr. De Lancey's power, by reducing him to his primitive private station, do I see any probability of the extinction of that party spirit, which hath so long disturbed the tranquility and injured the public weal of the colony.

If not the source, James De Lancey was thus the inspiration for Livingston's style, his energy, and imagery. The De Lancey image evoked in his writings a deep-felt sense of corruption, mystery, and intrigue, but politically it was a curse, for despite the untiring efforts of Livingston and his friends, the faction's assault on De Lancey's reputation and power made little headway. The Livingston's major political success in 1761 came only after De Lancey's death. The simple fact of the matter was that De Lancey was an unconvincing target. Unscrupulous, ambitious, and egotistical De Lancey may well have been, but he was hardly the sinister "American Stuart" of the Triumvirate's polemics. Moreover, the Livingston attack on De Lancey appeared so obviously tinged with self-interest and envy that the principles they espoused were inevitably rendered suspect.

Yet if the Livingston attack failed in the short run, it was to have in the long run consequences which could not have been guessed in the 1750s. If the taunts and denunciations hurled at De Lancey in the 1750's seemed unbelievable, a similar attack 20 years later on the next generation of De Lanceys would prove to be devastatingly effective when linked to an imagined broader scheme to destroy American liberty. Thus, though their ideology was rooted in a kind of private quarrel between rival figures within the governing elite, the Triumvirate managed to fashion a revolutionary ideology for the colony as a whole that would lead to independence. As for the De Lanceys, the lieutenant governor's imperial connections and his mastery of New York politics, once the pride of his family and the wonder of his enemies, proved in the end to be the political ruin of his heirs.

NOTES

1. Alfred F. Young, *The Democratic Republicans of New York: The Origins 1763-1797* (Chapel Hill, N.C., 1967), p. viii.
2. Undated charge to a grand jury; charge to a grand jury, 1748; Robert R. Livingston to Robert Livingston, April 12, 1766, Robert R. Livingston Papers, New York Historical Society.
3. William Smith, Jr. *The History of the Province of New York*, 2 vols., Michael Kammen, ed. (Cambridge, Mass., 1972), I, pp. 139-140.
4. Ibid., pp. 226-227; Anne Grant, *Memoirs of an American Lady* (Albany, N.Y., 1876), p. 28.
5. William Livingston, "History of the American Revolution commencing with the Settlement of the American Colonies and coming down to Novr 8, 1775," MSS Chapter I, John Jay Papers, Box I, New York Historical Society; Smith, *History of the Province of New York*, I, p. 226; "Mr. Colden's Account of the State of the Province of New York, December 6, 1765," *Documents Relative to the Colonial History of the State of New York*, 15 vols., Edmund B. O'Callaghan and Berthold Fernow, eds. (Albany, N.Y., 1853-1887), VII, p. 796 [hereafter cited as *New York Colonial Documents*].
6. Ibid.; Esther Singleton, *Social New York Under the Georges 1714-*

1776 (New York, 1902), p. 5; Arthur E. Peterson and George W. Edwards, *New York as an Eighteenth Century Muncipality* (New York, 1917), pp. 85-86.

7. "Mr. Colden's Account of the State of the Province of New York," *New York Colonial Documents*, VII, p. 796. The question of "democracy" in colonial New York is controversial. The great classic in the field is Carl L. Becker, *The History of Political Parties in the Province of New York, 1760-1776* [1909] (Madison, Wis., 1960). Becker argued strongly against a "democratic" interpretation of New York politics, and subsequent historiography has been largely concerned with defending or refuting Becker's thesis. The most able recent general study is Patricia U. Bonomi, *A Factious People: Politics and Society in Colonial New York* (New York, 1971). Two collections of essays are also valuable: Milton M. Klein, *Politics of Diversity: Essays in the History of Colonial New York* (Port Washington, N.Y., 1974); Jacob Judd and Irwin H. Polishook, eds., *Early New York Society and Politics* (Tarrytown, N.Y., 1974).

8. Nicholas Varga, "New York Government and Politics During the Mid-Eighteenth Century" (unpublished Ph.D. dissertation, Fordham University, 1960), pp. 277-291, 383-418; Beverly McAnear, "Politics in Provincial New York, 1689-1761" (unpublished Ph.D. dissertation, Stanford University 1935), pp. 721-734.

9. Smith, *History of the Province of New York*, I. p. 70.

10. Ibid.

11. Thomas E. Norton, *The Fur Trade in Colonial New York 1687-1776* (Madison, Wis., 1974), pp. 174-197. Also valuable on the role of the fur trade and the imperialist/anti-imperialist dispute are two biographical studies: Lawrence H. Leder, *Robert Livingston 1654-1728 and the Politics of Colonial New York* (Chapel Hill, N.C., 1961); and Alice P. Kenney, *The Gansevoorts of Albany: Dutch Patricians in the Upper Hudson Valley* (Syracuse, N.Y., 1969).

12. Smith, *History of the Province of New York*, I, p. 165.

13. Ibid., II, pp. 14-15.

14. Ibid., p. 23.

15. Two important assessments of De Lancey are Stanley N. Katz, "Between Scylla and Charybdis: James De Lancey and Anglo-American Politics in Early Eighteenth-Century New York," in *Anglo-American Political Relations 1675-1775*, Alison G. Olson and Richard M. Brown, eds. (New Brunswick, N.J., 1970), pp. 92-108; Bonomi, *A Factious People*, pp. 140-178.

16. Katz, "Between Scylla and Charybdis"; Katz, *Newcastle's New York: Anglo-American Politics, 1732-1753* (Cambridge, Mass., 1968).

17. Smith, *History of the Province of New York*, II, p. 61.

18. Clinton to Board of Trade, November 26, 1749, *New York Colonial Documents*, VI, p. 536.

19. Smith, *History of the Province of New York, II*, pp. 124-125.

20. Ibid., p. 125.

21. William Livingston, *A Review of Military Operations in North America . . .* [1756] (New York, 1770), pp. 36-37.

22. Smith, *History of the Province of New York*, II, pp. 245-247.

23. Thomas Jones, *History of New York During the Revolutionary War*, 2 vols., Edward F. De Lancey, ed. [1879] (New York, 1968), I., p. 2.

24. Smith, *History of the Province of New York*, II, p. 167.

25. Ibid., p. 166. According to Smith, De Lancey later refused to involve himself in the college's affairs, saying "that he had contributed enough to it by the loss of his reputation." Ibid., p. 208.

26. Jones, *History of New York*, I, pp. 3-6.

27. Ibid., pp. 6-7.

28. William Livingston, "History of the American Revolution commencing with the Settlement of the American Colonies and coming down to Nvr. 8, 1775," MSS Chapter I, John Jay Papers, Box I, New York Historical Society.

29. *Independent Reflector*, XXXIII, July 12, 1753; *The Independent Reflector*, Milton M. Klein, ed. (Cambridge, Mass., 1963), p. 288.

CHAPTER TWO

Liberty, Property, and No Stamps: The De Lancey Revival, 1765-1766

Implicit in the Livingston-De Lancey rivalry as it had developed during the 1750s was a division of opinion about the importance, the need, and the value of the imperial connection. For their part, the Livingstons increasingly looked to the imperial tie—whether in the form of war against New France, the presence of a strong governor such as Robert Monckton, or laws to enhance the power and independence of the colonial governor—as a means to curb the extraordinary influence of James De Lancey and his faction. In contrast, the De Lanceys tended to view the imperial connection with a certain indifference. Secure in the knowledge that their own ties to England's policy-making elite were more than a match for any colonial governor, the De Lanceys could afford to regard the imperial tie as a tool to be manipulated for personal advantage as the exigencies of New York politics required.

The Stamp Act crisis made this implicit division about the empire explicit. There was, of course, no division about the Stamp Act

22

itself, which both the Livingstons and De Lanceys opposed equally. But the Livingstons' opposition was tempered by an inherent respect for the law, for Parliament, and for the empire, and by their faith in the whig credentials and goodwill of a newly arrived governor. No similar considerations figured in the attitudes or actions of the De Lanceys. Their opposition was quite unrestrained; it was reckless and even dangerous. It was reckless in that the De Lanceys were not deterred by any concern about the effects that their protest might have on the empire, on the colony, and more significantly on themselves. Herein lay the danger. In order to gain an advantage over the Livingstons, the De Lanceys readily enlisted the support of middle- and lower-class popular leaders, with the result that the Livingston-De Lancey rivalry was transformed from an essentially private and gentlemanly quarrel between a few top leaders among the colony's governing elite into a broad dispute involving at one level a variety of political, economic, and social issues, and at another level the future of the empire itself. Viewed from the perspective of the popular leaders, this transformation meant that the way was open for outsiders to join in New York's key political rivalry and in joining make it their own.

In a colony heavily dependent upon trade and commerce it was not surprising that New Yorkers were quick to see in the Grenville ministry's plans for imperial reform a threat to their political and economic liberties.[1] From the outset of the Stamp Act crisis, New Yorkers led the American protest. The ministry's intentions were first made clear as early as March 1764, when Grenville introduced into the budget debate a plan for an American revenue. Consequently, for more than a year before the Stamp Act became law on March 22, 1765, the colonists had begun to make their views known in Whitehall. Even before the first of the new measures, the Sugar Act, had been laid before Parliament, New York's merchants had drafted a memorandum to the House of Commons explaining the adverse effects the new duties and a more rigorous enforcement of the navigation laws would have on New York's economy. The merchants' problem was an all too familiar one: the colony's continuing indebtedness to British creditors. Now, the merchants argued nothing less than that the proposed changes would destroy the commercial economy of the province, and they had some recent figures to back up their contention. For example, imports from the mother country for the year ending November 1763 exceeded New York's exports to Britain by £468,217. To survive economically, the merchants said, New York had to be free to trade its way out of debt, and this, in turn, required understanding from the authorities and a loose interpretation of the navigation laws. The most lucrative trade was to the French and Spanish Sugar Islands. In return for lumber and flour, New York's principal export commodities during the colonial period, the colonists received sugar, molasses, and most important, hard currency. These went to pay for British imports. The source of these goods or money, the merchants argued, not for the first or last time, was less important than the fact that the wealth they represented ultimately ended up in British hands, thus contributing to the national treasure. If the flow of these items was cut off by a literal reading of the navigation laws, the merchants warned, British imports into New York must also necessarily fall. In short, they concluded, Grenville's reforms spelled disaster for both the colony and Britain.[2]

The merchants' case received the full support of the House of Assembly when it gathered for the fall session. By now, however, the economic issue had become secondary to the more fundamental political one of the right of Americans to be taxed only by representatives of their own choosing. The Assembly, since the 1761 elections under the Livingstons' leadership, acted swiftly and boldly, drafting in October 1764 a petition addressed to the House of Commons sharply critical of Grenville's reform and revenue measures. It spelled out clearly and defiantly the right of Americans to self-taxation and the dependence of the colony's merchants on foreign markets.

The petition deserves careful consideration. Not only did it demonstrate the Livingstons' talent for political writing at its best. More importantly, it also pointed to the future by setting out a classic formulation of those ideas and principles which historians have come to regard as the essence of the "ideology" of the American Revolution. The petition began by asserting that the right of self-taxation was rooted in the history of the colony: "That from the year 1683, to this Day, there have been three Legislative Branches in this Colony; consisting of the Governor and Council appointed by the Crown, and the Representatives chosen by the People, who, besides the Power of making laws for the Colony, have enjoyed the Right of Taxing the Subject for the Support of the Government." Therefore, "it became our indispensable Duty," the petition continued, "to trouble you with a seasonable Representation of the Claim of our Constituents, to an Exemption from the Burthen of all Taxes not granted by themselves." The enjoyment of self-taxation, it was argued, was not merely a privilege but a right: "But an Exemption from the Burthen of ungranted, involuntary Taxes, must be the grand Principle of every free State,—Without such a Right vested in themselves, exclusive of all others, there can be no Liberty, no Happiness, no Security; it is inseparable from the very Idea of Property, for who can call that his own, which may be taken away at the Pleasure of another?" In short, the petition declared, the right of self-taxation was "the Natural Right of Mankind." [3]

These were fine-sounding words. Ultimately, the sentiments they expressed would become the rhetorical grist of a revolutionary ideology, but as events in New York would shortly make clear, the ideas contained in the Assembly's petition were of less immediate significance than was a more fundamental concern: namely, what should happen next? Dispatching petitions was one thing, but suppose the petition was rejected—and it was a virtual certainty that it would be—then what? What would happen would depend, as the colonists were about to find out, on the attitudes and behavior of the leaders of the Livingston faction, Lieutenant Governor Cadwallader Colden, and Captain James De Lancey, Jr.

Of the Livingstons much, perhaps too much, was expected. In dissenter circles the reputation of the Triumvirate as defenders of popular causes remained legendary. These were the men who had stood for freedom of the press and against the Cosby-De Lancey-Anglican establishment. Now, once again, they had, true to form, come to the rescue of the colony, defining with grace and wit the rights not only of New Yorkers but indeed of all mankind. The Livingstons had brilliantly seized the initiative. They controlled the Assembly and, for the moment, the hearts of the people. But could they keep the people's affections? For the Livingstons, the question, what next? was critical. The faction's talents were essentially intellectual. Significantly, its greatest leaders and the real brains of the faction, William Livingston and William Smith, Jr., were both painfully shy men, ill at ease in company. Both were poor public speakers, not the sort to rally crowds on street corners. If some bold action outside the polite bounds of law or parliamentary practice became called for, the Livingstons' position among the people might prove to be far from secure.

In a quite different way Lieutenant Governor Cadwallader Colden, head of the government since the departure of Major General Robert Monckton in June 1762, was also a legend. A first-rate scholar of international repute who deserves to be ranked with Jefferson and Franklin as a leader of the American Enlightenment, Colden was an aloof and somewhat sinister political figure in the eyes of many New Yorkers. Of Scottish descent, Colden was born in Ireland in 1688, the son of a clergyman. He was raised in Scotland, attended the University of Edinburgh, and later went to London, where he studied medicine. Colden removed to America in 1710, landing first at Philadelphia. Eight years later he moved to New York where he remained for the rest of his life. He devoted his career to public service, becoming surveyor general of lands in 1720 and a member of the governor's council from 1721. As the senior member of the Council he succeeded to the post of lieutenant governor in Monckton's absence. Colden saw himself as preeminently a servant of the crown, and he dedicated himself to advancing the imperial interest. An aggressive imperialist, he was for a time associated with the Morris-Livingston faction, but during most of his career he stood apart from the main factional alliances. Increasingly, Colden became alarmed by the extraordinary power of New York's great families, especially by their stranglehold on the land resources of the colony. He feared also the power of the legal profession and the great merchants whose influence, in combination with that of the land magnates, posed, Colden thought, a serious threat to the prerogatives of the crown. For a time Colden attempted to organize a popular party opposed to the interests of the great families and attached to the imperial interest, but this was at best only partially successful. Not surprisingly, Colden was hated by New York's elite. Whatever support he still commanded among the people was shortly also to be destroyed.

Captain James De Lancey, Jr. was something of an unknown

quantity in early 1765. Born in 1732, he was the eldest son of Lieutenant Governor James De Lancey. Like his father, he had had an English education, first at Eton and later Cambridge. He joined the army after university with the rank of captain. He may have served with General James Abercromby in the Lake George campaign of 1758, but he definitely participated in the 1759 capture of Fort Niagara. He left the army in 1760 to manage his family's political fortunes following his father's death. Gifted with his father's flamboyance, De Lancey was a sportsman of note, possibly the first man to import thoroughbred race horses into America. De Lancey's chief asset was his name, which, despite what the Livingstons might think, still commanded respect and a following. But how he would fare as a political leader was as yet unknown.

If the leaders of New York were content for the moment to watch and wait, the people were not. Events were rapidly unfolding that would limit the options open to the colony's leadership. The role of the colonial press in arousing popular sentiment against the Stamp Act was crucial. Especially significant were accounts of violence. Stories of violent protest against the Stamp Act began to appear in the New York press in July 1765. The intimidation and beating of stamp agents in other colonies was widely reported, as were the usually hasty resignations of these officials. The riot in Boston in August which forced the Massachusetts stamp commissioner, Andrew Oliver, to resign received detailed and extended coverage, and prompted New York's stamp commissioner, James McEvers, to follow Oliver's example.

These stories seem to have had two results, neither of which boded well for the future. On the one hand, they undoubtedly bolstered morale and the resolution of the colonists to oppose the Stamp Act. As well, the resignations of the stamp agents demonstrated that selective violence was an exciting, effective alternative to mere verbal protest. On the other hand, the stories of violent protest and rumors of more violence yet to come, which certainly lost nothing in the telling, persuaded jittery officials to prepare for the worst. No official anywhere was more jittery than Colden. Throughout the summer the lieutenant governor pressed the commander of British forces in the colonies, General Thomas Gage, to dispatch troops to New York to protect the city from "Negroes or a

Mob." Gage hesitated to comply, persuaded by the arguments of
city officials that the magistrates could keep the peace.[4] The situation was hardly helped by the apparently coincidental arrival at
the end of the summer of an English artillery company. Colden
was, of course, pleased, but the presence of soldiers in the city went
a long way to making the violence the lieutenant governor feared a
certainty.

But not yet; the avenues for respectable protest were not yet
closed. In October, New York played host to the Stamp Act Congress. The call for a meeting to plan and coordinate some form of
joint action had come from Massachusetts, and nine colonies responded. New Hampshire, Virginia, North Carolina, and Georgia
did not attend. New York was represented by the members of the
Assembly's committee of correspondence: Philip Livingston,
Robert R. Livingston, John Cruger, William Bayard, and Leonard
Lispenard. The latter three were merchants. All except Cruger
were Livingston supporters; Cruger, the mayor of New York, was a
friend of the De Lanceys.

Little was reported about the Congress. Its proceedings were
conducted in absolute secrecy, a decision that was probably a wise
one. Judge Robert R. Livingston's private correspondence indicates
that the sessions were rather dull and far from harmonious. Progress
toward some common ground was slow, and a week was wasted,
Livingston reported, before business was steered into "the Right
Channels." As Livingston put it: "An Irishman would say it is the
worse for so much mending."[5] Still, the Congress held together and
by October 19 the delegates had agreed upon 14 resolutions which
spelled out "the most Essential Rights and Liberties of the Colonists." During the next few days the resolutions were redrafted into
three petitions to the king, the Lords, and the Commons. The Congress' work was done.[6]

The end of the Stamp Act Congress coincided with the arrival on
October 22 of the ship, *Edward*, which carried fresh supplies of
stamps intended for use in New York and Connecticut. The *Edward*
dropped anchor that evening to the sound of ringing church bells
and booming cannon. The next morning the *Edward*'s controversial
cargo was brought ashore and deposited without incident at Fort

George, the official residence of New York's governors. According to Judge Livingston, the unloading was carefully observed by a large and "most furiously inraged" crowd.[7]

Rumors of impending trouble flooded the city. At the fort, Colden busied himself with various defensive preparations, with predictable effect on the public mood. His stand was taken as an "Insult," prompting "some rash men" to discuss openly an attack on the fort itself. November 1, 1765 was the date on which the Stamp Act became effective, and as "the last day of liberty" approached the city was flooded with broadsides threatening the life and property of anyone who attempted to use the stamps. The broadsides were signed *Vox Populi*. Who the author or authors might be was unknown, but the perceptive Judge Livingston noted that the writer's command of syntax marked him as "a person not very ill educated." [8]

On October 31 the merchants of New York City met. This meeting was to prove to be of the utmost importance. It signalled the beginning of a fresh De Lancey-led challenge to the Livingston ascendancy in the colony, and in so doing it laid the groundwork for the later divisions that were to divide New York between revolutionaries and loyalists. The immediate result of the meeting was the emergence of Captain James De Lancey as a first-class political leader and organizer of men. The Captain grasped perfectly, as the Livingstons did not, the colonists' desire for some bold, dramatic stroke against the detested stamps. Indeed, the Stamp Act crisis was made to order for De Lancey and his family, being exactly the sort of situation in which their flamboyance, their undoubted flair for popular politics, and their instinctive gift for public relations operated at their best.

Typical of De Lancey forethought was the location chosen for the merchants' meeting: Burns Tavern, once the home of James De Lancey, Sr. The merchants agreed to boycott all British imports until the Stamp Act was repealed. While the merchants and retailers, who also endorsed the pact, deliberated, a crowd of boys and sailors gathered outside the tavern, "imagining," Judge Livingston reported, "that there was a design to execute some foolish ceremony of burying Liberty." No such action was intended and the crowd soon dispersed, its anger directed to the breaking of windows. Amid rumors of more trouble, a confident Colden took an oath to execute the provisions of the Stamp Act.[9]

Tension in the city ran high on November 1, 1765. Handbills posted at the Merchants' Coffee House threatened Colden's life "as a memento to all wicked Governors." As evening fell a large crowd assembled in the city common, popularly called "The Fields." They carried large effigies of the lieutenant governor and the devil. "Colden" held the hated stamps in his hand, and "on his Breast was affix'd a Paper with the following Inscription, *The Rebel Drummer in the Year 1715,*" a witty reference to a popular charge—quite without foundation—that Colden had enlisted as a drummer boy in the 1715 Scottish uprising. The crowd paraded to Fort George and seized Colden's private coach and sleigh, dragging them "in Triumph" through the streets to the Bowling Green. Here, the coach, the sleigh, and the effigies, which were hastily executed on a makeshift gallows, were burned "midst the Acclamations of some Thousand Spectators." A gloomy and no doubt angry Colden suffered "the Mortification of viewing the Whole Proceedings from the Ramparts of the Fort." [10]

The excitement of the night had not yet run its course. The crowd "proceeded with the greatest Decency and good Order" to the house of Major Thomas James, commander of the recently arrived artillery company and a known "Friend to the Stamp Act." James' house was ransacked and its contents destroyed, a loss the Major put at £1500. A nearby whorehouse was also torn down, and a few more fires were set, but the worst had passed. A jubilant *New Mercury* reported that the "whole Affair was conducted with such Decorum, that not the least Accident happened." [11]

For the next few days the city was "Wild with Politics." On Saturday afternoon, November 2, Colden summoned the Council, who advised him to make a public declaration not to distribute any stamps. Meanwhile, in response to continuing rumors that an assault was planned to seize the stamps in Fort George, city officials were also attending an emergecy meeting. Judge Robert R. Livingston, who attended the meeting, found that "despondency and irresolution prevailed over all." Proposals to summon the militia or to organize viligante committees of leading citizens were debated, but finally the city fathers voted to put their trust in Colden "to quiet the minds of the people." But Colden's message, when it came, proved a disappointment. While promising to take no direct action to distribute stamps, the lieutenant governor nevertheless said he would provide stamps to anyone who asked for them. He did, however, promise to store the stamps on board a British warship in the harbor, if her captain would accept responsibility for them.[12]

Colden's message puzzled and angered Judge Livingston. As the lieutenant governor had freely acknowledged since mid-October that he was powerless to enforce the Stamp Act, why had he not simply made a declaration not to distribute the stamps? "Had he condescended to say this," Livingston wrote, ". . . all would have been quieted." James Duane, the son-in-law of Robert Livingston, the third manor lord, but also a political associate of the De Lancey family, now joined the Judge to suggest that, as many of the rioters were sailors, it might be possible to restore order by consulting with the masters of all ships in the port. Accordingly, accompanied by a privateer captain, Livingston and Duane set out to try to cool the public temper. Much to Livingston's surprise, the trio discovered about 200 seamen and mechanics actually preparing to attack the fort. The men were persuaded to abandon their "mad project" only after Colden, obviously under considerable pressure, agreed to send word that he "would not meddle with the Stamps at all." [13]

This assurance hardly mollified the militants, who responded by posting two notices. One threatened the life of any customs officer who tried to collect the stamp tax. The other, signed "the Sons of Neptune," warned the people that "they must not mind the peaceable orators, who had prevented them on Saturday night, that they should be resolute, they would be commanded by men, who had given proofs of their courage, in the defence of their country." They promised to attack the fort on Tuesday, November 5, Guy Fawkes Day, a notable date in the whig calendar and a fine time to strike a blow for the rights of Americans.[14]

It was this final threat which brought the crisis to an end. "It was high time, now, for those inclined to keep the peace of the City, to rouse their sleeping courage," Judge Livingston wrote. A large body of concerned citizens gathered at the Merchants' Coffee

House November 4th. By now it was clear that people were scared, "so intimidated were they at the secret unknown party which had threatened such bold things." Judge Livingston was one of the few to speak out, describing "in as strong a light as I could, all the terrors of a Mob Government." The result, after much hesitation, was that a vigilante committee of ship captains and leading citizens was formed to keep order. One last hurdle remained. The commander of the British man-of-war anchored in the harbor refused to accept responsibility for the stamps, fearful that his house would suffer a fate similar to James' home. As November 5 dawned New York faced the prospect of "Rebellion," Livingston reported. Trouble was averted, however, when the mayor and corporation of the city offered to store the stamps in the City Hall. On November 6 handbills appeared about the town urging public cooperation to keep the peace as the colonists had accomplished *"all we wanted."* [15]

Though the story of the November riot is a familiar one to students of the Revolution, it has deserved a careful retelling here because of the importance of the Stamp Act crisis in the evolution of the Livingston-De Lancey rivalry. The riot marked, with a precision rare in the historical process, the point at which that rivalry was transformed from a private to public quarrel, one involving New York's popular leaders and containing revolutionary implications. Unfortunately the historical evidence of these developments is not as full or clear as scholars would wish, and there remains now, as for contemporaries, an intriguing element of mystery about the November 1st riot and its immediate aftermath which cannot be satisfactorily resolved. How did the riot begin? Was it deliberately planned, or was it the result of a spontaneous outburst of emotion? Who were the rioters, and who were their leaders? And, most importantly, who were "the secret unknown party" or the men "who had given proofs of their courage, in the defence of their country," to whom Livingston referred, and who clearly terrorized much of the city?

Answers to these questions must be far from certain, but strong circumstantial evidence, especially inference drawn from the course of subsequent events, points to a number of conclusions. The easiest matter to clear up is the identity of the rioters themselves.

Various sources speak of sailors, Blacks, youths, mechanics and artisans as the principal participants. In short, the rioters represented a fairly accurate profile of a cross section of New York's middle and lower classes. These people were not a rabble of poor, unfed, revolutionary *sans culottes*, but they did have grievances about unemployment or high prices which occasionally manifested themselves in riotous behavior. The sailors were by reputation a particularly aggressive lot, perhaps because their grievances were the most serious. Impressment was a sore point in every port town, made worse by the rigors and harsh discipline of sea life. Unemployment was also always a problem on the docks, as were the familiar problems and grievances stemming from the sailors' traditional love of drinking, brawling, and whoring.[16]

The leaders of these people were typically men whose origins were of the middle class. Invariably, they owed their positions of leadership to their success in trade or commerce. Invariably too, they were gifted natural politicians, superb street-corner orators, broadside writers, and organizers. Though wealthy and popular, they were not, however, on the inside of the governing elite; they had allies and friends among the great families, but they remained outsiders, not insiders. But their day was coming. American history is in many ways the story of these men and the men and women who followed their lead. Those who survived the upheaval of revolution formed the nucleus of a new republican elite in the independent United States.

The three most prominent popular leaders in New York in the middle 1760s were Isaac Sears, John Lamb, and Alexander McDougall. Known as the "king" of the New York mob, Isaac Sears was the boss of the waterfront. Sears was born in Connecticut in 1730. A sailor from his early youth, Sears made his fortune and his reputation as a privateer captain in the French and Indian War. After the Revolutionary War, he served for a time in the state legislature. He died at Canton, China in 1786, while negotiating a trade deal. John Lamb, born 1735, was the son of a convicted burglar transported to the colonies in the 1720s. Upon completion of his sentence in Virginia, Lamb's father moved to New York, becoming an optician and instrument maker, in which trade John Lamb was also trained. After the Revolution, Lamb was appointed collector of customs for the Port of New York. He resigned his post in 1797, after his deputy was accused of defrauding the government of tax revenues. Lamb sold his assets to make up the loss and died in poverty in 1800. Alexander McDougall was born in Scotland in 1732. He arrived in New York as a boy and began his career by helping his father deliver milk. Like Lamb, he became a successful privateer in the French and Indian War. McDougall married money and established a large and profitable import business. He ended his career as the first president of the Bank of New York.[17]

Sears, Lamb, and McDougall were all active Presbyterians. They were attracted to politics in the 1750s in the heyday of the Livingston campaign against the De Lancey-Anglican establishment. The *Independent Reflector* became their political bible and their attachment to its principles was lifelong. Thomas Jones' description of McDougall's political philosophy was hostile but accurate, and it applied equally well to Sears and Lamb:

> Being a strong republican, a rigid presbyterian, extremely ambitious, a dabbler in politics, and having a pretty good genius, and by dint of application having obtained some knowledge in literature, his politics and religion paved the way to an intimacy with the triumvirate, and other leaders of the republican faction, with whom in a short time he became closely linked.[18]

The connection with the Triumvirate was not, however, quite as close or as simple as Jones implied. Sears, Lamb, and McDougall would remain close to the Livingstons only so long as they believed the Livingstons were pursuing the policies and principles to which they adhered. It is clear that in 1765 Sears, Lamb, and to a lesser degree McDougall, were far from satisfied with the Livingstons' performance.

The Livingstons' problems were problems of personality as much as anything else, but their implicit elitism was also damaging. Judge Livingston's careful and detailed account of the riot was evidence of his own distaste and alarm at, what was for him, an apparently unexpected turn of events. More important was the fact that the judge's view was also the view of the Livingston faction. William Smith perceptively noted: "The Ardor of the Populace on the subject of American Liberty outstripped the Zeal of the Assembly and the Livingstons lost Ground by the Moderation which their responsible Characters and the Novelty of the Dispute inspired." [19]

If the Livingstons were not involved in the riots, who then were the secret men who seemed to be directing affairs from behind the scenes? Though the evidence is circumstantial, it all points to the De Lancey family, especially to Captain James De Lancey and his uncle, Oliver De Lancey. Like the elder James De Lancey, both were said to prefer the company of men of lower estate. Oliver De Lancey was widely regarded as something of a delinquent, a rabble-rouser. Moreover, it was among the middle and lower ranks of the people that Chief Justice De Lancey had built his political base. Though the Livingstons had won the elections of 1758 and 1761, the majority of the middle and lower classes were attached during most of the 1750s to the De Lancey interest.

The most explicit evidence of De Lancey involvement in the riots and their aftermath is a remark of William Smith. According to Smith, the De Lanceys "had Agents without Doors who mixed with the Rabble for the Purpose of acquiring their Confidence." [20] The reference to "rabble" was an obvious and unnecessary slur, but one typical of the Livingstons' intellectual elitism. What it meant was that the De Lanceys were prepared to do what the Livingstons were not: mix with the people and demonstrate their solidarity with them over an issue of critical political importance. The long-term result was that the De Lanceys gained acclaim and a large public following that would endure to 1770.

A more immediate consequence of the De Lanceys' out-of-doors activity was the formation of the Sons of Liberty, in which were brought together the middle- and lower-class supporters of Sears and Lamb and the more affluent merchant friends of the De Lanceys. The origins of the Sons of Liberty remain obscure and are matters of controversy among scholars. Even more mysterious is the connection between the Sons of Liberty, or Liberty Boys, as they were popularly known, and Captain James De Lancey. The importance of the connection can be judged by the efforts made to keep the relationship secret. It was as a secret partner that De Lancey was most valuable, as an illuminating letter published by Isaac Sears in 1770 revealed. It read in part:

> I can call Numbers to Witness, that none of them [the De Lanceys] ever did publickly act in Opposition to the detestable Stamp-Act, or make their Appearance at our Associations, except once, when I think I saw Mr. John Alsop and Mr. James De Lancey there;—the latter opposed all the Plans we were going upon, which affronted many so much, that at a Meeting of the Sons of Liberty after the Repeal of the Stamp-Act, I had much to do to satisfy them and obtain their Consent, to choose him as our Representative. . . . Previous to interesting myself in Behalf of Mr. De Lancey, he, with several others were chosen a Committee to wait on the Lawyers, and desire them to go on with Business as usual, without Stamp Papers; this Service some of the Persons chosen, refused; but Mr. De Lancey declared that as he was one of the Persons intrusted with it, he thought himself obliged, and would perform it. This gave me a good Opinion of him: His not associating at our Meetings, I excused on the following Account, - That as his Family, and Connections were superior to any of those that assembled on those Occasions: Every Thing that should have been there transacted would have been principally imputed to his Influence; and if we had failed in our Attempt, we could not reasonably impose upon him.[21]

As the Sears letter pointed up, the Stamp Act riot in no way guaranteed that the Stamp Act would be repealed, nor did it guarantee that the colonists would resist paying the new tax. Thus, during mid-November there was a lull in the controversy. No stamps were issued, but at the same time business was idle. By the end of the month Judge Livingston was reporting that "all Business but public Business is at a Stand here." [22] With the crisis stalemated the De Lancey-Sears connection became firmer.

If the protest against the Stamp Act was to succeed, it was vital to mobilize the public to carry on its business as usual in defiance of the law. But how should this be done? One answer, proposed by some of the more militant Sons of Liberty, involved arranging for instructions to be sent to the Assembly, which resumed sitting November 12, directing the deputies to repeal the Stamp Act by provincial statute. The scheme was absurd, but the radicals were apparently quite serious, and a meeting for the purpose was called for November 26. Notices were posted about the town inviting persons "of all Ages, Ranks, and Conditions" to attend. The meeting drew a large crowd, among them such prominent De Lanceyites as James De Lancey, James Jauncey, John Alsop, Henry Cruger, and Whitehead Hicks, as well as several leading Livingston supporters, notably William Livingston. It was to this meeting that Isaac Sears referred in the letter quoted earlier. To many of those not aware of the secret De Lancey-Sears deal, it seemed that the meeting had been invaded and taken over by men "not privy to the Design." In view of Sears' letter, however, it is most unlikely that De Lancey's appearance was unexpected. At any rate, the question of repealing the Stamp Act—"the Thing now most wanted"—was quickly and quietly dropped. Instead, a committee was formed of men of such "unexceptional characters, Respect to them prevented any of the company from Objecting to the Method of Proceeding." Membership on the committee was balanced between De Lancey and Livingston supporters. It adopted several resolutions, later drafted by William Smith into a formal address to the Assembly, denouncing the Stamp Act, the extended jurisdiction of the vice-admiralty courts, the non-jury courts designated by Parliament to hear future cases involving violations of the trade laws, and the strict enforcement of the navigation act.[23]

Further proofs of the De Lancey-Sears alliance were forthcoming. Three incidents were particularly revealing. The first concerned Peter De Lancey, a brother of the elder James De Lancey, and the son-in-law of Cadwallader Colden, who arrived in New York at the end of November bearing a commission appointing him stamp inspector for Canada and Nova Scotia. Though the appointment predated the wave of American protest against the Stamp Act, it was nevertheless an acute embarrassment to the De Lanceys. They skilfully avoided trouble, however, by adroitly turning a potential disaster into a minor triumph. In a well-staged public ceremony Peter De Lancey resigned his commission. The Sons of Liberty applauded his "patriotic Spirit" and that of his family.[24]

The second incident, to which Sears briefly alluded in his 1770 letter, concerned the colony's lawyers. The campaign against the lawyers had been building for some time. As the Livingstons were nominally the leaders of the bar, it seems certain that the attacks against lawyers were deliberately fomented by the De Lanceys and their allies. As well, the colonists were angered by the refusal of the attorneys to process contracts or file suits for the collection of debts while legal documents were subject to the stamp tax. The climax to several nights of public demonstrations came on December 14 when a mob rallied in the streets against the lawyers. Directed by Sears and James De Lancey, the crowd did "no Mischief," but voted to send a delegation headed by De Lancey to meet with representatives of the attornies. Within the week the lawyers resolved to resume their duties "without using stamps." [25]

The last incident involved two merchants, Lewis Pintard and Charles Williams, both De Lancey supporters. In February 1766 Pintard and Williams purchased stamps from customs officials. A committee of irate Liberty Boys immediately summoned the two "Culprits," who were forced to burn the stamps before a crowd of several thousand. The crowd marched on Williams' house determined to pull it down, but were restrained "owing to some Gentlemen present and as Mr. Williams [house] belonged to Mr. De Lancey." [26]

Up to the end of 1765 the Stamp Act disturbances had been confined largely to New York City, but early in the New Year the protest spread north to Albany. The Stamp Act had caused little initial concern here. Albany merchants had not bothered to cancel their regular orders of English imports, and five of them had applied for the job of stamp distributor for the Albany district. But when Albany's representatives in the Assembly returned home in January with accounts of the New York riots, the Sons of Liberty in Albany decided it was high time the people of their town were more attentive to the defense of their rights. A group of "tenants" accordingly visited each of the five merchants, requiring each to sign a pledge not to distribute stamps or assist in any way the execution of the act. One of the five, Henry Van Schaack, refused to cooperate. On January 4 he was summoned to appear before a committee of Albany Sons of Liberty to explain his conduct. Confronted by what he later termed "a druncken Set of Man," Van Schaack again refused to sign any documents on the grounds that the committee lacked any legal authority. Van Schaack shortly discovered, however, as others before him had, that the Liberty Boys enjoyed an unofficial authority which was considerable. Two days after his appearance before the Sons of Liberty, on January 6, a mob chased Van Schaack through the town, forcing him to flee to the protection of Albany's fort. The next day Van Schaack capitulated. The Sons of Liberty had bluntly informed him that his house would be destroyed and its contents ransacked if he failed to cooperate.[27]

In New York City the protest also continued into 1766. The Liberty Boys boldly declared their determination to "go to the last Extremity, and venture our Lives and Fortunes, effectually to prevent the said Stamp-Act from ever taking place in this City and Province." Twice in January it looked as though their nerve might be put to the test. January 7 the ship *Polly* dropped anchor bearing packages of stamps consigned for use in Connecticut. The next night the *Polly* was boarded by persons unknown and her offensive cargo burned. Later in the month the arrival of more stamps drew large and angry crowds, who were dissuaded from taking direct action against the stamps only by the urgent pleas of Governor Henry Moore, who had arrived in New York the previous November two weeks after the riot, and the mayor and corporation of the city.[28]

Fresh rumors at the end of January that plans were being laid to force compliance with the Stamp Act triggered a new round of demonstrations. The high point was a procession in which a cannon, upon which an effigy of Lieutenant Governor Colden was mounted, was pulled into the Commons and destroyed. These demonstrations were, however, the last gasps of an ebbing radical mood. Increasingly, riotous behavior was confined to the lower classes. The spirit and bravado of the previous few months, so well captured in the Liberty Boys' promise to "fight up to their knees in blood," was plainly losing its appeal. The more radical of the Sons of Liberty began to express concern "that the Gentlemen of Property don't publickly join them." [29]

The reason for the changing mood was not difficult to identify. Since at least as early as February news from England pointed to a repeal of the Stamp Act by the new ministry of the Marquis of Rockingham. A bill to repeal received royal assent March 18, 1766, though news of the repeal did not reach the colony until late April. The joy of New Yorkers was unrestrained. The Sons of Liberty led the celebrations. They published notices thanking the public for its cooperation and attended a thanksgiving service at Trinity Church, after which there was a 21-gun salute and a commemorative banquet. A grateful Assembly voted to commission statues honoring George III and William Pitt.

Amid the celebrations the colonists paid little attention to the Declaratory Act, passed with the Stamp Act repeal, which asserted Parliament's absolute authority over the colonies, and which would ultimately be the fundamental cause of the American Revolution. The general reaction was expressed by Judge Robert R. Livingston. He thought the repeal a glorious moment in British history, a triumph for the whig principle of individual liberty, which was "the foundation of the grandest empire in the universe." The De Lancey view was similar. James De Lancey was at particular pains to identify himself with the Rockingham whigs. Rockingham and his friends, De Lancey later wrote Rockingham, were the "only real Friends of the Colonies," and he proudly added that he had patterned his ideas and career after the Marquis.[30]

Close on the heels of the Stamp Act protest, widespread disturbances, in the form of tenant uprisings, broke out in the countryside north of New York City. The problem of explaining these disorders, which were centered on the large Livingston estates in Westchester and Dutchess counties, has perplexed historians and provoked controversy.[31] Debate about whether the riots should be seen in the larger context of the Stamp Act protest and the struggle for popular rights, has obscured the important fact that in the broader context of the development of the revolutionary movement in New York, the tenant uprisings do shed significant light on the Livingston-De Lancey rivalry. In particular, the tenant riots revealed the

Livingstons' ambiguous relationship with the imperial authorities. They especially emphasized the Livingston tendency—so evident during the heyday of the elder James De Lancey—to appeal to imperial authority, in this case in the form of the army and the courts, to maintain their property interests in the face of opposition they could neither comprehend nor control. A brief consideration of the riots is therefore useful to an understanding of the Livingston-De Lancey rivalry as it developed between 1766 and 1769.

The leading student of New York's colonial land system and the 1766 land riots is Patricia Bonomi, whose study of the colony's land problems is the most authoritative now available. Bonomi eschews an interpretation of the riots based on a tenant v. landlord formula. To be sure, the tenants had legitimate grievances, especially concerning the extensive, if somewhat indirect, control landlords were able to exert over the running and management of their farms. At the same time, however, it is evident that the economic viability of the manors depended to a large degree on the ability and willingness of the landlords to compete with cheap land available elsewhere by offering potential tenants attractive terms of tenancy. Consequently, the tenants were far from being a poor, exploited, economically oppressed peasantry. They constituted a respectable, and often moderately wealthy, rural middle class. The key to understanding the riots is not to be found among these people, but rather among numerous outsiders and squatters who were not tenants, and whose numbers in the course of the eighteenth century increasingly grew. For the most part these intruders came from New England. They were of English stock in contrast to the tenants, most of whom were of Dutch origin. The squatters were encouraged to emigrate westward with the blessing of imperial authorities whose long-range policy was to cut down the size of the larger manorial estates. They were also supported by local New York figures like Cadwallader Colden, who had his own reasons for seeing the powers of the great land magnates reduced, and by various New England land speculators, who believed with good reason that the often imprecise land claims of the large landholders could be successfully challenged in the courts. In short, Bonomi observes: "Vacant lands, overlapping colonial boundaries, unextinguished Indian titles, and an unsympathetic government all conspired to make New York land titles among the most assailable in North America." [32]

If Bonomi is correct, then the riots of 1766 must be viewed as not primarily conflicts between tenants and landlords, but more properly as conflicts between opposing groups of land speculators, the New York landlords, and their legal tenants on one side and squatters supported by New England land promoters, and indirectly, by some imperial authorities, on the other. In demanding outright ownership of their land, or the renewal "forever" of all leases, the rioters were in effect demanding that New York adopt the New England pattern of land distribution and ownership.

Not surprisingly, therefore, the efforts of some of the leaders of the riots to muster support for their cause by an appeal to a radical whig or even revolutionary rhetoric were singularly unsuccessful. A case in point was the march on New York in the spring of 1766 by Westchester rioters. Robert R. Livingston reported that they confidently expected the Sons of Liberty to rally to their cause. Instead, they found the roads to the city blocked by armed Liberty Boys and themselves hunted criminals. In Dutchess County the story was the same. There, the leader of the riots, William Prendergast, was tried for high treason by a specially selected court dominated by Livingston interests. Prendergast's argument that the rioters' cause resembled the cause of the colonies against the Stamp Act made no impression on the court or the jury, which quickly reached a verdict of guilty. Although William Smith reported that the verdict was criticized in some quarters, "the Tumultuousness of the Time inducing many to discountenance all severity in this Instance," the verdict was evidence that the sympathies of most of New York's townsfolk were with the land magnates in drawing a sharp distinction between protests against unpopular imperial policies and matters of domestic law and order, especially if the sources of disorder were aggressive New Englanders. In contrast, the qualified sympathy of imperial authorities for the rioters' attempts to break the monopoly of the landowners was suggested by the king's decision in December 1766 to pardon Prendergast.[33]

The Stamp Act crisis triggered a revolution in New York politics which heralded the revolution to come in 1776. At the center of this revolution stood New York's two most important political families, the Livingstons and the De Lanceys, whose rivalry had dominated public affairs for two decades. As I have said, the Stamp Act transformed their rivalry into a public quarrel involving fundamental political and constitutional issues of interest to everyone in New York. The evidence of this transformation was dramatically manifested in the upsurge of violence and the intimidation of public officials; in the sudden and unexpected collapse of the Livingstons, a reversal of political fortune that was unprecedented in the colony; and in the forging of the semisecret De Lancey-Sears alliance. The De Lancey-Sears connection was of the utmost importance. It was, indeed, the key to the De Lanceys' new success and they did everything they could to promote and maintain it. Specifically the De Lanceys undertook to develop two conceptions of themselves: On the one hand, they encouraged the belief that they supported violence or other radical action in the defense of American liberties; and on the other hand, they claimed credit for the repeal of the Stamp Act by fostering the impression that they were close associates, and indeed the American representatives, of the Rockingham whigs. For the moment the De Lanceys were overwhelmingly successful, but in the general elation felt by everyone over the repeal of the Stamp Act the point was missed that the De Lanceys' claimed association with the Rockingham party also went a long way toward committing the De Lanceys to the terms of the Declaratory Act. The significance of this committment was as yet unperceived.

NOTES

1. The standard account of the Stamp Act crisis is Edmund S. and Helen M. Morgan, *The Stamp Act Crisis: Prologue to Revolution* (Chapel Hill, N.C., 1953). Also very important is P.D.G. Thomas, *British Politics and the Stamp Act Crisis: The First Phase of the American Revolution, 1763-1767* (Oxford, 1975).
2. "Memorial of the New York merchants, April 20, 1764," in *Journal of the Votes and Proceedings of the General Assembly of the Colony of New York* [1691-1765], 2 vols. (New York, 1764-1765), II, pp. 740-744.
3. New York Petition to the House of Commons, October 18, 1764 in

Prologue to Revolution: Sources and Documents on the Stamp Act Crisis, 1764-1766, Edmund S. Morgan, ed. (Chapel Hill, N.C., 1959), pp. 8-14.

4. Colden to Gage, July 8, 1765, *The Colden Letter Books 1760-1775. New York Historical Society Collections* IX-X (New York, 1877-1878), II, p. 23; Gage to Conway, September 23, 1765, *The Correspondence of General Thomas Gage with the Secretaries of State, 1763-1775,* 2 vols., Clarence E. Carter, ed. (New Haven, Conn., 1931), I, p. 68.

5. Robert R. Livingston to Robert Livingston, October 7, 1765, in *Revolution Letters of Importance: The Unpublished Correspondence of Robert R. Livingston, First Chancellor of New York* [Catalogue of a sale by the American Art Association, January 18, 1918] (New York, 1918), item 39.

6. "Resolutions of the Stamp Act Congress, and petitions to the King and Parliament, October 7-24, 1765," in *Prologue to Revolution,* pp. 62-69.

7. Robert R. Livingston to Robert Monckton, November 8, 1765, in *Aspinwall Papers: Collections of the Massachusetts Historical Society,* 4th series, IX-X (Boston, 1871), X, pp. 559-560.

8. Ibid., p. 560.

9. Ibid., pp. 560-561.

10. Ibid., p. 561; Colden to John Cruger, October 31, 1765, in *Colden Letter Books,* II, p. 53; *New York Gazette, or, the Weekly Post Boy,* October 31, 1765; *New York Mercury,* November 4, 1765.

11. Livingston to Monckton, November 8, 1765, *Aspinwall Papers,* X, pp. 561-562; *New York Mercury,* November 4, 1765.

12. Livingston to Monckton, November 8, 1765, *Aspinwall Papers,* X, pp. 562-563.

13. Ibid., p. 564.

14. Ibid., pp. 564-565.

15. Ibid., pp. 565-567; Statement of Robert R. Livingston, John Cruger, Beverly Robinson, John Stevens, November 4, 1765, Chalmers Papers, IV, p. 58, New York Public Library; "Council minutes, November 5, 1765," in *Letters and Papers of Codwallader Colden. New York Historical Society Collections* L-LVI, LXVII-LXVIII (New York, 1918-1937), VII, pp. 66-71; Handbill, November 6, 1765, ibid., p. 91; "Proceedings of the Common Council, November 5, 1765," in *Minutes of the Common Council of the City of New York,* 8 vols (New York, 1905), VI, pp. 438-439.

16. See Jesse Lemisch, "Jack Tar in the Streets: Merchant Seamen in the

Politics of Revolutionary America," *William and Mary Quarterly*, 3d series, XXV (July, 1968), pp. 371-407.

17. For biographical studies see Robert J. Christen, "King Sears: Politician and Patriot in a Decade of Revolution" (unpublished Ph.D. dissertation, Columbia University, 1968); Isaac Q. Leake, *Memoir of the Life and Times of General John Lamb* (Albany, 1850); especially valuable is Roger J. Champagne's recent, *Alexander McDougall and The American Revolution in New York* (Schenectady, N.Y., 1975).

18. Jones, *History of New York During the Revolutionary War* I, p. 26.

19. *Historical Memoirs from 16 March 1763 to 25 July 1778 of William Smith*, 2 vols., William H.W. Sabine, ed. (reprint edition, New York, 1969), I, p. 95.

20. Ibid.

21. Sears to Holt, May 5, 1770, *New York Journal; or, the General Advertiser*, May 10, 1770.

22. Robert R. Livingston to Robert Livingston, November 20, 1765, *Revolution Letters of Importance*, item 42. In a similar vein, see John Watts to Robert Monckton, November 22, 1765, *Aspinwall Papers*, X, p. 585. Watts, a New York merchant, was married to Anne De Lancey, sister of Chief Justice De Lancey.

23. *New York Gazette, or, Weekly Post-Boy*, November 28, 1765; *New York Mercury*, December 2, 1765; William Smith Papers, No. 197 (9), New York Public Library; *Journals of Captain John Montresor, Collections of the New York Historical Society*, XIV (New York, 1882), pp. 336-337. For a conflicting interpretation from the one advanced here, see Jesse Lemisch, "New York's Petitions and Resolves of December 1765: Liberals vs. Radicals," *New York Historical Society Quarterly*, XLIX (October, 1965), pp. 313-326.

24. *New York Gazette, or, Weekly Post-Boy*, November 28, 1765; *New York Mercury*, December 9, 1765.

25. Goldsbrow Banyar to George Clarke, December 21, 1765, Goldsbrow Banyar Papers, Box I, New York Historical Society; Sears to Holt, May 5, 1770, *New York Journal; or, the General Advertiser*, May 10, 1770.

26. *Journals of Captain John Montresor*, p. 350; John Holt to Mrs. Benjamin Franklin, February 15, 1766, quoted in Morgan, *Stamp Act Crisis*, pp. 250-251.

27. For various accounts of the Stamp Act protest in Albany see Sir William Johnson to Thomas Gage, January 17, 1766, *The Papers of Sir William Johnson*, 14 vols., James Sullivan and others, eds. (Albany,

N.Y., 1921-1965), V, p. 5; Abraham Yates to Robert Livingston, Jr., January 13, 1766, in Livingston-Redmond Papers, microfilm, reel 6; Cadwallader Colden to Conway, February 21, 1766, *New York Colonial Documents,* VII, p. 812; Albany Sons of Liberty to Hugh Gaine, January 3, 1766, *New York Mercury,* January 27, 1766. See also Beverly McAnear, ed., "The Albany Stamp Act Riots," *William and Mary Quarterly,* 3d series, IV (October, 1947), pp. 486-498.

28. *New York Mercury,* January 13, 1766; *Journals of Captain John Montresor,* pp. 344-345; "Resolutions of Sons of Liberty," *Prologue to Revolution,* p. 115; Council Minutes, January 11, 1766, *Calendar of Council Minutes 1668-1783; New York State Library Bulletin,* VIII (Albany, N.Y., 1902), p. 470; *Corporation of the City of New York to the Freemen and Freeholders,* January 1766, Broadside Collection, New York Public Library; Roger J. Champagne, "The Military Association of the Sons of Liberty," *New York Historical Society Quarterly,* XLI (July, 1957), pp. 338-350.

29. Robert R. Livingston to Robert Livingston, February 18, 1766, Robert R. Livingston Papers, Box 1, New York Historical Society; *Journals of Captain John Montresor,* p. 350.

30. *New York Mercury,* May 26, 1766; Robert R. Livingston to John Sargent, May 2, 1766, Livingston Papers, Bancroft Collection, p. 57, New York Public Library; James De Lancey to Rockingham, undated, *Correspondence of Edmund Burke,* 9 vols., Thomas Copeland, general ed. (Chicago, 1958-1971), II, p. 215 note.

31. The older standard work is Irving Mark, *Agrarian Conflicts in Colonial New York, 1711-1775* (New York, 1940). The most penetrating modern analysis is Patricia U. Bonomi, *A Factious People: Politics and Society in Colonial New York,* pp. 179-228. Also valuable is Sung Bok Kim, "A New Look at the Great Landlords of Eighteenth-Century New York," *William and Mary Quarterly,* 3d series, XXVII (October, 1970), pp. 581-614. For an interpretation opposed to the Bonomi thesis see Edward Countryman, " 'Out of the Bounds of the Law': Northern Land Rioters in the Eighteenth Century," *The American Revolution: Explorations in the History of American Radicalism,* Alfred F. Young, ed. (De Kalb, Ill., 1976), pp. 39-69.

32. Bonomi, *A Factious People,* pp. 180-211. Bonomi's thesis about the social background and aims of the rioters is supported in detail by Sung Bok Kim, whose study of landlord-tenant relations in New York appeared after my study was substantially completed. See Kim, *Landlord and Tenant in Colonial New York: Manorial Society, 1664-1775* (Chapel Hill, N.C., 1978), especially chapter 8.

33. *Journals of Captain John Mortresor*, pp. 361-384; Colden to Jeffrey Amherst, June, 1766, *Colden Letter Books*, X, pp. 111-112; Henry Moore to Conway, April 30, 1766, *New York Colonial Documents*, VII, p. 825; Gage to Conway, May 6, 1766, *Thomas Gage Correspondence*, I, p. 91; Council minutes, *Calendar of Council Minutes 1668-1783*, p. 471; Smith, *Memoirs*, I, p. 34; Bonomi, *A Factious People*, pp. 218-224; Mark, *Agrarian Conflicts*, pp. 131-163.

CHAPTER THREE

The De Lancey Ascendancy, 1766-1769

By the end of 1766 the De Lanceys were firmly in control of New York. James De Lancey was the hero of the Sons of Liberty and the most popular man in the colony. Whether De Lancey and his friends would retain their ascendancy would depend on how they responded to the continuing imperial crisis.

Though undoubtedly the most important, the Stamp Act was only one of several reforms planned for the American colonies by the Grenville administration. Other changes included an extension and strengthening of Whitehall's control over colonial judicial decisions. The latter development touched New York directly. In October 1765 Whitehall authorized Lieutenant Governor Colden to hear an appeal against a jury verdict, a decision which New Yorkers interpreted as an attack on the time-honored jury system. The case in question dated back to October 1764 and rose from an assault charge brought against a New York merchant, Waddel Cunningham, by another merchant, Thomas Forsey. Found guilty, Cunningham appealed to the Council through Colden. The colony's

lawyers were united in holding that appeals to Council were justified only in cases of error by the court, but the lieutenant governor
used a loophole in the governor's instructions to allow the appeal.
Clearly, Colden had little interest in Cunningham's fate; from the
outset, as the colony's leaders appreciated only too well, his first
concern was to establish a legal precedent for imperial review of
cases touching on the interests of the crown, and in particular those
affecting the legal status of land grants. By admitting Cunningham's appeal, Colden frankly told home authorities, the stage
would be set to curb what he termed the "dangerous influence" of
New York's great families.[1]

Coinciding with the Stamp Act crisis, the appeals controversy
seemed to offer convincing proof of London's intentions to reduce
American liberty. What worried New Yorkers especially was the
fact that the Cunningham case seemed to demonstrate that appeals
to English precedent or procedure apparently now counted for little in disputes involving fundamental questions of imperial control
over the colonies. Judge Robert R. Livingston's reaction was typical: "This attack on us, and the stamp act on back of it, has raised
such a flame here that except we are relieved by a sudden repeal of
the last, I can't tell to what extremities they may go." [2] Finally, in
September 1765 the Privy Council reversed its earlier decision,
declaring that henceforth appeals to the Council should be admitted only in cases of error. But the damage done to imperial relations by the controversy was not to be easily repaired or forgotten.

Even more explosive were Grenville's plans for army reform and
imperial defense, which also directly affected New York. From his
predecessors Grenville inherited a scheme, developed in the last
years of the French and Indian War and approved by Parliament
March 4, 1763, to place a regular British army of 20 regiments in
the American colonies to police and defend the back country. The
enabling legislation took the form of a quartering act, appended to
the annual Mutiny Act for 1765, which required colonial legisla-
tures to provide quarters and supplies for His Majesty's soldiers
stationed in America. It was anticipated that the Stamp Act revenues would cover the costs of this new policy.

As in the case of the appeals controversy, reaction to the Quartering Act was largely overshadowed by the more important ques-

tion of the Stamp Act. Nevertheless, the Quartering Act received some attention. John Watts, brother-in-law of the elder James De Lancey, wrote sarcastically: "If Administration . . . put the Troops by Act of Parliament into Private Houses, it will be extremely kind and Constitutional in the Bargain, they intend it wou'd seem, that the Colonys sho'd either love or fear them, one of the two, but not both surely." To another correspondent Watts wrote: "This same Billeting Bill on the Carpet is a new Matter of serious Speculation, People say they had rather part with their Money, tho' rather unconstitutionally than to have a parcel of Military Masters put by Act of Parliament a bed to their Wifes and Daughters." [3]

It is far from certain, however, that Watts' remarks were representative of public opinion in New York. In fact, the Quartering Act appears to have stirred little controversy. For example, the same Assembly which met in November 1765 to adopt resolutions against the Stamp Act, ignored the quartering legislation altogether. The deputies did reject a request from the army commander, Thomas Gage, for additional funds, but the rejection was not linked to the Quartering Act, nor was the constitutionality of the placing of a standing army in America raised. The Assembly merely pleaded a shortage of money, and directed the general's attention to money set aside in 1762 for the commander-in-chief's use.

The truth was that the attitude of New Yorkers to the army was ambivalent. Like other Anglo-Americans they were deeply imbued with a whiggish prejudice against standing armies, but at the same time the army's presence was clearly not unwelcome. The tenant riots of 1766 dramatically demonstrated the need for a police force in the colony. Not surprisingly, the Livingston-led Assembly hurried through a quartering bill in July 1766. The bill, whch did not conform to the letter of the 1765 parliamentary statute, was, however, close enough to it to more than satisfy General Gage and Governor Henry Moore. The Assembly undertook to supply the royal barracks at New York and Albany with sufficient bedding, firewood, and cooking utensils for two infantry regiments and one artillery company. Reporting the Assembly's decision, Moore wrote that "altho' it appeared plainly that they did not choose to shew that obedience which was due to an Act of Parliament it was as evident that they were too apprehensive of the ill consequences which would attend their refusing to comply with it." [4]

For the Livingstons the quartering bill was a source of acute embarrassment. As the principal sufferers in the tenant riots, their self-interest in the legislation was all too obvious, but even more damaging was the widespread feeling that troops might be used to enforce the Stamp Act, an issue on which the Livingstons were already thoroughly compromised. So anxious were the Livingstons about the bill that Judge Robert Livingston paid a visit to Governor Moore, generally regarded as a Livingston ally, to make sure the measure got executive approval. The Livingstons' chief worry was that Moore would veto the bill, which he was required to do if he followed the letter of his instructions, and call a snap election which the Livingstons calculated they must surely lose. William Smith saw matters this way: "I was apprehensive that the De Lanceys wanted a Quarrel that they might revenge the Governor's Neglect of them ever since he has been here, and so raise their Significancy[;] besides James De Lancey would probably get into the Assembly now as he was among the Sons of Liberty." [5]

Meanwhile in London there were more serious problems brewing for the Livingstons. In July 1766, the same month the Assembly passed the quartering bill, New York received official permission to issue £260,000 local currency in the form of nonlegal tender bills of credit. When the news of this decision reached New York in November 1766 it should have been welcome. Ready money was always in short supply; what little there was in circulation was scheduled for redemption in November 1768, and under the terms of the Currency Act of 1764 new issues of paper were to be halted. But this latest instruction contained an important qualification to which the Assembly strongly objected. This was the requirement that any paper money bill contain a clause suspending its operation until royal assent had been given. The Assembly refused to pass a money bill with a suspending clause. Instead, they proposed a bill for the issuing of £130,000 without the suspending clause. Moore, attempting to put the proposal in a favorable light, explained it this way in a letter to the Lords of Trade: "I find upon enquiry that it was not their intention to strike Bills for more than one half of the sum mentioned in the Instruction, as they were sensible of the evil

tendency of paper currency in general, and would have been glad
as soon as they possibly could to have laid aside entirely all emis-
sions of paper money ... and it is imagined that if they had a
liberty of emitting the sum of one hundred and thirty Thousand
pounds without any restriction and the time enlarged from five to
eight years for doing it, that it would be the last time that Province
would strike Bills for any such purpose." For the moment, the
money question was stalemated.[6]

The ministry's stubbornness on the money issue reflected an increasingly hostility at Whitehall toward New York. The Chatham
Ministry, which succeeded Rockingham in July 1766, was angered
with the behavior of New Yorkers on a number of counts. First, was
the matter of the Quartering Act, the terms of which, Chatham
insisted, the assembly must meet "in the full extent and meaning of
the Act." [7] Second, was a petition sent to Parliament by the merchants of New York late in 1766 demanding a reduction in customs
duties and easier access to the French and Spanish Sugar Islands.
Coming at the same time as news of the Assembly's refusal to pass
the Quartering Act, and against the continuing demand for paper
money, the New York petition infuriated the ministry and Parliament. Lord George Sackville well expressed the mood in ministerial circles:

> The Colonys are growing worse and worse. Some of the prov-
> inces refuse obedience to the Act of Parliament about quarter-
> ing the troops.... This refusal added to the ill grace with
> which they have granted money for indemnifying the sufferers
> by the late riots [Stamp Act riots], and a petition just arrived
> from New York praying relief from the chief points in the Act
> of Navigation, has sour'd the minds of people here in general,
> and occasions a good deal of distress among the ministers, who
> must perceive how ill they are requited for that extraordinary
> lenity and indulgence with which they treated the last year
> these undutiful children. These affairs must come into Parlia-
> ment, and will afford matter of triumph to those who foretold
> the fatal consequences of yielding to riot and ill-grounded
> clamour, and may perhaps oblige Administration to exert a
> degree of rigour.[8]

It was against this background that the ministry turned its attention to the problems of devising new measures for finance and imperial control which were to culminate in the Townshend Acts. While Charles Townshend, chancellor of the exchequer since August 1766, thought about the general problem of imperial revenues, his cabinet colleagues took up the question of the New York Assembly's conduct. "It is the general opinion," secretary of state for the southern department, Lord Shelburne wrote in mid-February, "that the present packet should not go to America without some determination of government, after the imprudent conduct of New York, as well on account of appearance here as effect there." [9] Agreement, however, was not forthcoming. A proposal to appoint a general governor of New York was considered, as were suggestions to reenact the Declaratory Act as an amendment to the Mutiny Act, and to impose a special tax on shipping using New York harbor.

The cabinet's indecision paved the way for Townshend to exert his fateful influence on colonial policy. He proposed that the New York Assembly be suspended until the colonists agreed to comply with all the terms of the Quartering Act. Though the connection between this proposal and the chancellor's tax measures was at best tenuous, the suspension of the New York Assembly and a new schedule of American customs duties were presented to Parliament as a package. As no one in Parliament questioned the need to assert parliamentary authority in the colonies, both proposals easily passed, receiving royal assent June 29, 1767.

As New York had, quite unintentionally, played a large role in the shaping of the Townshend Acts, it could be expected that reaction to the new measures in that colony would be especially sharp. In particular, the Townshend legislation presented the Livingstons with a crisis similar to that of the Stamp Act, and a chance to reestablish themselves as popular leaders. But once again as in 1765 the Livingstons' response was curiously ambiguous. This time, however, the ambiguity was to cost them dearly.

As always, the De Lanceys were quick to respond to the crisis. In late December 1767 the merchants and mechanics, the twin pillars of the Sons of Liberty, formed a committee to promote "Frugality, Industry, and Employment of our Tradesmen and Poor," and in

April 1768 the merchants founded the New York Chamber of Commerce, one of the chief purposes of which was "adjusting disputes relative to trade and commerce." The campaign against the Townshend Acts had scarcely begun, however, when Governor Moore dissolved the House of Assembly February 6, 1768. A month later New Yorkers went to the polls to elect a new Assembly.

The election of 1768 was of profound significance in the history of the revolutionary movement in New York. The most important result was the evidence the election provided of an inherent radicalism in the protest against the Stamp Act and the Townshend duties, and in the demands for local autonomy in such matters as paper money, defense spending, and judicial procedures. In the short run the moderate Livingstons were the principal losers, but the radicalism of the populace on the subject of imperial control of the colony also contained hidden dangers for the De Lanceys, whose ascendancy in New York was for the moment guaranteed by the drift of events.

As the campaign opened, therefore, the De Lanceys' most important asset was their radical image. Captain James De Lancey was uniquely positioned to take advantage of the situation. His record as a friend of American liberty was unimpeachable and he possessed one other additional asset: his father's name. The news that the Captain intended to contest one of New York City's four seats prompted his uncle, John Watts, to observe that "his father's character and memory will be a Rock he may build upon all his life." [10]

In sharp contrast were the gloomy electoral prospects of the Livingstons and their allies. On every major issue that had risen in the colony since 1764 they were acutely vulnerable. Their most recent blunder had occurred in June 1767, when the Assembly had grudgingly agreed to pass a quartering bill in line with Whitehall's requirements. That the suspending act would not now take effect was hardly reassuring; if the Livingstons wanted to retain control of the Assembly, they would have to do much better in future. As well, other more fundamental issues were working against Livingston candidates. Most important was the Livingstons' prominence in the New York bar. New Yorkers as a whole were suspicious of lawyers. Partly, this was due to their overly cautious—their enemies said sympathetic—reaction to the Stamp Act, but equally significant factors were the superior education, wealth, and influence of most lawyers, which made them objects of popular envy and distrust.

Given these considerations, the election strategy of the De Lanceys was simple: attack the character and record of the Livingstons by playing on the popular prejudice against the legal profession. Early in the campaign De Lancey pamphleteers called attention to the high fees lawyers charged clients. "Are not *pettifogging Attornies,*" one writer asked, "the *bane* of Society? And does not *this* Country as much swarm with *them* as *Norway* does with Rats?" The selfish greed of the lawyers was contrasted to the disinterested behavior of the colony's merchants who were described as "Men whose only interest it *can* be to promote the Interest of the Community; and who do not depend for subsistence, upon the *Quarrels of their Neighbours.*" 11

An important indicator of popular feeling was the widespread support given the De Lanceys by the Sears-Lamb wing of the Sons of Liberty. Typical of the Liberty Boys' support, was this statement printed on cards handed to potential voters: "That the good People of this City are supported by Trade and the Merchants. That the Lawyers are supported by the People. The Difference here given will plainly point the Course they out to Steer." Similar sentiments were expressed in verse:

Beware my good Friends of the Wolf's gripping Paw,
And the Man who will rob, under Sanction of Law;
Nor trust your dear Rights in the Hands of a Knave,
Who will sell them for Gold, and your Persons enslave—
Consider before—Hand, mark well his Intent,
Or you'll find it—perhaps, when too late to repent.12

Under this kind of fire, the Livingston campaign withered. In an effort to stir memories of the Triumvirate's greatest days, the Livingstons tried to exploit the De Lancey-Anglican connection. In other times this issue might have roused more support. The long battle by churchmen to secure the appointment of an American bishop gained new life in 1767 with the publication of Thomas Bradbury Chandler's *Appeal to the Public in Behalf of the Church of England in America,* undoubtedly the most able tract of its kind. The Livingstons charged that James De Lancey, who was in England when the Assembly was dissolved, had undertaken to solicit official support for an American bishop, an accusation that was adroitly dismissed as nonsense by the De Lanceys. On March 8th the Captain's friends announced:

> The Son of the Most upright Judge, the best of Governors, and the greatest Patriot ever known in this Country, being accused of soliciting in London an Episcopal Establishment for the Colonies, and procuring appointments for himself that must be odious to you: His Friends beg leave to declare, that these Imputations are utterly groundless, and propagated only to injure him whilst a Candidate for the Favour of your Suffrages during the Poll. They have indubitable Evidence of his lately refusing a Post of great Profit, merely as an Acceptance of it would have been incompatible with his invariable Attachment to the Liberty and Interest of America, which he is duly employed in defending and promoting; emulous to imitate the amiable and disinterested Qualities of his honourable Ancestor, whose Memory should ever be dear to the Good People of this Province.[13]

The Livingstons had also tried to exploit the Captain's love of horse racing. He was accused of neglecting the interests of America while wasting his time at the Newmarket race track. A De Lancey supporter replied: "I believe that any Man who is foolish enough to believe that a certain Person continues this Winter in Great Britain for the Sake of the Diversions at *New-Market,* and not with Design to influence the august Parliament of the Nation in Favour of America, is an obstinate Heretic, and is only fit for the flames." [14]

Control of New York City's four Assembly seats was the key to victory, and it was in the city that the political battle was hardest fought. Six men contested the four seats. They were Philip Livingston, James De Lancey, Jacob Walton, James Jauncey, John Morin Scott, and Amos Dodge. Walton and Jauncey were successful merchants, attached to the De Lancey interest. Dodge was high constable of New York, and something of an independent. Scott, one of the Triumvirate, was a Livingston man. Scott was also a lawyer, and it was against him that most of the barbs against the legal profession were aimed. The campaign reached its height during the five days of polling from March 7 through 11, 1768. De Lancey supporters were everywhere evident among the people. Oliver De Lancey patrolled the Broad-Way, while other De Lancey men stationed themselves at the city hall, or mingled among the tenants on the Trinity Church estate. The De Lanceys spent lavishly. For example, James De Lancey was billed by one saloon keeper for nearly 250 meals and large quantities of liquor.[15]

Despite the liveliness of the campaign, the result was not decisive. Cadwallader Colden's opinion that "the general cry of the People both in Town and Country was *No Lawyer in the Assembly*," accurately describes one aspect of the result, but in other respects generalizations about the outcome are of dubious value. Most interesting was the apparent failure of voters to perceive, in New York City at least, a clear distinction between the Livingston and De Lancey interests. In New York the results were Philip Livingston, 1320; James De Lancey, 1204; Jacob Walton, 1175; James Jauncey, 1052; John Morin Scott, 870; Amos Dodge, 257.[16] The De Lanceys took the city with three out of four seats. Livingston's fine showing was an indication of the continuing strength of anti-Anglican feeling, and, of course, of the personal popularity of the candidate, who, unlike most of the Livingston faction leadership, was not a lawyer. Little is known about the contest outside New York City, and given the absence of formal party ties, the results are open to conflicting interpretations. Historians are agreed, however, that the De Lanceys failed to gain a majority. Probably the balance of forces between the De Lanceys and Livingstons was about even. The De Lanceys' most notable gain outside the city was in the Livingston stronghold of Dutchess County, where Judge Robert R. Livingston, the most prominent victim of the attack on the legal profession, was unseated.

With the election out of the way attention again turned to the Townshend Acts. Buoyed by the election returns, the De Lanceys easily kept up the initiative they had established in October 1767. Most interest now centered on the Massachusetts Circular Letter, voted by the Massachusetts Assembly February 11, 1768 at the behest of Samuel Adams, which called on other American colonies to join Massachusetts in opposing the Townshend legislation by agreeing to a universal boycott of British imports. As authorities regarded the Letter as seditious, the reaction of other colonies to it assumed great significance for the future of imperial relations. Few on either side of the Atlantic doubted the significance of the Circular Letter. At stake were conflicting interpretations of two fundamental issues: sovereignty, and the American claim to the right of self-taxation. So far as the Ministry was concerned, an endorsement of the Circular Letter by the House would amount to an official sanctioning of sedition; if the Assembly voted approval for the Letter, Moore was obligated by special instruction from Colonial Secretary Hillsborough immediately to declare a dissolution. The Ministry had cleverly seized the initiative from the colonists by stating its policy in advance of any American reaction. By interpreting the Circular Letter as a challenge to British sovereignty in the colonies, the Ministry had given notice that opposition would not be tolerated, and might well lead to retaliatory measures. The threat was unprecedented, and, American bravado notwithstanding, not one to be taken lightly.

The great importance of the Circular Letter seems, however, to have been completely missed by the Livingstons. If William Smith is to be believed, the Livingstons apparently expected little resistance to the Townshend Acts. The Circular Letter they dismissed as a piece of political propaganda related more to internal quarrels in Massachusetts than to significant principles. The Livingstons' attitude was made clear at a meeting of the governor's Council April 6, 1768. Governor Moore asked Smith how he thought New York's merchants would react to the proposed boycott. Smith answered, "That I had Reason to think our Merchants would not come into the Measure—that the late Revenue Act had never been remonstrated against—That this ought to be first done before any other violent steps were taken—That a New Parliament might be better affected to the Colony Claims than the last—That our people were Suspicious of Philadelphia and that Boston having a Quarrel with [Governor Francis] Bernard separate from that with Great Britain, we saw less Reason to follow their heated Example." [17]

Moore was disinclined to put much store in Smith's opinion. Noting that efforts were already well underway to draw up a nonimportation pact similar to the agreement reached at Boston in early March, he replied that he thought nonimportation inevitable. Of greater concern to the governor was the prospect of violence in the city should serious opposition to the boycott develop. Moore said that "he knew of Persons who would refuse if they could be protected but that they apprehended Violence if they objected to sign the proposed Agreement." No protests materialized, however, and a few days later the merchants agreed to a boycott from October 1, 1768 on condition that similar agreements were upheld at Boston and Philadelphia. As the public calm continued into early summer, Moore came around to Smith's earlier assessment of the popular mood. Though he reported the continuing publication of various "inflammatory Papers" supporting nonimportation, he wrote that he could discover "No Disposition . . . to follow the Example of Boston; and as far as I have been able to learn, the scandalous Behavior of the People there, is generally condemned in this Place." [18]

The apparent calm was quite misleading. With the commencement of the Assembly session, evidence of the intense behind-the-scenes activity that had marked the recess began to emerge. The groundwork for positive action was laid in mid-September when the city's merchants, with the backing of the mechanics and artisans, reaffirmed their boycott of British imports. More dramatic was the riot which erupted on the night of November 14, and which was immediately followed by a parade of merchants who descended on the Assembly "in a Body" to demand legislative support for nonimportation.

As in the case of the Stamp Act riots, this disturbance again highlighted the different styles and attitudes of the Livingstons and De Lanceys. True to form, the Livingstons adopted a moderate whig posture which was legalistic, scholarly, and elitist, and which reflected their belief that colonial rights must be tempered by respect for perogative and authority. In contrast were the De Lanceys. Impatient in discussion, bored by the Council, and supremely confident in their English connections, they could easily ignore the governor and their peers to act instead as "radicals" in the popular interest, a role well suited to their temperaments, ideas, and ambitions.

The Council met November 19 to discuss the disturbance. Smith hoped that the De Lanceys might be goaded into admitting their part in the riot, and he was not disappointed. The governor asked the Council to issue a proclamation condemning the rioters, but was opposed by three De Lanceyite councillors, Oliver De Lancey, John Watts, and Henry Cruger. Watts protested so strongly that Moore was obliged to adjourn the meeting.

Two days later an angry Moore announced he had prepared a proclamation of his own, a decision apparently influenced by Smith, who had managed to persuade the governor that the De Lanceys were behind the trouble. Moore bluntly told the Council he suspected that "the Rioters were set up by People of Property, and the grand End to destroy the Harmony subsisting between the several Branches by intimidating the Assembly." He added, "that he believed the Riot was preparatory to the Instructions to the City Members now as he heard carried about to be signed." Delighted by the governor's stand, Smith reported that the De Lanceys had now lost the support of all New York's "weighty Citizens."

Given the recent election results, it is not clear why Smith should have thought that the De Lanceys' support of the riot or any other aspect of their conduct was detrimental to their position, but Smith and other leaders of the Livingston faction proceeded on the assumption that Moore had exposed a De Lancey weakness. When the Assembly received Moore's proclamation denouncing the riot, Speaker Philip Livingston directed it to a committee headed by a Livingston ally and confident, Philip Schuyler of Albany. The committee, working from a draft prepared by William Smith, hastily produced a report which was almost identical to the governor's proclamation. It blamed the riot on "the Indiscretion of a very few Persons of the lowest Class," and recommended the posting of a reward of £100 for information about the ringleaders.

Backed by the Sons of Liberty, the De Lanceys tried to have the report quashed. Rough tactics were used without hesitation. On the night of November 21, for example, one deputy, Judge John Thomas of Westchester, was visited by some Liberty Boys. What transpired is not exactly clear, but the visit was enough to change the judge's vote on the report. As William Smith somewhat circumspectly put it: "Mr. Thomas got a Panick. . . . Thomas was not for it on the Committee but having been visited by the Sons of Liberty as they stile themselves he now moved to have it rejected." Thomas' vote was hardly significant, however, and the report easily passed the House. Its author, Smith, was understandably pleased. "Never," he wrote, "did the De Lanceys act with less Craft. They lost Credit with the Government and now gave Proof of what I had told Sir Harry of their wanting to Head the Mob to disturb his Administration. . . . The Mob was now stunned and the Power to disturb the public Repose all over." [19]

At best, Smith's interpretation was wishful thinking; at worst, it was nonsense. From the outset of the session the rising De Lancey ascendancy in the Assembly had been evident. The cases of Lewis Morris and John Morin Scott were suggestive. When the Assembly opened, Morris and Scott, defeated candidates in the Borough of Westchester and New York City respectively, brought charges of election bribery against the winners, John De Lancey, the Captain's cousin, and James Jauncey. During November and December the House heard witnesses and examined lists of voters. It is difficult to judge with any certainty where the truth lay, but from the evidence gathered it appears that both the successful and losing candidates engaged in what one witness termed "irregular, unfair, and riotous" tactics. What really mattered from the De Lanceys' point of view was that by the middle of December they had mustered sufficient support to confirm De Lancey and Jauncey in their seats.[20] The way was now clear for a consideration of the Massachusetts Circular Letter.

Since everyone knew that favorable consideration of the Letter must immediately result in a dissolution of the House, the first concern in the minds of the deputies was the prospect of another election. As in the case of the November riot, the Livingstons again completely misread the public temper. Remarkably, they persuaded themselves that it was they and not the De Lanceys who had the most to gain from another poll. If Smith is to be believed, the Livingstons thought James De Lancey was playing a clever double game. Posing as "the Oracle of the Sons of Liberty," Smith reported, De Lancey "frequently threatened" to introduce a motion approving the Circular Letter, and indeed, he went so far as to arrange for the freeholders and freemen of New York City to draft instructions directing the House to reply to the Letter "with Respect." But in fact, Smith argued, these were mere empty threats. De Lancey did not want another poll, only the applause of the Liberty Boys, and he was afraid of offending the governor and the home authorities. In a lengthy and somewhat confused passage in his memoirs, Smith explained De Lancey's complicated maneuvers this way:

> As the De Lanceys had evidently a Design of Influencing the House . . . and that if accomplished it must be done by inducing the Members to believe that he was the Oracle of the Sons of Liberty and Instructions had been lately given to the City Members to treat Lord Hillsborough's Circular Letter with Contempt and the Boston Circular Letter with Respect. James De Lancey frequently threatened the House with a Motion for that Purpose. It appears to Colonel Schuyler that the House in the Main were desirous to take no Notice of the Matter of the Instructions but yet that if a Motion was made they would join in it for Fear of the Populace Though a Dissolution was to be the Consequence and as he had shewn the Governor the Resolves and learn't from his that those against the Statute for Declaring the Supremacy of Great Britain and the Suspension of our Legislature would necessarily create a Dissolution and that De Lancey Walton and Jauncey were fearful of a Dissolution and only wanted to gain Credit with the Sons of Liberty as Friends to the Instructions and yet wished they might be overruled for the Sake of exposing others to the popular Odium.

It is not difficult to appreciate that De Lancey hoped to manage proceedings so as to place the Livingstons in a bad light, but it is hard to see why the Captain and his friends should have been fearful of another election, in which they could surely expect to do well. Unfortunately, we have only Smith's word for what the De Lanceys' thought. One thing, however, seems clear. Since 1765 the

De Lanceys had had a continuous record of opposition to the administration, so why they should now care what Sir Henry Moore thought of them is not easily explained. Smith himself noted elsewhere in his diary: "Every Body knows that the De Lancey Family were no Friends to Sir Henry Moore, and that they were impatient under a want of Power to distress him and reduce him to a Subserviancy to their Ambitious Desire of Ruling the Colony under an Absolute Sway." Confrontation with British authority was, admittedly, a more serious matter, but it was not the sort of issue about which a man of De Lancey's character or English contacts worried.

Undaunted, the Livingstons therefore counterattacked in an effort to force a dissolution of the Assembly on their own terms. Philip Schuyler surprised the House on December 10 by moving resolutions in support of the Massachusetts Circular Letter. It was a brilliant stroke, and it caught the De Lanceys, who were reportedly "thunderstruck," completely off guard. The Schuyler resolutions were fiercely debated. With the opposing forces nearly balanced, only a bipartisan set of motions stood a chance of passing. Finally, on December 13, after "much Altercation," a compromise was reached. An election was now inevitable, but the resolutions agreed to would give neither side an advantage, permitting, Smith observed, "all the Members to fare alike in Point of Reputation." [21]

The resolutions were the work of John Morin Scott, and replaced other resolves, phrased in "high terms," laid before the House in November by James De Lancey. The Scott resolutions asserted that Americans were entitled to self-taxation, that colonial assemblies had the right to correspond with one another about matters of mutual interest, and that Parliament's act suspending the Assembly was unconstitutional as only the King or his governor could dissolve a popularly elected legislature. As expected, Governor Moore declared the resolutions to be "flatly repugnant" to the laws of England, and on January 2, 1769 he dissolved the Assembly.[22]

Contemporary opinion of the 1769 election was varied. Peter Van Schaack thought it a most "decently conducted election," but Peter R. Livingston's characterization "hott and pepper" was probably closer to the truth. Cadwallader Colden believed personal enmity and ambition were the only important issues. "Tho' in the late spirited contest in the late Elections," the lieutenant governor wrote, "Patriotism the Church and the Dissenting Interests were made the Pretences the true motive was whether the De Lancey or the Livingstone Interest should have the Lead in the Assembly for the future." All things considered, it was, one colonist declared, "the Strongest Election ever known." [23]

Though the Livingstons had performed well in the Assembly, their fundamental weakness was now exposed. Consider, for example, the case of Philip Livingston. As the standing of the four city members was high, most New Yorkers expected to vote the same ticket as in 1768, namely, Livingston, De Lancey, Walton, and Jauncey. But Philip Livingston unexpectedly announced he would not stand. Instead, a broad-based committee of dissenters recommended on January 4 the creation of a bipartisan ticket composed of two Anglicans and two Presbyterians.

The proposal, which amounted to a suggestion to form a new political party, was unprecedented and caught the De Lanceys by surprise. Obviously, a chance to eliminate Livingston was attractive, but such a step would be risky. Livingston was a popular man, who shared with the De Lanceys whatever credit was due for the vote on the Circular Letter. James De Lancey's first thought was therefore to keep the team of Livingston, Walton, Jauncey, and himself together. He approached Livingston through James Duane, Philip's nephew, but a political ally of the De Lanceys. According to Duane, De Lancey "sent me to Solicit a union, and offered to do it in person, *at any time and place He should appoint.*" Livingston's decision puzzled Duane, as it may have other Livingston supporters. Livingston's announcement that he had withdrawn because he believed only a balanced bipartisan slate could guarantee a "peaceable" election was hardly convincing. In fact, as Duane noted, only the candidature of the four 1768 candidates would assure an easy election.[24]

It soon became transparently evident that Philip Livingston had acted less than candidly. The De Lanceys turned down the proposal for a balanced ticket and named four candidates of their own: James De Lancey, James Jauncey, Jacob Walton, and John Cruger, a member of the Council who had been mayor of New York during the Stamp Act crisis. The dissenters in turn nominated Philip Livingston, Peter Van Brugh Livingston, John Morin Scott, and Theodorus Van Wyck. Livingston reiterated that he was not a candidate but coyly added that if elected he would serve. It now appeared that Livingston's original statement had been nothing but a poorly executed trick to win approval for a slate of four dissenters. The De Lanceys charged that the bipartisan proposal was nothing more than a "settled, preconcerted plan" to embarrass their family and deceive voters.[25] John Jay, a De Lancey supporter and law partner of Robert R. Livingston, Jr., the future chancellor of the state of New York, noted: "Ph Livingston is shaky. He is said to have played a double game. Appearances are against him." Duane put a kinder interpretation on his uncle's actions, observing that he had become committed to the dissenters' ticket "whether he meant to do it or not" because his "Conduct had that Colour." [26]

Philip Livingston's problems reflected the larger difficulties facing the Livingston faction. An attempt to stir anti-Anglican passions met with as little success as it had in 1768. As one De Lancey supporter answered in reply: "Like People in a Storm, let us not dismiss our Pilot [De Lancey] because he *kneels down when he prays.*" A more hopeful issue for the Livingstons was the Assembly's support of the Massachusetts Circular Letter. With justice, the Livingstons claimed most of the credit for the Assembly's positive response, and they fought hard to establish their important role in the debate. The key to their strategy, and really their only hope of success, was the charge that the De Lanceys had tried to block dissolution:

> The Courage of some of the present Candidates, who were in the last Assembly, is the less to be applauded; because it is well known, that a Dissolution was so far from being apprehended, that two of them laid wagers, that the House would not be dissolved; and the greatest EVIL they dreaded, was only, as one of them expressed it, a *Prorogation.*[27]

The De Lanceys responded masterfully. It was quite true, they conceded, that Philip Schuyler introduced the patriotic resolutions voted by the House, but at the same time they reminded voters that the Schuyler motions had replaced Captain De Lancey's more strongly worded alternative proposals. Moreover, the De Lanceys skillfully insinuated that the Schuyler resolutions were the result of instructions sent to the Assembly by the freemen and freeholders of New York City, for which the De Lanceys were of course responsible. They agreed with the Livingstons that the instructions were not signed by anything like a majority of the legal voters, but they asserted they were in no doubt that the instructions were supported by a large majority of the colonists. As to the Livingston charge that the three De Lanceyite city members had bet among themselves there would be no dissolution, the De Lanceys answered:

> It is acknowledged that some of the late three Members did lay Wagers, that the House would not be dissolved, and it is very true that a Dissolution *"was so far from being apprehended,"* that they regarded the many Threats which were then thrown out, calculated only to intimidate them from persisting in certain Measures, which some Persons supposed to be in the *Secrets* of the Court, asserted would infallibly bring on a Dissoluiton.—But that the three late Members could not be diverted from their steady Purpose by any such Threats hath been fully evinced by the whole Tenor of their Conduct.[28]

Once again the De Lanceys counted on the help of Isaac Sears and John Lamb. As in 1768 the De Lancey campaign appealed to the mechanics' pocketbooks. The "Leather Aprons" were reminded that they "never got Sixpence from riding Law-books, but many pounds of the Merchants." The merchants' contribution to the prosperity of the New York was stressed again and again. "Philio Patria," for example, declared:

> *Three* of these reputable Gentlemen, respectable not only on Account of their Families and independent fortunes, which ever ought in so important a choice, to be averted to; whose Actions have evidenced their warm Attachment to the Good and Welfare of the Community in general, and of this opulent *Commercial* City in particular; must appear in a conspicuous Light to every impartial and sensible Voter—*These*, I say, are

surely the most proper Persons to represent us, in the General Assembly. . . .[29]

This time, however, the Sons of Liberty were not united behind one ticket. John Morin Scott, defeated in the previous election, came out strongly for the Livingston-Presbyterian candidates and was supported by such prominent Liberty Boys as Alexander McDougall, Abraham Brasher, and Robert Murray. How many of the rank-and-file Liberty Boys joined Scott cannot be determined. On January 17 the Freemasons announced their support of the Livingstons, but it seems that a majority of the Sons of Liberty remained loyal to the Sears-De Lancey interest.

At Sears' direction, the anti-Sears group was bitterly attacked. The Livingston leadership, especially the old Triumvirate stalwart, John Morin Scott, bore the brunt of the attack. Scott was accused of condemning the protest against the Stamp Act. His professional standing and his character were also smeared. He was accused of being a homosexual: he "dances with, and *kisses (filthy beast!)* those of his own sex." Scott replied, "I am truly of revolutionary principles," and he in turn accused Sears of bribing voters. Thomas Smith, brother of William Smith, was said to have slandered the Irish voters: *"That they came into this Country upon Straws."* Philip Livingston was described by one opponent as "a Snake in the Grass," and by another as "a great Prerogative Man, and bound up within the Walls of the Fort." [30]

When the furor of the campaign ended in late January voters in New York City and the colony swept James De Lancey and his friends to power with a comfortable majority. The results, Peter Van Schaack wrote, were "what the Churchmen call a complete victory." The triumphant De Lanceys organized a victory parade:

The four Candidates who had the Majority of Votes in their Favour (three of whom had remarkably distinguished themselves in the late spirited Measures for supporting the Rights and Liberties of their Country, and the other Gentleman, who has always proved himself a steady Friend to its true Interest and Prosperity) were attended from the City-Hall, in a vast

Concourse of People, with Music playing, and Colours displayed; in this Manner the main Street to the Coffee-House, being repeatedly saluted with loud Huzzas, and with every other Demonstration of Joy, that could be shewn upon this happy and interesting Occasion.[31]

The election of 1769 was the crowning achievement of the public career of Captain James De Lancey. However, in less than a year after his election triumph, the ascendancy of the De Lancey faction was shattered. In the De Lancey collapse lay the foundations of New York's independence.

NOTES

1. Colden to the Lords of Trade, November 7, 1764, *The Colden Letter Books 1760-1775*, I, pp. 395-398.
2. Robert R. Livingston to ?, December 20, 1765, Livingston Papers, Bancroft Collection, pp. 41-43, New York Public Library.
3. Watts to John Napier, June 1, 1765; Watts to Moses Frank, June 1, 1765, *Letter Book of John Watts, Merchant and Councillor of New York, January 1, 1762-December 22, 1765. New York Historical Society Collections*, LXI (New York, 1928), p. 354. For a general discussion of the quartering issue, see John Shy, *Toward Lexington: The Role of the British Army in the Coming of the American Revolution* (Princeton, N.J., 1965), pp. 45-83.
4. Moore to Conway, June 20, 1766, *New York Colonial Documents*, VII, p. 831.
5. Smith, *Historical Memoirs*, I, p. 33.
6. Moore to Lords of Trade, November 15, 1766, *New York Colonial Documents*, VII, p. 878. For a first-class analysis, see Joseph A. Ernst, *Money and Politics in America 1755-1775: A Study in the Currency Act of 1764 and the Political Economy of Revolution* (Chapel Hill, N.C., 1973), pp. 108-109.
7. Shelburne to Moore, August 9, 1766, *New York Colonial Documents*, VII, p. 848.
8. Sackville to Sir John Irwin, February 13, 1767, Historical Manuscripts Commission. Report IX, Part III. *The Manuscripts of Mrs. Stopford-Sackville, of Drayton House, Northamptonshire*, 2 vols. (London, 1904-1910), I, p. 122.
9. Shelburne to Chatham, February 16, 1767, *The Correspondence of*

William Pitt, Earl of Chatham, 4 vols. (London, 1838-1840), III, pp. 206-207.

10. Watts to Robert Monckton, January 23, 1768, Chalmers Papers, II, p. 18, New York Public Library.

11. *New York Journal,* February 18, 25 and March 3, 1768.

12. Political card, Broadside Collection, New York Public Library.

13. *To the Worthy Freeholders and Freemen,* March 8, 1768, Broadside Collection, New York Public Library. It is not clear what appointment De Lancey may have rejected, but on January 20, 1769 the Captain turned down an appointment to the governor's Council, much to the surprise of the Livingstons. Council minutes, XXVI, p. 144, New York State Library.

14. *A Political Creed for the Day,* New York, 1768, Broadside Collection, New York Public Library.

15. Roger Champagne, "Family Politics versus Constitutional Principles: The New York Assembly Elections of 1768 and 1769," *William and Mary Quarterly,* 3d series, XX (January, 1963), pp. 67-68; Bonomi, *A Factious People,* pp. 243-244.

16. Colden to Hillsborough, April 25, 1768, *New York Colonial Documents,* VIII, p. 61; *New York Gazette, and Weekly Mercury,* March 14, 1768.

17. Smith, *Historical Memoirs,* I, p. 44.

18. Gage to Shelburne, June 28, 1768, *Thomas Gage Correspondence,* I, pp. 182-183.

19. Smith, *Historical Memoirs,* I, pp. 46-48.

20. The case of Lewis Morris sheds light on the extent of political democracy in colonial New York. The question at issue was whether freemen of the Borough of Westchester who were not also freeholders could vote in Assembly elections, as was the practice in the counties of New York and Albany. The De Lanceyites stated that the votes of the freemen were rejected "Because it appeared to be contrary to the usage of the borough, to admit freemen to vote in the choice of a burger," but Morris' supporters charged that the freemen's votes were disallowed only because they announced that they would vote for Morris. The freemen claimed a right to vote on the grounds that the election writs were directed to the freeholders and freemen of the Borough. In the Assembly, only Peter R. Livingston, Abraham Ten Broeck, George Clinton, Pierre Van Cortlandt, and Philip Schuyler supported the freemen, and on November 18 the House declared John De Lancey the winner by one vote. The charges of election irregularities were by no means one-sided. Joshua Bishop, who pos-

sessed the required £40 freehold and had always voted in the past, claimed Morris told him he could not vote after he declared his support for De Lancey. See *New York Assembly Journal*, October 29, November 9, 15, 17, 18, December 15, 1768; *New York Gazette, and Weekly Mercury*, March 7, 1768.

21. Smith, *Historical Memoirs*, I, pp. 46-48, 59-60. On the role of Philip Schuyler, see Don R. Gerlach, *Philip Schuyler and the American Revolution in New York, 1733-1775* (Lincoln, Neb., 1964), pp. 163-164.

22. *New York Gazette, and Weekly Mercury*, January 9, 1769.

23. Van Schaack to Henry Van Schaack, January 27, 1769, Henry C. Van Schaack, *The Life of Peter Van Schaack* (New York, 1842), pp. 10-11; Livingston to Oliver Wendall, January 19, 1769, Livingston Family Papers, Museum of the City of New York; Colden to William Johnson February 26, 1769, *Sir William Johnson Papers*, XII, p. 699; Richard Cartwright to Johnson, January 15, 1769, ibid., VI, p. 586.

24. *New York Gazette; or Weekly Post-Boy*, January 9, 1769; *Philip Livingston to the Freeholders and Freemen of the City and County of New York*, January 7, 1769, Broadside Collection, New York Public Library; Duane to Robert Livingston, Jr., June 1, 1969, Livingston-Redmond Papers, microfilm, reel 6.

25. "Honestus," *An Anecdote of a Certain Candidate* (New York, 1769), *New York Gazette, or Weekly Post-Boy*, January 9, 1769; *Reasons for the present Glorious Combination of the Dissenters in this City against the farther Encroachments and Strategems of the Episcopalians* (New York, 1769), New York Public Library; *New York Journal*, January 5, 1769; *Declaration of James De Lancey and Jacob Walton*, January 6, 1769; *John Cruger to the Freeholders and Freemen of the City and County of New York*, January 9, 1769, Broadside Collection, New York Historical Society; Affidavit of *George Harison, Anthony Rutgers, Jr., and R. Nassau Stevens*, January 6, 1769, Broadside Collection, New York Public Library.

26. Jay to Robert Livingston, Jr., January - 1769, Livingston Papers, Bancroft Collection, 19, New York Public Library; *New York Gazette, and Weekly Mercury*, January 16, 1769; Duane to Robert Livingston, Jr., June 1, 1769, Livingston-Redmond Papers, microfilm, reel 6.

27. *Reasons for the Present Glorious Combination of the Dissenters in this City. . .* , New York, 1769, Broadside Collection, New York Public Library; "The American Whig XLVI," *New York Gazette, or Weekly Post-Boy*, January 23, 1769; *Observations on the Reasons for the Malicious Combination of Several Presbyterian Dissenters*, New York, 1769; *The Old Dutchman to the Freeholders and Freemen of the City*

and County of New York, New York, 1769, *"Impartial," to the Dissenting Electors of all Denominations*, New York, 1769, Cruger, De Lancey, Jauncey, and Walton, *To the Freeholders and Freemen, of the City and County of New York*, January 9, 1769, *The Querist, Number 1*, New York, 1769, *The Freeholder, Number 1*, New York, 1769, Broadside Collection, New York Public Library; *An Answer to the Foolish Reason that Is Given for Re-choosing the Old Members*, New York, 1769, Broadside Collection, New York Historical Society.

28. *As a Scandalous Paper Appeared stiled An Answer to the foolish Reasons for Re-choosing the Old Members*, New York, 1769, Broadside Collection, New York Public Library.

29. *A Card*, New York, 1769, Broadside Collection, New York Public Library; *New York Gazette, and Weekly Mercury*, January 16, 1769.

30. *A Contrast*, New York, 1769, Broadside Collection, New York Public Library; *New York Journal*, April 19, 1769. The reference was to Fort George, the governor's official residence and the seat of government.

31. *New York Gazette, and Weekly Mercury*, February 6, 1769.

CHAPTER FOUR

The Great Betrayal, 1769-1770:
The De Lancey Collapse

The De Lanceys' collapse resulted from their stand on three issues: one, the exclusion from the Assembly of nonresident deputies and judges of the Supreme Court; two, the granting by the House in the fall of 1769 of £2000 for the support of English soldiers stationed in New York; and three, the decision of the merchants of New York City in July 1770 to end their boycott of British imports. James De Lancey's active support for these measures met strong resistance from the Sons of Liberty, who soon rejected his leadership in favor of a fresh rapprochement with the Livingstons, who joined the Liberty Boys' protest against the Assembly and the merchants. The breakup of the De Lancey-Sears alliance had the effect of casting the Captain and his supporters in the unfamiliar role of friends of government, from which position they were unable to recover leadership of the colony. Partisanship, ambition, and imperial politics—the factors that had promoted De Lancey's rise—now precipitated his fall and provided the Livingstons with an opportunity again to assume an ascendancy in New York's political affairs.

Of the three issues—which were closely related—the most important was the decision to provide money for the troops. However, to appreciate its significance it is necessary to consider all three in some detail.

At the root of the De Lanceys' political difficulties lay a deteriorating economy which continued to go from bad to worse. The chief source of trouble was the money supply. Beginning in November 1768 the Treasury began the recall of all paper money in circulation, and the prospects for a new money issue were far from encouraging. The crisis which the recall would trigger had of course been anticipated. Governor Henry Moore had warned of the "Distresses" facing the colony, and correctly predicted that "Commerce here as well as the ordinary Services of Government must very shortly be exposed to great inconvenience." [1] By spring 1769 New York was in the throes of a major depression. "The declining Condition of Trade and the Scarsity of Money here," one Albany merchant reported, "is not to be Exprest if frugality and Industry do not increase I do not know what will be the Event." [2] Another merchant, James Beekman of New York, observed that many persons of "undoubted Estates" were unable to meet their debts.[3]

Adding to the problem was the continuing boycott of British imports. Since October 1, 1768 a nonimportation agreement had been in force. Its terms were strict. In effect nearly all trade with Europe was cut off, with resulting hardship on the entire community. By early 1769 business in New York was at a standstill. The merchants, whose businesses centered about the import trade, faced bankruptcy, while the seamen, artisans, and other laborers whose livelihoods depended on prosperity on the waterfront, looked to a bleak future of prolonged unemployment. Not surprisingly, the boycott became an issue of controversy. General Thomas Gage reported:

New York has kept up to the Agreement with the most punctuality, and is consequently the greatest Sufferer by it; Some rich Merchants have made Advantage, but the Traders in general are greatly hurt. Many testify their Dissatisfaction, and the Country People begin to complain of the dearness of the Commodities, they stand in Need of.[4]

New Yorkers might have borne their hardship with stoic resignation had they believed Americans in the other colonies were suffering with them, but such was far from being the case. The success of the policy of nonimportation at New York was in sharp contrast to the open disregard of the boycott at the ports of Philadelphia, Boston, and Newport. Adding insult to injury was the fact that merchants from these and other neighboring towns were taking advantage of New York's steadfastness, competing for a share of the New York market by supplying the imports New Yorkers were denying entry to. Philadelphia traders were particularly busy, disposing, General Gage reported, of "very large Quantities of Goods" throughout New York.

Understandably, merchants demanded the termination, or at least easing, of the nonimportation pact. The more radical leaders of the shopkeepers, mechanics, and artisans who had led the boycott campaign from its inception insisted, however, that so long as it was the "fixed determination" of Parliament to impose taxes on the colonies the continuation of the boycott was essential to the preservation of American liberty. The division between the merchants and mechanics was of fundamental importance. Less dependent for their livelihood on imports, the mechanics could perhaps more easily afford stubborn principles, but their sentiments were also probably genuinely sincere. The truth was that the imposition of the Townshend Duties had had the effect of significantly radicalizing the mechanics, an inclination toward which their dissenting religion and the boisterous style of popular politics may well have predisposed them.[5] Repeal of the Stamp Act had suggested, at least to those who ignored the Declaratory Act, a restoration of balance in the imperial system, a respect in Whitehall for American rights as the colonists understood them. But with the passage of the Townshend Duties, an enormous amount of trust, not to mention that vital sense of Anglo-American community upon which the empire in the final analysis rested, was destroyed. That the problem resulted from colonial self-deception about England's intentions was irrelevant. The militants hesitated to enter into fresh conciliatory measures. For the time being their views prevailed, and in March 1769 the mechanics persuaded the merchants to agree to the formation of a committee of inspection to enforce the suspension. The committee solved nothing. The merchants remained unhappy because the boycott was too strong; the mechanics worried that it was too weak. Both expected the De Lanceys to endorse their respective positions. If the De Lanceys were to retain their ascendancy in the Assembly and in the colony, they would have to find a way to reconcile the conflicting interests of their allies. As events unfolded it became evident that they were unequal to the task.

From the outset of the April 1769 session of the House of Assembly, the De Lanceys seemed curiously unwilling or unable to come to grips with the pressing problems which beset the colony. For the moment their first concern was with their own political security, to ensure which they determined to destroy the remaining Livingston forces in the Assembly. Their plan was twofold: to persuade the House to pass two pieces of legislation, the first excluding deputies who did not actually reside in the counties, towns, or manors they represented, the second disqualifying judges of the colonial Supreme Court from sitting in the Assembly. The former law would unseat Philip Livingston, who had been chosen to represent the Manor of Livingston following his defeat in New York City, and Colonel Lewis Morris, Jr., a Livingston ally returned for the Borough of Westchester. The latter law would effectively prevent the return to the Assembly of Judge Robert R. Livingston, the defeated candidate in Dutchess County, who had represented the county from 1759 to 1768.

For a long time the election of nonresident deputies in the Assembly had been a matter of dispute. The controversy illuminates some aspects of contemporary opinion about the role of class, economic, and regional interests in politics. Because the election of nonresident freeholders gave an undoubted advantage to wealthy families, who usually owned property in several counties, historians have often cited nonresidency as one example of the undemocratic way New York's aristocracy perpetuated its influence. The undemocratic features of nonresidency or the wealth of individual deputies failed, however, to arouse much if any opposition in the colony. Indeed, as extant election literature makes abundantly evident, contemporaries regarded an independent fortune as a mark in a candidate's favor. More important to the colonists, and the main cause of complaint, was the fact that most nonresidents had close ties with New York City. Country folk and their representatives complained that the growing numbers of nonresident deputies unfairly increased the influence of New York City in the Assembly. The Livingstons were particularly vulnerable on this point. Long accustomed to a decisive say in the politics of Livingston Manor, Dutchess County, Albany, and New York City, it is no exaggeration to argue that no family had benefited more from the absence of strictly enforced residency requirements than the Livingstons. Moreover, since the mid-1750s the most politically active Livingstons were all men closely associated in one way or another with the interests of New York City. By taking up the nonresidency question the De Lanceys could assure themselves of the firm support of the country deputies, and at the same time deal a sharp blow to the power and prestige of their great rivals.[6]

The assault on the Livingstons began in early April. Pro-De Lancey freeholders in the Borough of Westchester petitioned the House to disqualify Lewis Morris on the grounds that he failed to meet the residency requirements specified in the Election Law of 1699. A week after the petition was received, the De Lanceys moved for the exclusion of both Morris and Philip Livingston. A bitter debate ensued. Custom was on the side of Morris and Livingston, and eight deputies, led by Philip Schuyler, tried without success to block the exclusion motion, debate on which was postponed to the end of April. Meanwhile the Livingstons worked to rally support, charging that the exclusion motion was "vexacious and frivolous." [7] At the same time they moved to exploit a fundamental contradiction in the De Lanceys' position: namely, their willingness to allow nonresident voting. To allow nonresidents the vote but not the right to sit for their own freeholds was to adopt, the Livingstons asserted, the mischievous doctrine of virtual representation. Charles De Witt, representative for Ulster County, put the Livingstons' case most strongly. He argued before the House that "the Exclusion of a Member having a Freehold in the County or Place for which he is returned, from having a Seat in this House, on Account of his Non-Residence there, may draw into Question the Rights of Electors to the Choice of Representatives in Places where they do not Reside, and the Taxation of the Estates of such Persons will consequently strongly imply the Approbation of this House of the odious and dangerous Principle assumed by the enemies of the Colonies." De Witt therefore urged his colleagues to "avow their Abhorrence of the Principle of a virtual Representation asserted in England against the Colonies." But the De Lanceys blocked debate on the matter by moving the previous question, a device by which controversial issues could be set aside without a formal division.[8]

While debate on the Morris case continued, support for Philip Livingston was received in the form of a petition dated April 18 signed by the freeholders of Livingston Manor. Charging that the attack on Livingston "originated from party Spirit," they demanded Livingston's seating. For 53 years, they noted, the Manor had been represented by nonresidents except in three cases. The argument that possession of a freehold did not constitute a residency was, the petitioners asserted, "a Pernicious Doctrine . . . invented by the Enemies of *America* and manifestly tending to the Subversion of that most invaluable Privilege of not being taxed without our own Consent." [9]

Debate on nonresidency reached a climax on April 26. "Convince me," Philip Schuyler demanded, "that there is a just distinction between non-resident *electors* and *elected*. People out of doors will complain. They will censure this House when it is *no more* . . . they will stigmatize you, when they are not afraid of your resentment." Schuyler's outburst failed to impress the anti-Livingston country deputies. John De Noyelles, a De Lancey supporter and member for Orange County, told Schuyler "your speech is more calculated for the bye-standers than for any *information* to this House." De Noyelles continued:

A freehold should give a right of representation. Every man who has such an interest in the community as the law prescribes, should be entitled to vote[,] whether resident or not. From this no evil can result. But to admit non-resident representatives is pregnant with many evils. The landed interest in time will be disregarded and our boroughs, manors, &c, will be bought. This is the case in England. The city of London furnishes representatives for two thirds of the kingdom.[10]

The opponents of nonresidency carried the day. On May 12 the Assembly voted legislation excluding nonresidents, and the next day writs were issued for a new election in the Manor of Livingston. As late as May 18th, Philip Livingston was assuring friends that Moore would not sign the bill, but on May 20th the governor signed it into law, an action, Smith reported, which "staggered the Livingstons." Privately, Moore professed his friendship and confidence in the Livingstons. According to Smith, the governor claimed he was "forced" to consent to it, but he promised Peter Van Brugh Livingston that "he would get it damned in England." [11]

Attention now turned to the eligibility of judges to sit in the Assembly. The most likely successor to Philip Livingston as manor representative was Judge Robert R. Livingston. He was a veteran of ten years in the Assembly and a formidable politician who the De Lanceys were eager to get rid of. On May 17th, De Noyelles moved in the House for the exclusion of judges, on the grounds that judges were barred from sitting in the English House of Commons. Unlike the residency question, this motion produced neither debate nor discussion, but was immediately passed without controversy. On this note the Assembly adjourned.[12]

If the De Lancey position in the House seemed completely secure, their position outside was far from safe. Basically their problems came down to the poor state of New York's economy and the unrest which the continuing depression was producing. This deteriorating state of affairs favored the Livingstons, who, excluded from the Assembly, now formed a powerful natural center of opposition, drawing to it a number of dissident elements. This turn of events requires close scrutiny, as its effects on the coming of the Revolution in New York were to be profound.

Of particular significance was the renewed contact between the Livingstons and the popular leaders of the Sons of Liberty. The groundwork for a rapprochement was laid with the formation in February 1769 of the Society of Dissenters, the founders of which included two of the old Triumvirate, William Livingston and John

Morin Scott. Other members associated with either the Livingstons or the Sons of Liberty included Peter Van Brugh Livingston, Alexander McDougall, and Thomas Smith, William's brother. Formed to advance religious liberty and the interests of dissenters, this group revived the alliance between the Livingstons and the dissenters which had been the key to Livingston power in the 1750s.[13] At the same time the Livingstons came out strongly for a continuation of the nonimportation agreement. On April 10th, Philip Livingston, still a member of the Assembly, asked the House to record its thanks to the colony's merchants for their patriotic adherence to the suspension of trade. Two days later, again at Livingston's insistance, the Assembly repassed the controversial resolutions of December 31th, 1768 which had produced the dissolution of January 1769.

But the most important development in the evolution of the alliance between the Livingstons and the Sons of Liberty was the reuniting of the Liberty Boys under Livingston patronage. Easing the way to reunion, and an important boost to the radicals' morale, was the news of the passage of the so-called Virginia Resolves, a series of resolutions passed by the House of Burgesses in May, which supported nonimportation and denounced recent British policy, especially a Ministry proposal that Americans charged with political crimes be sent to England for trial. By June, plans to reunite the Liberty Boys were well advanced. Peter R. Livingston told correspondents that he and his friends planned soon to form a new organization to encourage the cause of American liberty, and in July the Livingstons and such erstwhile De Lanceyites as Sears and Lamb joined with the McDougall faction of the Sons of Liberty—which had always remained loyal to the Livingstons—to announce formation of the "United Sons Of Liberty." The rejuvenated Liberty Boys promised to drop "all Party Distinction that may have originated from a Difference in Sentiments in other Matters," and to support "by all legal means in our Power" the continuation of nonimportation.[14]

The alliance between the Livingstons and the Sons of Liberty was not the only significant political change in the colony, however. Equally important for the future was a new understanding between Cadwallader Colden and Captain James De Lancey. The death of Governor Henry Moore on September 11, 1769 put the administration of the colony once again in Colden's hands. The lieutenant governor's position was extremely weak. Hated on all sides, Colden undertook to form a connection with his old enemies, the De Lanceys. For their part, the De Lanceys were probably more ready to receive Colden, in view of their recent rebuff at the hands of the Liberty Boys. William Smith believed that the De Lanceys faced two contradictory and hence insoluble problems: the need to win back the Sons of Liberty while at the same time showing a proper regard for the authorities in England, whose power over the colony, in theory at least, was enormous. In a long passage, which is worth quoting at length, Smith presented a challenging, if not unbiased, interpretation of the motives of the two parties:

> The De Lancey Family . . . had so weeded the House as to be sure of a Majority for the purpose of humbling the Governor and yet as they dreaded the Indignation of the Crown, it was necessary to make Compliance to recover the Reputation they had lost to gain the Sons of Liberty on their side . . . To the Day of Sir Henry Moore's Death on the 11th of September 1769, there subsisted the most inveterate Animosity between the De Lanceys and Lieutenant Governor Colden. In an Instant of which those old Enemies became intimate Friends, and to conceal the conversion of the De Lanceys to the Lieutenant Governor it was given out that he himself had changed his Principles. The Truth is that he had no Regard for the Crown in his Attachment to the Prerogative nor they to the Liberties of the Country both moved as private Interest dictated and a Bargain was struck between them . . . The Contract was advantageous to both Parties. He had to look for a short Administration, and with them against him every thing to fear from the popular Abhorrence of a Man who had armed the Fort against the Town to preserve the Stamp Paper in 1765. The Sweets of Dominion and the Gratification of private Pique were their Aims, though it must be confessed that to regain Credit with the Crown they ran the risk of losing what they had with the People, yet it was hoped that before a Dissolution would take place their Faults would be forgotten

and intoxicated with the present State of their Interest they were willing to venture the dangerous Association of Interests with a most unpopular Governor.[15]

From Colden the De Lanceys extracted a promise to drive the Livingstons and their friends from the local colonial service. Within days of Moore's passing, the shakeup began, and Livingston men were systematically turned out of office. Philip Livingston, son of Peter Van Brugh Livingston, lost his job as private secretary to the governor to Colden's son, David Colden. Lewis Graham, a Livingston ally, lost the post of sheriff of Westchester County to James De Lancey. When Graham objected and produced petitions signed by 600 freeholders protesting the change, "he was told," Smith wrote, "that the People had no Right to interfere in such Appointments and that because they had he must be removed." Thomas Jones got the post of Recorder of New York City, an appointment that must have upset Colden as "not a Man in the Colony had been louder in his Clamours against Mr. Colden." Stephen De Lancey, eldest son of Peter De Lancey, was named Clerk of Albany, while another De Lancey man, Goldsbrow Banyar, was appointed Deputy Secretary of the colony. There was no exaggeration in Smith's remark that Colden's past "Friendship to the Livingstons was incompatible with the new Contract with the De Lanceys." [16]

Even more remarkable, in view of the past relations between the two, was the De Lancey effort to refurbish Cadwallader Colden's public image. Not surprisingly, the effort failed absolutely, though the fact that it was made at all is suggestive of the devastating impact the loss of the Liberty Boys' support had had on the De Lanceys. As Smith put it: "But all Scandal now ceased and upon the Presumption that every Man in the Colony had lost his Memory or that the De Lanceys possessed as uncontroulable an Influence over the People as a Scotch Lord over his Clan Mr. Colden was held up as an Object of Confidence and ready to promote the best Interests of the Country." [17]

Such were the circumstances that lay behind the political crisis of December 1769.

In that month the De Lanceys tried to force passage of a paper currency bill. The trouble lay in their tactics: They made a bargain with Lieutenant Governor Cadwallader Colden to grant the army the support it needed in return for Colden's signature on a bill to issue £120,000 local currency. To make sure Colden kept to his part of the deal, the De Lanceys stipulated that half the army grant would be paid from the paper emission. The De Lanceys probably thought they had struck a good political bargain. Since 1761 every Assembly had provided English troops stationed in New York with food and board, and the Livingstons had proposed a bill to issue paper money in the spring of 1769. Now, it was hoped, the army would get its money, the colony would get a badly needed currency, and, most important, Colden, who had violated specific instructions from Whitehall against signing any agreement relating to paper currency, would now be more or less dependent on the support of the Assembly. The deal could thus be viewed as another step in the rise of the Assembly, as another blow for American autonomy at the expense of the colony's traditional ties with England. Smith noted that the De Lanceys "to gain Popularity sacrificed poor Colden to the Resentment of the Sovereign." [18]

If New Yorkers had viewed the De Lancey-Colden deal in this light, the De Lanceys might well have found themselves once more regarded as heroes in the cause of American liberty. As it was, the deal, which was widely regarded as an act of the basest villainy, failed absolutely.

Two days after the Assembly granted the army money, a broadside, entitled *To the Betrayed Inhabitants of the City and Colony of New York,* and signed "A Son of Liberty," appeared on the streets of New York. Its author was Alexander McDougall. The paper, which must rank as one of the finest pieces of political propaganda produced in the revolutionary era, was a brilliant denunciation of the De Lanceys. McDougall's charge was simple. The De Lanceys, he said, had "betrayed the Liberties of the People" by "implicitly acknowledging the Authority that enacted the Revenue-Acts." McDougall called on the people to resist "the Minions of Tyranny and Despotism." [19]

The impact of the broadside was enormous, and its significance in the history of the revolutionary movement in New York can scarcely be exaggerated. With hindsight it is clear that the broadside confirmed the new alliance of the Livingstons and the Sons of Liberty and set in motion events that would within five years make that faction a revolutionary party. It is therefore necessary to consider *To the Betrayed Inhabitants* at some length.

To the Betrayed Inhabitants was important not only for what it said, but also for the language and style its author employed. In ways that are only clear with hindsight, McDougall brought together and exploited the colonists' deep-rooted fears about corruption in high places, the army's presence in America, and the ministry's intention to tax or regulate the colonies. McDougall owed much to the influence of the Livingston Triumvirate. Like *The Independent Reflector*, *To the Betrayed Inhabitants* subtly evoked an atmosphere of political corruption, of secret and sinister intrigues. McDougall's opening sentence set the mood of the entire piece. It read:

In a Day when the Minions of Tyranny and Despotism in the Mother Country, and the Colonies, are indefatigable in laying every Snare that their malevolent and corrupt Hearts can suggest, to enslave a free People, when this unfortunate Country has been striving under many Disadvantages for three Years past, to preserve their Freedom; which to an Englishman is as dear as his Life,—when the Merchants of this City and the Capital Towns on the Continent, have nobly and cheerfully sacrificed their private interest to the public Good, rather than to promote the Designs of the Enemies of our happy Constitution: It might justly be expected, that in this Day of Constitutional Light, the Representatives of this Colony would not be so hardy, nor be so lost to all sense of Duty to their Constituents . . . as to betray the Trust committed to them.[20]

What was the nature of the "betrayal"? The second sentence provided the answer. "This they have done in passing the Vote to give the Troops a Thousand Pounds out of any Monies that may be in the Treasury, and another Thousand out of the Money that may be issued, to be put out on Loan. . . ." [21]

McDougall then explained why the Assembly's action betrayed

the "common Cause of Liberty." "Our granting Money to the Troops," McDougall asserted, "is implicitly acknowledging the Authority that enacted the Revenue-Acts, and their being obligatory on us As these Acts were enacted for the express Purpose of taking Money out of our Pockets without our Consent. . . ." McDougall continued: "And what makes the Assembly's granting this Money the more grevious, is, that it goes to the Support of Troops kept here, not to protect, but to enslave us." If this was true, and McDougall confidently asserted that no one would disagree, then why had the measure been adopted? "Hence it follows," McDougall wrote, "that the Assembly have not been attentive to the Liberties of the Continent, nor to the Property of the good People of this Colony, in particular We must therefore attribute this Sacrifice of the public Interest to some corrupt Source." The guilty parties, McDougall stated, were Lieutenant Governor Cadwallader Colden and the De Lancey family. Their corruption sprang from their desire to rule the colony indefinitely. McDougall described their attitude this way: "Mr. Colden knows, from the Nature of Things, that he cannot have the least Prospect to be in Administration again; and therefore, that he may make Hay while the Sun shines, and get a full Salary from the Assembly, flatters the ignorant Members of it, with the Consideration of the Success of a Bill to emit a Paper Currency, when he and his artful Coadjutors must know, that it is only a snare to impose on the simple; for it will not obtain the Royal Assent." Of the De Lanceys, McDougall wrote: "The De Lancey Family knowing the Ascendency they have in the present House of Assembly, and how useful that Influence will be to their ambitious Designs, to manage a new Governor, have left no Stone upturned to prevent a dissolution. . . . the De Lancey Family, like true Politicians, altho' they were to all Appearance, at mortal Odds with Mr. Colden, and represented him in all Companies, as an enemy to his country; yet a Coalition is now formed in order to secure to them the Sovereign Lordship of this Colony." McDougall concluded that the people should rally to protest and "to prevent the Accomplishment of the Design of Tyrants." [22]

McDougall's challenge to the De Lanceys was one they could not ignore. Two days after publication, on December 19, the Assembly voted overwhelmingly for a motion proposed by James De

Lancey that declared the broadside "an infamous and scandalous libel." [23] Plans were quickly laid to prosecute the author of the piece for seditiously libelling the lieutenant governor and the Assembly.

Meanwhile, events were rapidly developing that would shortly render prosecution futile. The broadside brought to a head a long-smouldering quarrel between soldiers and civilians in the city. Ever since the passage of the Quartering Act of 1765 tensions between the two had been running high. Too much drink, too few women, an unlucky turn at cards were familiar sources of trouble, but with the bitterness aroused by the Townshend measures and the discontent induced by the depressed state of the economy, tensions in early 1770 reached the boiling point. On January 17 British soldiers chopped down the local Liberty Pole, raised in 1766 to commemorate the repeal of the Stamp Act. Two days later Sons of Liberty and off-duty soldiers fought each other in an affair known as the "Battle of Golden Hill."[24] The behavior of the redcoats confirmed beyond doubt in the popular mind the apparent truth of McDougall's charges.

The weight of the Livingston faction was now fully behind McDougall. On February 8, the day McDougall was arrested for libel, the first number of a new series of pamphlets, *The Watchman*, made its appearance on the streets of New York. They were largely the work of William Livingston. All shared a common theme: a defense of liberty of the press combined with a bitter attack on Colden and De Lancey. Much of *The Watchman* was clever bombast, but the first number spelled out a simple political truth which the De Lanceys and their friends seemed unwilling or unable to grasp: "In a day when the American pulse beats very high for liberty; when it is the theme of almost every public paper; it might justly be expected, that no American assembly would be so hardy as to violate the rights of their constitutents." [25] In other words, politically, prosecution of McDougall was now a practical impossibility.

In the Council Livingston influence was also asserting itself. William Smith was the key figure. At a meeting of the Council in February he artfully implied his support for bringing charges against McDougall. "I told them" he confided to his diary, "the Path was plain if they chose to prosecute—That the Paper was a

Libel." This was a trap, and Colden and the De Lanceys were only too ready to fall into it. A month later Smith was anonymously writing in a New York newspaper:

> I rejoice at the Attack upon Captain McDougall. Whatever was the Design of your old Lieutenant Governor and his Adherents in stirring up a Prosecution against that gallant Son of Liberty it will rather advance than injure the grand Cause of America. The Stroke meant at him will prove to be a fatal one to the Mutiny Act for a Spirit of Jealousy and Enquiry is gone forth and no future wheedling to procure fresh Compliances with that Statute will succeed. Before this Alarm our Zeal for Liberty began to Languish, Uniformity of Sentiment induced a degree of Stupidity and as every Man trusted to the Vigilance of his Neighbour we were all composing ourselves for a Nap of Security. There was a Necessity for fresh Oil to quicken that expiring Lamp, and let the Minstry restrain their Gratitude if they please, certainly we should be forward in a sort of Thanks to Mr. Colden and the Politicians of his Train. They have done a good Service to the Continent in sending a Son of Liberty to Jail, and I hope they will increase the Obligation by bringing him to Trial.[26]

From the public response it was clear that further prosecution of McDougall would be politically unwise. In July 1770, just as McDougall's case was about to come before the courts, fate gave the De Lanceys a possible way out of their difficulties. James Parker, printer of McDougall's broadside, died. As McDougall had steadfastly refused to incriminate himself, it was now inevitable that the Crown would lose its case, for, without Parker, McDougall's authorship could not be proved. The De Lanceys could have dropped the matter without loss of face. Maybe, with luck, the affair might have soon been forgotten. But the De Lanceys threw away their last chance to retreat. Toward the end of the year, the Assembly resumed the attack on McDougall. He was again arrested. Interrogation and a citation for contempt of the Assembly followed. McDougall was sent to jail, where he remained until April 1771.

The third factor in the De Lanceys' downfall was the decision of the New York merchants in July 1770 to resume trade with England, which followed the news received in April that Parliament intended to repeal most of the Townshend Duties except the small tax of threepence per pound on tea, and to permit New York to issue paper currency worth £120,000.[27] Reactions to the news were mixed, and its effects were bitterly divisive. The merchants were understandably pleased, but the Sons of Liberty and their supporters were furious at what they viewed as a surrender of principle. The arrival in New York on May 10 of the Boston merchant, Nathaniel Rogers, reportedly a leading proponent of trade resumption, provided an excuse for some positive action. Convinced that Rogers' visit was undertaken "to poison the minds of the merchants here, and influence them, if possible, to break the non-importation agreement," the Sons of Liberty launched a broadside attack against the merchant "Dons." It was nonsense, the Liberty Boys declared, to suppose that nonimportation was an issue of concern to the merchants alone: "Spurn at the assuming Upstart who dares to assert that in a Question of such universal Concern, none but the Merchants have a Right to decide." On the night of May 10 a crowd of some 4000 burned an effigy of Rogers "amidst the acclamations of the people." Rogers could take a hint: On May 11 he "ordered his carriage out at 2 o'clock this morning, and immediately decamped for Boston."[28]

The Rogers incident gave the merchants pause to think. For the moment they postponed further direct action, announcing on May 18 a decision to defer resumption of trade pending confirmation of the repeal of the Townshend Duties. But as the Sons of Liberty recognized only too well, deferral meant little, especially in the face of news that merchants in other American coastal towns were rapidly moving to reestablish their English contacts.[29]

Maneuvering by both sides was frantic and not a little desperate, clearly revealing the rift that had come between the erstwhile allies. At the end of May the Liberty Boys staged a public rally, there solemnly vowing: "We will, to the utmost of our power, by all legal means, preserve the non-importation agreement inviolate in this city and colony . . . we will not buy any goods from any person or persons, who shall transgress that salutary agreement; and . . . we will use our utmost influence to prevent others from purchasing goods from them." [30] This statement drew an immediate and angry reply from the merchants. On May 31, the day after the rally, the membership of the merchant-dominated Committee of Inspection, formed in March 1769 to police nonimportation, resigned, charging the Liberty Boys with interference "on a Matter settled the Evening before to the intire Satisfaction of the Persons chosen for that Purpose." [31] The matter in question was, of course, the reopening of trade, and the Sons of Liberty were being told bluntly not to interfere. The merchants promptly reelected the Committee.

A precise account of the events of the next few days cannot be given with any certainty, but it is evident that the Committee regarded its reelection as a mandate to proceed with plans to reestablish trade. Accordingly, letters were dispatched to Boston, Philadelphia, and other neighboring towns, proposing a meeting of merchants to discuss the termination of the nonimportation agreement. Meanwhile, merchants in other cities, notably Philadelphia, had lost some of their previous enthusiasm for a resumption, with the result that the proposal was generally rejected.

This negative response seems to have caught the New Yorkers by surprise. Their earlier arrogance somewhat blunted, they proceeded with greater caution. At a meeting on June 11 the merchants resolved to conduct a poll among themselves to gauge support for a reopening of trade. Responses were sought to two questions: "Do you approve of a general importation of goods from Great Britain except teas and any other articles which are or may be subject to an importation duty? Or do you approve of our nonimportation agreement continuing in the manner it now is?" The poll began June 12, 1770.[32]

Not surprisingly, in view of the state of the economy, the poll resulted in a decisive triumph for the advocates of resumption. Angry speeches by the leaders of the Sons of Liberty and dire warnings by the radicals that the poll should be ignored "till a general Determination upon this Matter" counted for little, especially among the unemployed. Few doubted that the pocketbook argument carried the day. "It is," one merchant wrote, "for the interest of the city in particular, but not for the country in general, that we should import; and it is upon this principle, making proper allowances for party spirit, that I account for a majority of subscriptions in this city." Cadwallader Colden reported that support for the merchants ran to a total of 1180, among whom were numbered all the "principal Inhabitants"; 300 expressed no opinion; and, concluded Colden, "few of any distinction declared in the opposition." On June 14 two Liberty Boys on the Committee of Inspection, Isaac Sears and Peter Van Devoort, resigned from the Committee in protest against the merchants' actions.[33]

The Sons of Liberty made one last attempt to prevent the resumption of trade. At noon July 7 they and their supporters rallied outside the City Hall. Sears, McDougall, "and others of the same kidney" directed proceedings. The highlight was a speech by Isaac Sears, who reportedly "publicly declared if any Merchant, or number of Merchants presumed to break through the non-importation agreement till the several Provinces had agreed to do the same, he would lose his life in the attempt, or the goods imported should be burnt as soon as landed." Meanwhile, the merchants were assembled at the Merchants' Coffee House. Sensitive to the charge that "no private Set of Men" had the right to end the nonimportation agreement, the merchants voted to carry out a second poll of the city. This time nothing was left to chance. Bipartisan committees were hastily organized to canvass the wards. Colden wrote that "Persons on both sides of the question, were appointed to go from house to house." The results of this poll were like the first. Despite what Colden termed the "Riots, Clamour, and threats" of the Liberty Boys, New Yorkers once more overwhelmingly endorsed the reopening of trade. It was with the undoubted approbation of "a great majority" that the ship, the *Earl of Halifax*, set sail for England on July 11, her mail pouches bulging with orders.[34]

For the moment the merchants' victory seemed complete. They organized a grand victory parade, which was not without overtones of political symbolism. "De Lancey and Walton," McDougall reported, "headed the importers from the Coffee House." The Liberty Boys were temporarily in disrepute. "It is high time for us—my fellow citizens!" a writer in the *New York Gazette, and Weekly Mercury* declared, "to despise that fondness for *bawling out the word freedom, and sporting with liberty colours, liberty caps, and liberty poles, which no more become men than the tops, marbles, paper kites, and other playthings of children.*" Reflecting the public

mood was the fact, reported by Colden, that even those "who appeared most zealous to prevent the importation of British Manufac-
tures, have, notwithstanding, sent orders for large quantities of
goods." [35] But for the merchants there was a high price to pay:
Never again would the Sons of Liberty trust them. The alliance
upon which the De Lancey ascendancy had depended was forever
shattered.

It is tempting in reviewing the events that led to the De Lanceys' collapse and the Livingstons' resurgence to see yet another
variation in the familiar pattern of political struggle that had characterized New York public life since at least the 1750s. But something much more profound was involved in the upheaval of 1769
and 1770 than merely a contest between "ins" and "outs." The
McDougall controversy holds the key. While the events of 1769
and 1770 opened the way for an understanding between the Liberty Boys and the Livingstons, the McDougall affair—undoubtedly
the most significant event in New York political history from 1765
to 1776—and the reopening of trade also revealed underlying conflict between the new allies. This reflected the tension and contradiction between the inherent "radicalism" of the leaders of the
Sons of Liberty and the moderate whiggism of the Livingstons. The
Livingstons' enthusiasm for McDougall's cause suggests that they
did not perceive any serious division over either ideas or purpose
between themselves and their new friends, but the Sons of Liberty
certainly did. The critical point which the Liberty Boys recognized, and which was to shape significantly New York's response to
the coming of independence, was that McDougall's attack on the
De Lanceys was in large measure an attack on the whole of the
colony's elite, and a challenge to traditional customs of deference
and to accepted political practices. From this perspective McDougall's broadside *To the Betrayed Inhabitants* was quite unprecedented, and it was for this reason that it was so important. Quite
possibly, the De Lanceys perceived McDougall's challenge, and if
so, their prosecution of him in the face of incredible legal and
political obstacles was, from the point of view of their class, entirely justified. Any doubts about McDougall's intent were surely
dispelled by a second broadside which appeared the day after
McDougall's celebrated paper. Entitled *Union, Activity and Free-*

dom, or Division, Supineness and Slavery, it was probably the work of McDougall himself, or of John Lamb. This broadside followed up McDougall's earlier arguments against the army grant by asserting that the continued stationing of soldiers in New York unnecessarily strained the colony's meager resources by promoting useless "luxury." The writer called upon the population to assemble at the Liberty Pole to protest the Assembly's actions, and he issued this pointed direction to the aristocracy:

> As the Design of this Meeting is to get the free and unbiased Sentiments of the People, on this important Head, all such who are contending for Power, are desired to stay at Home, that the People be uninfluenced in their Deliberations; therefore the De Lanceys, the Livingstons, and Waltons, are hereby requested not to give the People any Uneasiness by their Appearance, least they should be insulted.[36]

Even more striking evidence of widespread dissatisfaction with elite-dominated politics was the move to introduce the secret ballot into provincial elections. The issue was not a new one, though there is little doubt that the McDougall affair gave it an urgency it had hitherto lacked. The challenge to the time-honored practice of voting *viva voce* began on December 22, 1769, five days after publication of *To the Betrayed Inhabitants*, when John Thomas, deputy for Westchester, introduced in the Assembly a bill to establish the secret ballot. The Sons of Liberty quickly rallied behind the cause of secrecy. At a public meeting called at the end of December by Sears, Lamb, McDougall, and other popular leaders a "vast majority" endorsed secret voting.[37]

Arguments by both sides were bitter. The demands for change were accompanied by an unprecedented outburst of class hostility. One writer, for example, complained of "bribery and Corruption . . . the most brutal Debauchery and Riot; and many of the poorer People having deeply felt the Aristocratic Power, or rather the intolerable Tyranny of the great and the opulent, who (such is the shocking Depravity of the Times, and their utter Contempt of all public Virtue and Patriotism) have openly threatened them with the Loss of their Employment, and to arrest them for Debt, unless they gave their Votes as they were directed." [38] Opponents of the measure denounced it as "a dangerous innovation, directly contrary to the old Laws and Customs of the Realm, and unknown in any royal British government." It was, they asserted, "a strange and new plea for an Englishman that he is afraid openly to declare his choice, altho' legally authorized to do so." [39] Both sides met on January 5, 1770. The opponents turned out in force, and to some frustrated Sons of Liberty it seemed that the full weight of New York's "Aristocratic Power" was set against them. One Liberty Boy later complained, with perhaps only a little exaggeration: "Here, the grand and the mighty, and the rich, and the long Whiggs and Squaretoes, and all Manner of Wickedness in high Places, had ranged themselves in Body compact and tremendous, hoping by the very Appearance of their Magnosities to over awe and intimidate." The meeting was a fiasco. Both sides accused each other of thwarting the popular will. Efforts to take a poll of those present failed, though the Sons of Liberty later stated that a majority of three to two favored the secret ballot. The end came on January 9, when the bill was narrowly defeated in the Assembly by a vote of 13 to 12, the deciding vote being the Speaker's.[40]

In a less obvious way, the reopening of trade had impressed on the minds of the leading Liberty Boys the gulf that existed between themselves and the colony's elite. As the secret ballot tended to draw the elite together—whatever their differences, they shared a common opinion about how society and the political system should operate—so too did the reopening of trade, from which the De Lanceys and Livingstons and their respective supporters all stood to gain. The result was a massive loss of trust, a breaking of those intimate ties and connections between men upon which deferential societies were based. "Imagine," wrote New York's disillusioned Sons of Liberty to their friends in Boston in August 1770, "how is our Grief and Indignation heightened when we find just Reason to suspect that those who pretended to be mighty Sticklers for the Rights of America are guilty of the vilest Collusion that any human creatures, instigated by the Devil, could devise." [41]

The events of 1769 and 1770 were of the utmost significance in the making of the Revolution in New York. The De Lanceys were now discredited, and though their support for the cause of American liberty had by no means waned, their future as loyalist supporters of the old order was to a great degree now determined. In reviewing the McDougall controversy and the De Lanceys' disastrous part in it, the question inevitably arises, why did the De Lanceys ally themselves to Colden in a project that was surely doomed to failure from the outset? There are no clear answers. Possibly McDougall's explanation, as contained in his famous broadside, was the correct one. Maybe the De Lanceys simply blundered, on the one hand, underestimating public contempt for Colden and, on the other hand, overestimating their own popularity and ability to make palatable a dubious political deal. A third possibility is less easily defended, though it merits consideration. It is that the De Lanceys' conduct reflected and anticipated what only later would be identified as the De Lancey's fundamental commitment to what has been termed "whig loyalism." The De Lanceys were certainly whiggish in their attitude to the questions of taxation and American political autonomy, but they were not basically hostile to the empire, to English institutions, or to those entrusted to exercise English power in the American colonies. When it seemed expedient to do so, as in the case of the army grant, or when confronted with a political crisis of the first magnitude, as in 1776, they naturally turned to the familiar agencies of the empire for aid and comfort.

The De Lancey setback did not immediately redound to the Livingstons' advantage. Their position and their future remained ambiguous. Among the Sons of Liberty the place of the Livingstons now seemed strong, though appearances were somewhat illusory. For their ideology the Liberty Boys owed the Livingstons a profound intellectual debt, but their acceptance of the inherent radicalism of the Triumvirate's ideas suggested the possibility of conflict between themselves and the Livingstons. McDougall's attack was not simply an assault on the De Lanceys; it also demonstrated how the Triumvirate's ideology could form the basis for a radical critique of the whole provincial elite. If the Livingstons were to have a decisive influence on future developments, they would first have to accept fully the implications of their own ideas and of the radicalism of McDougall and his friends.

NOTES

1. Moore to Shelburne, January 3, 1768, *New York Colonial Documents,* VIII, p. 1.
2. Gerrit Lansing to James Beekman, April 24, 1769, *The Beekman Mercantile Papers,* 3 vols., Philip L. White, ed. (New York, 1956), II, p. 973.
3. Beekman to Fludyer, Marsh, and Hudson, July 22, 1769, ibid., pp. 720-721.
4. Gage to Hillsborough, December 4, 1769, *Thomas Gage Correspondence,* I, p. 242.
5. This process of radicalization is admirably analyzed in Pauline Maier, *From Resistance to Revolution: Colonial Radicals and the Development of American Opposition to Britain, 1765-1776* (New York, 1972), especially chapter five. On New York, see Champagne, *Alexander McDougall,* pp. 11-26; Lee R. Boyer, "Lobster Backs, Liberty Boys, and Laborers in the Streets," *New York Historical Society Quarterly,* LVII (October 1973), pp. 281-308.
6. Smith, *Historical Memoirs,* I, p. 51.
7. *New York Assembly Journal,* April 12, 1769.
8. Lawrence H. Leder, "The New York Elections of 1769: An Assault on Privilege," *Mississippi Valley Historical Review,* XLIX (March, 1963), pp. 678-679.
9. Petition of the freeholders of Livingston Manor, April 18, 1769, *New York Assembly Journal,* May 12, 1769.
10. Reported in Peter Van Schaack to Henry Van Schaack, May 14, 1769, Henry C. Van Schaack, Memoirs of the Life of Henry Van Schaack, MSS copy, pp. 39-40, New York Historical Society.
11. Smith, *Historical Memoirs,* I, p. 52; Albert E. McKinley, *The Suffrage Franchise in the Thirteen English Colonies in America* (Philadelphia, 1905), p. 216, note 2; *The Colonial Laws of New York from the Year 1664 to the Revolution,* 5 vols. (Albany, N.Y., 1894), V, pp. 1094-1096; *New York Assembly Journal,* May 18, 1769.
12. Ibid., May 17, 1769. At the same time the De Lanceys also spread the rumor that they planned to challenge the right of Livingston Manor to separate representation in the Assembly. See James Duane to Robert Livingston, Jr., May 17 and June 1, 1769, Livingston-Redmond Papers, microfilm, reel 6, New York Historical Society.
13. Herbert L. Osgood, ed., "The Society of Dissenters founded at New

York in 1769," *American Historical Review*, VI (April, 1901), pp. 498-507.

14. *Resolves of the United Sons of Liberty*, July 7, 1769, Broadside Collection, New York Public Library; Peter R. Livingston to Robert Livingston, Jr., June 15, 1769, Livingston-Redmond Papers, microfilm, reel 6, New York Historical Society; Philip Davidson, *Propaganda and the American Revolution, 1763-1883* (Chapel Hill, N.C., 1941), pp. 75-76.

15. Smith, *Historical Memoirs*, I, p. 67.

16. Ibid.

17. Ibid., p. 68.

18. Ibid., p. 96. Colden, of course, vigorously defended his part in the deal. He told Hillsborough in a letter of January 6, 1770 "that the Bill for supplying the Troops, was carried by a very small majority, and it could not have been carried, had I not given the Friends of Administration expectations that I would assent to the Bill for emitting Bills of Credit." *New York Colonial Documents*, VIII, p. 199.

19. The broadside is printed in Jones, *History of New York*, I, pp. 426-430. It was dated December 16, 1769.

20. Ibid., pp. 426-427.

21. Ibid., p. 427.

22. Ibid., pp. 427-430.

23. Smith, *Historical Memoirs*, I, p. 72. An excellent, detailed account of McDougall's trial is Champagne, *Alexander McDougall*, pp. 27-40.

24. Boyer, "Lobster Backs," pp. 291-292.

25. *The Watchman*, I, February 8, 1770.

26. Smith, *Historical Memoirs*, I, pp. 73, 76. Though he rejected Smith's conclusions, the De Lanceyite, Thomas Jones, interestingly shared Smith's view of the importance of McDougall. Jones did not, however, accept the argument that McDougall was a sufferer in the cause of colonial liberty. As Jones saw matters, the public outcry over McDougall only proved the ridiculousness of the Liberty Boys. See Jones, *History of New York*, I, pp. 27-28.

27. On the paper question see Ernst, *Money and Politics*, pp. 277-280.

28. McDougall Notebook May-July 1770, McDougall Papers, Box 1, New York Historical Society; James Rivington to Sir William Johnson, May 15, 1770, *Sir William-Johnson Papers*, VII, p. 671; Sons of Liberty to Philadelphia Sons of Liberty, May 11, 1770, in Leake, *Memoir of the Life and Times of General John Lamb*, p. 64; *To the Free and Loyal Inhabitants*, May 10, 1770, Broadside Collection, New York Public Library.

29. McDougall Notebook, May-July 1770, McDougall Papers, Box 1, New York Historical Society; *New York Gazette, or Weekly Post-Boy,* May 21, 1770.

30. Resolves, May 30, 1770, Lamb Papers, Box 1, New York Historical Society. The resolutions are printed in Leake, *Memoir of the Life and Times of General John Lamb,* pp. 56-57.

31. *Advertisement,* May 31, 1770, Broadside Collection, New York Public Library; McDougall Notebook, May-July, 1770, McDougall Papers, Box 1, New York Historical Society.

32. Ibid.; *New York Gazette, and Weekly Mercury,* June 18, 1770. Becker, *A History of Political Parties,* p. 90.

33. Colden to Hillsborough, July 7, 1770, *New York Colonial Documents,* VIII, p. 217; *Advertisement,* June 12, 1770, Broadside Collection, New York Public Library; *New York Gazette, and Weekly Mercury,* June 18, 1770; Egbert Benson to Peter Van Schaack, June 21, 1770. Henry C. Van Schaack, *Life of Peter Van Schaack.* (New York, 1842), pp. 12-13.

34. McDougall Notebook, May-July 1770, McDougall Papers, Box 1, New York Historical Society; Colden to Hillsborough, July 10, 1770, and Alexander Colden to Anthony Todd, July 11, 1770, *New York Colonial Documents,* VIII, pp. 218-220; *Advertisement By Order of a Number of Inhabitants,* July 7, 1770, Broadside Collection, New York Public Library.

35. *New York Gazette, and Weekly Mercury,* August 18, 1770; Colden to Hillsborough, August 18, 1770, *New York Colonial Documents,* VIII, p. 245; McDougall to Joseph Reed, November 21, 1770, Joseph Reed Papers, II, New York Historical Society.

36. *Union, Activity and Freedom, or Division, Supineness and Slavery,* December 18, 1769, Broadside Collection New York Historical Society.

37. *New York Gazette, or Weekly Post-Boy,* January 1, 1770; *New York Journal,* January 4, 1770; *To the Public,* December 28, 1769; *To the Freeholders and Freemen,* January 4, 1770, Broadside Collection, New York Public Library.

38. *New York Journal,* January 11, 1770.

39. *To the Independent Freeholders and Freemen,* January 11, 1770, Broadside Collection, New York Historical Society.

40. *New York Gazette, or Weekly Post-Boy,* January 8, 1770; *New York Assembly Journal,* January 9. 1770.

41. New York Inspectors to the Trade of the Town of Boston, August 6, 1770, Samuel Adams Papers, Box 1, New York Public Library.

CHAPTER FIVE

Our Domestic Parties Will Die: Making Radicals, 1770-1774

The events of 1769 and 1770 formed a watershed in the political history of New York, dividing its colonial past from its independent and republican future. Nothing indicated the change that was taking place more clearly than the old rivalry of the Livingstons and De Lanceys, on the one hand, and the emergence of Alexander McDougall, on the other. The former symbolized the politics of New York's colonial era, the latter the thrust toward independence. Increasingly from 1770 to 1774 the old rivalry between the Livingstons and the De Lanceys was superseded by a new and more significant rivalry between the De Lanceys, the Livingstons, and the radical popular leaders. By 1774 the De Lanceys were effectively isolated from the colony's political mainstream; the Livingstons meanwhile moved steadily ever closer to the radicals. In short, the years from 1770 to 1774 comprised the crucial period of transition from colonial to independent status, during which the foundations for revolution were laid.

Although the months following the reopening of the English trade were free of the turmoil that had marked the recent past, the "domestick tranquillity" which General Thomas Gage reported was very deceptive.[1] A general malaise, not to say a good deal of unrest, prevailed, and, as previously, continuing economic problems were at the root of it. The lifting of the trading suspension had not had the salutary effects on the economy which the advocates of resumption had predicted. Quite the reverse. The slump continued, with no sign that conditions would soon improve. Optimistic merchants continued to import heavily, taking advantage of generous credit arrangements offered by their British suppliers, but, far from ameliorating the situation, the large volume of imports drove prices even lower. By November 1772 knowledgeable observers had concluded that imports were no longer a paying proposition. Cutthroat competition and price-cutting resulted. James Beekman reported that many desperate merchants found themselves "obliged to sell at any rate" to avoid imprisonment for debt.[2] For those with money to spend, the slump had its brighter side.

Politically, the outlook was equally uncertain. The shock waves of the McDougall controversy continued to be felt, though the political future of the colony remained unclear. On the one hand, the De Lanceys' position outside the Assembly had steadily eroded, yet, on the other, it was far from certain who would replace them as popular leaders. There was some evidence of growing Livingston strength. The continued exclusion of Judge Robert R. Livingston from the House of Assembly kept alive the partisan issues of 1769 and 1770 to the detriment of the De Lancey interest: Judge Livingston himself reported that growing numbers of people in New York City, and the counties of Queens, Suffolk, and Dutchess were now persuaded that he had been "ill-used." [3] The old quarrel was exacerbated by a fresh struggle to win favor with New York's newly appointed governor, William Tryon, who assumed his duties in the summer of 1771. The De Lanceys tried to maneuver Tryon much as they had Colden, though this time without success. In January 1773 they proposed a new paper money bill worth £120,000, ostensibly to counteract widespread counterfeiting. The Livingstons feared a De Lancey trap, however, and moved smartly to save Tryon from Colden's error by advancing a scheme to affix special stamps to all bills in circulation. What made this suggestion all the more attractive was that it would not only put the counterfeiters out of business, but also effectively extend the currency supply, without violating either parliamentary statute or the king's instructions. The Assembly seized upon the Livingstons' proposal "to the Disgrace of the De Lancey Interest," William Smith wrote.[4]

Even more indicative of the De Lanceys' declining prestige and influence than their failure to befriend or intimidate the governor was their failure to keep the support of the merchants. The break between the two occurred early in 1773, when the New York City merchants petitioned the Assembly to reduce the number of flour inspectors at the port of New York from two to one, a change that would bring New York into line with its principal competitor in the flour trade, Philadelphia. As well, by effectively reducing the enforcement of regulations governing the processing of flour, the New York product would become more competitive. The De Lanceys resisted any change, however. At the insistence of John Cruger, speaker of the House, the deputies voted to retain two inspectors. The merchants were furious. According to William Smith, "All the Coffee House was in an Uproar and an open Quarrel ensued." The merchants soon had a chance to retaliate. In the spring of 1773 city elections for aldermen were held, and, among others, the anti-De Lancey candidate, Benjamin Blaggs, was elected coroner in the De Lancey stronghold of the Montgomerie ward, "in Spite of all the Interest that could be made for William Walton," the De Lanceys' choice. Smith believed the lesson was obvious: "This taught both the Assembly and People without Doors that the old Despotism was broke." [5]

These issues were of only minor significance, however. For the moment New York drifted, caught between a crippled economy and a paralyzed political leadership. In England, meanwhile, events were unfolding that would abruptly end the drift, destroy the familiar pattern of politics, and set New York on a course toward revolution and independence.

The sudden collapse of a number of prominent banking houses in June 1772 triggered a panic which quickly spread through London financial and commercial circles. Caught in the middle of the crisis was the huge East India Company, which faced debts amounting to

£300,000 which the company's directors could not now repay. Though it ranked as one of the major business concerns of the realm, the recent financial history of the company was far from encouraging. Money problems had led to government intervention in the company's affairs in 1767 and 1769. The latest crisis again brought in the government, led since March 1770 by Lord North. In November 1772 the Ministry launched an extensive inquiry into the management of the company. The result was a loan to the directors worth nearly one and a half million pounds, extended on the understanding that the government would gradually take over the administration of the firm's territories in India.

East India directors meanwhile turned their attention to the matter of restoring the company's profitability. One recommendation urged the Ministry to permit the company, which hitherto had confined its activities to wholesale dealings with importers, to retail its surplus tea, currently amounting to about 18,000,000 pounds, directly in Europe. What made this scheme particularly attractive to the directors was the added suggestion that the government remit all customs duties on tea exported to the Continent. But this plan got a poor response from the company's European agents, with the result that in February the directors petitioned the Ministry to grant them the same privileges with respect to the American colonies. Thus amended, this request passed Parliament as the Tea Act of May 10, 1773.[6]

Given the enormous popularity of tea in the colonies, neither Parliament nor the company had reason to anticipate much opposition in America to the tea legislation. Initially, the only Americans who appeared to be seriously interested in it were the tea importers. They welcomed the measure and during the summer of 1773 scrambled for the lucrative East India agencies. By the fall, however, the situation had changed considerably, and it was clear that a major crisis was building. On the one hand, honest merchants and smugglers, whose operations were widespread and more or less respectable, began to realize that the tax concessions granted the East India Company would enable it to monopolize the tea business by charging prices even the smugglers could not match. On the other hand, Americans resented what they saw as a clever scheme to induce them to pay unconstitutional taxes. William

Smith caught the mood in New York perfectly. In mid-October he wrote in his diary:

> A New Flame is apparently kindling in America . . . we have Intelligence that the East India Company resolved to send Tea to America to be sold they paying the Duty on Importation . . . The Fact is that ever since the Duty of 3d per Pound had been laid, by the 7 George III, all Tea had been Smuggled from Holland, to the great Detriment of the India House. And now the Sons of Liberty and the Dutch Smugglers set up the Cry of Liberty. . . . I suppose we shall repeat all the Confusions of 1765 and 1766. Time will shew the Event. Our Domestic Parties will probably die, and be swallowed up in the general Opposition to the Parliamentary Project of raising the Arm of Government by Revenue Laws.[7]

Smith wrote with more truth than he could possibly have imagined. New York's old factions did die, and the result was revolution.

From the outset of the protest against the Tea Act, it was evident that the initiative in the campaign had passed for the first time to the militant leaders of the Sons of Liberty. The De Lanceys were not completely without influence; the Livingstons retained prestige and some authority, but not, as would become increasingly evident, as leaders so much as followers scrambling to find a place on the Sons of Liberty bandwagon.

In October the Livingstons backed resolutions drafted by the militants thanking the English shipmasters who had refused to carry East India tea to the colonies, and in November they joined in public demonstrations against the Tea Act. On November 5, Guy Fawkes Day, a mob gathered outside the Merchants' Coffee House. They burned an effigy of William Kelly, a New Yorker now resident in London and a partner of Abraham Lott, one of the East India Company's New York agents, who was supposed to have assured Lord North that Governor Tryon would "cram Tea down their Throats." But the most important development in the radicalizing of the population was the publication on November 29 of the *Association of the Sons of Liberty of New York*. This document, which formalized the alliance between the Livingstons and the radicals, called upon the public to boycott any importer of dutied tea. It asserted that "whoever shall aid or abet, or in any manner assist in the introduction of tea from any place whatsoever into this Colony, while it is subject by a British act of Parliament to the payment of a duty for the purpose of raising a revenue in America, he shall be deemed an enemy to the liberties of America." One effect of the *Association* was immediate: The day after its publication the New York East India agents—Abraham Lott, Henry White, and Benjamin Booth—resigned.[8]

The resignations brought the government into the controversy for the first time. It was a significant measure of the radicals' popular authority that the government did not for a moment question the assertion of quasi-legal powers contained in the *Association*. Governor Tryon's first concern was merely to avoid at all costs a repeat of the Stamp Act turmoil; that his caution was itself making some sort of extreme response inevitable was not yet evident.

The issue before the Council when it met December 1, 1773 was what should happen when the first tea ship arrived in New York. As there were now no consignees to receive the shipment, the government would have to act. But how?

It seems clear from Smith's report of the meeting that the Council still failed to grasp the gravity of this latest crisis. After some discussion, the Council agreed to provide the tea ship with a naval escort to guarantee its safe docking and to store the tea in the barracks at Fort George. Tryon thought the decision should be kept secret, but was persuaded by Smith to make it public. According to Smith, "Secrecy would create Jealousy, and bring a Mob together at the Landing; Whereas if our Advice was public, the People would be indifferent." [9]

Smith's comment remains something of a puzzle. Smith was not above a little intrigue, especially if he thought it would cast the De Lanceys in a bad light. Smith's opinion that the people would be "indifferent" to the storing of the tea, may have been an attempt to draw the De Lanceys into unpopular policies. If, however, Smith's advice was sincere, it may provide more evidence of the Livingston tendency, so often apparent in the past, to misunderstand or underestimate popular feelings about public issues.

Whatever the truth may have been, within a week it was abundantly clear that the radicals at least were far from indifferent and indeed were prepared to take extreme measures. Their attitude was apparently affected by a number of considerations. First was the arrival on December 10 of a letter addressed to Philip Livingston, Sears, and McDougall, informing the New Yorkers that the Boston town meeting had resolved to prevent the landing of any tea in that city. New York's Liberty Boys immediately made this policy their own, and a committee, which included Livingston, Sears, McDougall, the moderate merchant Isaac Low, and a few other radical leaders, David Van Horne and the brothers, Samuel and John Broome, told Smith to advise the governor "not to concern himself about the Tea." Second, and more important, was the radicals' fear that if the tea were landed, a thirsty populace would demand its distribution for retail. According to Smith, the Liberty Boys were worried because the *Association* was not attracting the support expected, and because tea was now in very short supply.

Smith was the radicals' key contact on the governor's Council, and they went to great lengths to impress on him their point of view. As Smith reported it, the radical argument went something as follows:

> The Inhabitants heard of the Governor's Intention to land and stow the Tea, and approved it as a good and moderate Measure. They suppose it was founded upon a Belief that it was his Duty to take Care of it. This was apprehended to be a Mistake. The Governors of Boston and Philadelphia and Admiral Montague conceive that Government have nothing to do with Merchants' Goods, if their Agents will not take Care of it. We think so too. The Inhabitants wish Mr. Tryon would not charge himself with it. If he does not go Home of Course. If he does not it will not be Safe. If we land it here they will elsewhere, and we can't be sure it will not be vended, and immense animosities may arise from it.

The meeting was critical for Smith and the Livingstons. It brought them for the first time face to face with militant men and radical policy, a confrontation that revealed both the gulf that had developed between the Livingstons and their more radical allies and the decline of Livingston influence among the popular leaders. Sears and McDougall objected strongly to Tryon's plan to store the tea, and talked vaguely of organizing 10,000 protesters to bring the port to a standstill. Their threats worried the now suspicious Smith. He urged moderation, especially as Tryon's intentions had not yet been made public. "I could not say," Smith recalled, "that I knew the People were, *at all Events,* averse to the Plan before published." If Sears or McDougall apprehended or perhaps knew that bloodshed would result from any attempt to land the tea, they should inform the governor, Smith thought. He warned the radicals not to push Tryon too hard. As the governor was about to return to England, it was certain that he would not risk his reputation with the home authorities by backing away from trouble. Livingston and Low readily agreed with Smith, "but Sears remained unaltered, and McDougall rather silent; except that he put the Question What if we prevent the Landing, and kill [the] Governor and all the Council. Philip Livingston started and said I won't think half so far." Well might Livingston be shocked, but his response was curiously ambiguous, and the radicals now moved quickly to take advantage of his uncertainty and the uncertainty and ambivalence of other moderates.[10]

The Liberty Boys wasted no time capitalizing on their momentum, announcing plans to hold a large public rally on the afternoon of December 17. This news prompted an emergency meeting of the governor's Council. The Council adopted a moderate posture; all agreed on the necessity of storing the tea. Smith urged Tryon to attend the meeting in person, a tactic, Smith believed, that would "insure a Vote for the Storing of the Tea." Oliver De Lancey and John Watts suggested that the entire Council attend. Finally the Council voted to send Whitehead Hicks, the mayor. Hicks was ordered to relay the governor's intention to protect the tea.[11]

The meeting, held one day after the Boston Tea Party, turned into a spectacular triumph for the radicals. When Hicks read out the governor's message, he was shouted down by "a general no! no!" Instead, the meeting was persuaded to approve the *Association* and to adopt the radicals' policy of resisting forcibly, if necessary, the landing of any East India tea in New York. What was really significant, however, was the fact that no formal vote was taken or called for. The Liberty Boys merely announced that a majority supported them, an assertion the crowd of some 3000, including the governor's representative, prominent members of the De Lancey and Livingston families, and members of the Council, accepted apparently without question. Smith found the conduct of the elite remarkable. The failure of the "Principal Inhabitants" to "exert themselves," Smith attributed to three causes: "(1) That some were fearful of the Populace (2) Some courting the People against Elections (3) That the De Lanceys rather fell in with the Multitude to save Interest, and out of Pique to the Governor who is too Independently Spirited for them." The importance of the elite's failure and of the radicals' success did not escape Smith's notice. "The Gentlemen," he concluded, "who came for the Call of the Question and did not call for it made an egregious Error for the Body of the Common People take their Presence to be a Countenance of the Vote, and thus Sears and McDougall and their Partisans gained an immense Advantage, of which I find they are very sensible." The next evening over drinks at Simmons' Tavern Smith rebuked Sears and McDougall for failing to take a proper poll, pointedly adding he doubted that they had a majority behind them:

> I rallied them upon their unfair State of the Question, and suggesting that I thought it owing to their Fears of not having a Majority they smiled, and expressed only very soft and jocular Negatives; and seemed to own that if they knew as now, that the Majority was so great, they would have had the Credit of a Division upon the Question, are you for opposing or for storing? and got the Yeas and Nays to separate in two Bodies to expose the Weakness of those who are for Storing the Tea.[12]

Comments of other observers indicate, however, that support for the radicals' position may have been greater than either Smith or the Liberty Boys believed. Governor Tryon, for example, thought that the *Association* of November 29 was "universally approved by all the better sort of inhabitants," and the appearance on December 20 of a moderate petition probably inspired by the De Lanceys, and signed by two future loyalist merchants, Jacob Walton and

Isaac Low, suggests that Tryon's judgment may well have been true. Was it "the general sense" of the *Association,* the petition asked, "that the landing or storing of the said tea should be opposed by force?" Moderation was urged, though it was nevertheless stated "That we do concur with the parties to the association, that the said tea ought not, on any account, to be suffered to be sold or purchased while it remains subject to a duty imposed by the authority of Parliament, for the purpose of an American Revenue." The petition concluded that "we do not conceive it necessary or expedient to hazard the peace of the city, by opposing the landing or storing the said tea with force." The petition attracted little, if any, support. "Brutus," writing in the *New York Gazetteer,* reported that "the general sense of the citizens ran . . . much against the last resolve." Historians have generally regarded the document's strictures against the use of violence as indicative of an increasing "conservative" reaction against the drift of radical policy. For example, New York's most distinguished historian, Carl Becker, argued that "the failure [of the petition] at least served to define the position of the radicals: if force was found necessary, force would be used." The view that the petition was "conservative" rests essentially upon an analysis of its final point. Viewed in its entirety, the petition was far from being moderate; certainly it did not either directly or indirectly rule out the use of force. Quite the reverse. Far from being a last desperate stand of New York's conservatives, it was, within the context of the times, strong evidence of the radicalization of all sectors of the community.[13]

News of the Boston Tea Party reached New York December 21. "The Boston News astonished the Town," Smith reported, but it was not until April 1774 that New Yorkers had a chance to have a tea party of their own. After the drama in Boston the New York affair was decidedly anticlimactic. It began on April 18 when word arrived from Philadelphia that Captain James Chambers had departed London for New York with 18 chests of tea. This intelligence was initially treated with a good deal of skepticism. Chambers was held in high esteem in New York; he had been "one of the first" to refuse publicly to carry East India tea to America. As a result, many New Yorkers "supposed it to have been shipped by some Ministerial tool, under another denomination, in order to injure the owners, or the reputation of the master, or to make an experiment of this mode of introducing the teas to America." Nevertheless, the colonists made it clear that they were "determined to examine into the matter with great vigilance."

Word of Chambers' sailing coincided with the arrival of another tea ship, the *Nancy*, commanded by Captain Benjamin Lockyer. Lockyer was told he could repair his ship, which had suffered extensive damage in a stormy crossing, and take on fresh supplies, but he was warned not to attempt to land his tea or to "go near the customhouse." Lockyer was agreeable to this arrangement, and a committee of inspection was dispatched to watch over the ship until her departure, Saturday, April 23.

Chambers dropped anchor off Sandy Hook in the Lower Bay the following Friday. He denied he was carrying tea, which appeared to be confirmed by a close examination of the cargo manifest. Accordingly, Chambers was allowed to proceed up the Narrows into the harbor, where he docked at Murray's wharf at the foot of Wall Street. Chambers was now subjected to a second interrogation "by a great number of citizens" who admonished that he "had better be open and candid" about his cargo. An unnerved Chambers reluctantly admitted to carrying 18 tea chests of which he himself was the owner. "After the most mature deliberation" the Committee of Inspection informed the large crowd assembled at the wharf of Chambers' perfidy. With the example of Boston before them, the Liberty Boys acted promptly:

> The *Mohawks* were prepared to do their duty at a proper hour; but the body of the people were so impatient that before it arrived a number of them entered the ship, about 8 p.m., took out the tea, which was at hand, broke the cases, and started their contents into the river, without doing any damage to the ship or cargo. Several persons of reputation were placed below to keep tally, and about the companion to prevent ill-disposed persons from going below the deck.

On Saturday morning Lockyer and Chambers set sail for England. New York celebrated their departure. Church bells rang out, cannon boomed, the colonists cheered. "Thus, to the great mor-

itification of the secret and open enemies of America, and to the joy
of all the friends of liberty and human nature," declared a jubilant
New York Gazette, and Weekly Mercury, "the union of these Colonies is maintained in a contest of the utmost importance to their
safety and felicity." [14]

The bravado was short-lived, however. The tea had scarcely had
time to settle on the harbor's muddy bottom when New York was
rocked by a new crisis more serious than any since the Stamp Act.
On May 12 New Yorkers learned the first stage of the price Boston
was to pay for the Tea Party: Parliament closed the port of Boston
to imperial shipping and the king appointed General Thomas Gage
governor of Massachusetts.[15] "This intelligence," Alexander Mc-
Dougall wrote, "was received with Great Abborrance by the Sons
of Freedom." [16]

News of the Boston Port Act had significant, and by no means
predictable, effects on New York politics. For one thing, it advanced considerably the process of the radicalization of public
opinion. Related to this, was the fact that the Port Act temporarily
reunited the colony's political leadership—for the first and last time
since 1765. This new unity, and the parallels between this and the
Stamp Act crisis, for a brief moment provided the De Lanceys with
their last chance to influence once again the course of affairs in
New York, and they made the most of their opportunity. It will not
do, however, to be too cynical about the De Lanceys' motives. The
truth is that the De Lanceys were as alarmed by the implications of
the Port Act as anyone in the colony. In this fact lies the real
significance of the Port Act: It united New York, and in so doing
created conditions which made revolution a certainty.

Expressions of alarm at the turn of events came from every quarter. Oliver De Lancey dramatically declared that he "would rather
spend every shilling of his Fortune than that the Boston Port Bill
should be compiled with." To be sure, this was curious sacrifice, the
value of which to the colonial cause was far from clear, but it was
no doubt genuinely meant. More to the point, William Smith noted
that "we shall lose all that attachment we once had to so great a
Degree for the Parent Country." [17]

The rank and file of the Liberty Boys—the mechanics, artisans,
and shopkeepers—immediately called for a resumption of the trad-

ing boycott against England, but the suggestion met sharp resistance from the big importers. The Sons of Liberty therefore altered their tactics: Isaac Sears announced that an open meeting would be held on Monday, May 16, at Fraunces Tavern to discuss nonimportation, the setting up of a committee of correspondence to communicate with other colonies, and the convening of a general congress of the Thirteen Colonies. At the same time, however, Sears and McDougall wrote privately to Boston May 15 to assure Sam Adams and his friends that New York would back any trade boycott adopted by the other colonies. New York's future, it seemed, had already been decided.[18]

Still, no chances were taken that matters might go awry. In particular, the radicals were at pains to avoid a repeat of the accusation that they had manipulated a meeting for their own ends. McDougall was assigned the job of publicizing the meeting, in order to "prevent any charge of design or chicane." On the morning of the sixteenth he posted two notices in the Merchants' Coffee House inviting the Sons of Liberty to assemble that evening to consider "the expediency of a non-importation agreement" and the setting up of an "impartial" committee of correspondence.

The meeting stirred more interest than probably the Liberty Boys had bargained for. After a period of public silence and inactivity, the De Lanceys turned out in force, skillfully mustering impressive support among the merchants. A worried McDougall made this not unbiased assessment: "the De Lancey Faction, although the advertisements were to the Merchants only, were at great Pains all the Day to collect every tool who was under their influence as well as those in Trade as out of it." Among the De Lanceyites who attended were Oliver and John De Lancey, Isaac Low, Roger Morris, and "all the Waltons." Morris was a retired army officer who had become a wealthy landowner in Dutchess County through marriage into the Philipse family; the others were New York City merchants. The large turnout overflowed the Merchants' Coffee House, necessitating an adjournment to the Exchange at the foot of Broad Street.

The De Lanceys succeeded in dominating the proceedings, with the result that the radicals' momentum was for the moment blunted. A decision on nonimportation was postponed, pending a poll of the people to ascertain the extent of popular support for a boycott. More important, a committee of correspondence was nominated on which De Lancey men were in a majority. On the issue of the size and composition of the committee, order broke down completely. The radicals asserted that "the majority" favored the creation of a small committee numbering 25 members at most, but the De Lanceys proposed one of 50, 15 of whom would make up a quorum. If McDougall is to be believed, the figure of 15 was misunderstood, much to the De Lanceys' advantage. Amid shouting and a confusing show of hands the committee of 50 was chosen, but only, McDougall reported, because many who voted for it did so in the mistaken belief that they were voting for a committee of 15, which was, of course, in line with radical policy. In the end the Liberty Boys secured about 14 places on the committee. More radical popular leaders like John Lamb were excluded, despite McDougall's contention that he had the votes of "a vast majority of impartial persons." [19]

As the Sons of Liberty recognized all too clearly, the significance of the meeting lay in the obvious reassertion of De Lancey influence. Particularly alarming to the Liberty Boys was the continuing evidence of De Lancey support among the mechanics, whose support the radicals had to have. McDougall saw the conduct of the De Lanceys this way:

> The whole of the Business of this meeting so far as the De Lanceys had any agency in it, Evidenced, a design to get such a [committee] nominated as would be under their direction, with a view to gain credit with people if any thing was done to advance the Liberty cause, or to prevent any thing be done in which case they would make a merit of it with administration, to procure places for themselves and their children.

William Smith's assessment echoed McDougall's. Smith wrote: "Two motives give rise to so large a Committee (1) Many People of Property dread the Violence of the lower Sort and a small Number (2) the De Lanceys urged their Friends to attend and pushed them in to mix with the Liberty Boys, as well to drown the latter as to gain their confidence again lost in the late Party Struggles." [20]

McDougall and Smith exaggerated the De Lancey threat. The

De Lanceys had hardly won a victory—not yet, anyway. The nominees elected by the meeting still had to be approved by the colonists at large, and approval was by no means certain. On May 17 advertisements went up about the city urging people to endorse the Committee of Fifty at a meeting scheduled for that purpose two days later. On the same day the Liberty Boys got word from Boston that the Sons of Liberty there had voted for nonimportation. They also heard a rumor that a convention of Anglican clergy then meeting in New York had also endorsed nonimportation. "If this be true" a somewhat surprised McDougall recorded, "the Body of Episcopalians will favour the measure whenever it's proposed." Thus encouraged, "a Number of respectable Merchants and the Body of Mechanics" proceeded independently to nominate a rival committee of 25 members. Although all but two of the nominees for this committee were also on the Committee of Fifty, the exclusion of conservatives and moderates gave this committee a complexion more favorable to the radicals' viewpoint. These nominations raise another point which is not easily clarified: this is the confused relationship between the Liberty Boys, led by Sears and McDougall, and the apparently new Committee of Mechanics. Were there, in fact, two distinct groups? It is far from certain. Smith refers occasionally in his *Memoirs* to the "Liberty Boys and mechanics" as two separate identities, but more often he makes no clear distinction between the two, implying that the terms "Liberty Boys" and "mechanics" were more or less interchangeable. The issue is additionally complicated by Smith's statement that New York's "Cartmen and some Mechanics" remained under the influence of the merchants and De Lancey—not surprising, as the cartmen depended on the merchants for their livelihood. Nevertheless, Smith wrote on May 18: "The Mechanics meet to reduce the Committees to chosen Men, fearing the Languor of the Chief Citizens and being betrayed again by the De Lanceys." Generalizations about the new group are therefore quite speculative. It seems clear, however, that the mechanics' committee, in fact probably a subcommittee of the Sons of Liberty, was more "radical" on the question of resistance to Britain than were the majority of Liberty Boys who followed the somewhat more moderate lead of Sears and McDougall. Certainly it was anti-De Lancey.[21]

Predictably, the merchants met this challenge by counterappeals to unity. On the morning of May 19, Isaac Low, the quintessential moderate who had chaired the May 16 meeting, issued a plea for harmony: " 'Tis therefore anxiously hoped, that at the general meeting to be assembled this day, to declare the universal assent to the choice of the body who made the nomination, all partial attachments and private animosities will be laid aside, and the choice be confirmed without any sinister opposition from narrow and ungenerous sentiments." Later, Low reiterated this view in a speech to the crowd assembled outside the Coffee House. "It is but charitable," Low told his audience, "to suppose that we all mean the same thing, and that the only difference amongst us is, or at least ought to be, the mode of effecting it, I mean the preserving of our just rights and liberties." [22]

Low's was the classically moderate statement: It was meaningless. Of course, what Low said was true enough, but the divisions between the factions were deep and fundamental. If unity was to be achieved, it would be only after some very hard bargaining. The De Lancey-merchant faction was prepared only to approve or reject the Committee of Fifty, but the leaders of the Liberty Boys were determined also to force a vote on the additional issue of nonimportation. Unfortunately for the Liberty Boys, the turnout at the Coffee House was small, and the merchants easily carried the day. As the official record put it: "The nomination of the Fifty Gentlemen, made at the Exchange on the 16th inst., was then submitted by Mr. Low, and confirmed by the Meeting, and Mr. Francis Lewis was added [to] the number by unanimous consent." The record seemed straightforward, but in fact it was highly misleading, hiding entirely the bitter feud between the merchants and the Liberty Boys. McDougall's private notes provide a good glimpse of the sense of the meeting, unrevealed in the official report. Isaac Sears repeatedly attempted to introduce resolutions calling for nonimportation but was shouted down each time by Chairman Low and the Waltons. Attempts to conduct a poll were as unsuccessful as they had been at the May 16 meeting: A call to separate supporters of the Fifty and the Twenty-Five into two bodies failed utterly. Accordingly to McDougall the friends of the Fifty "artfully thro' [sic] the meeting into such confusion that the Majority could not be well known." Sears insisted on a careful body count of everyone present, but was frustrated by the mechanics, who said they would lose a day's pay if they did not get back to work immediately. A compromise suggestion to conduct a poll of the wards that evening also had to be dropped because the meeting "could not get any persons to go." Francis Lewis was added to the roster of committee members to conciliate the mechanics, with the result that the next day the Liberty Boys and the mechanics agreed to endorse the committee, now consisting of 51 members, "upon the Principle that we should appear to be united." This decision was confirmed publicly a week later in an announcement in the *New York Journal:* "Since the Meeting at the Coffee House on Thursday last, the Merchants and Mechanics who were opposed to the Committee of Correspondence, consisting of Fifty-one Persons, have, for the Salutary Purpose of Union among ourselves, agreed to that Number; and that the Gentlemen whose names were published in Mr. Gaine's last Paper, be the Committee for this city." [23]

At the first session of the Committee of Fifty-One the members immediately found themselves facing an issue of fundamental importance to the crisis and to New York's future conduct: the drafting of a reply to the appeal from Boston, received May 17, for a general nonimportation agreement. The significance of the kind of reply sent was not lost on the Committee. The merchants remained, as they had since 1770, opposed to nonimportation, but this time the radicals were determined to bring New York into line with the other colonies, especially as it was now widely believed in the colony that an extension of the boycott of 1768-1770 by another six months would have resulted in the total repeal of the Townshend Duties. According to McDougall, several of the merchants advised that the Committee should state clearly in its response the opinion that Boston was not "suffering the Cause of American Liberty." This was unacceptable to the radicals, and for that matter, to most of the moderates. James Duane, certainly no radical, argued persuasively that if the cause of Boston was not the cause of all the colonies then any reply was "useless." [24]

Duane's view prevailed. The Committee of Fifty-One adopted a response acknowledging that Boston was "suffering in the defence of the rights of America" and proposing a general convention of the colonies to plan future action. The reply read in part:

The cause is general, and concerns a whole Continent, who are equally interested with you and us; and we foresee that no remedy can be of avail unless it proceeds from the joint act and approbation of all; from a virtuous and spirited union which may be expected while the feeble efforts of a few will only be attended with mischief and disappointment to themselves and triumph to the adversaries of our liberty. Upon these reasons we conclude that a Congress of Deputies from all the Colonies in general is of the utmost moment; that it ought to be assembled without delay, and some unanimous resolutions formed in this fatal emergency, not only respecting your deplorable circumstances, but for the security of our common rights.[25]

Because the Committee's answer left open the question of non-importation, historians have generally been inclined to take the view, first suggested by Carl Becker, that the Committee's decision provides further evidence of a conservative backlash against a rising tide of radicalism. In addition, Becker stressed the Committee's conservatism with respect to a second point: the call for a continental congress, which Becker regarded as an attempt by "conservatives" to check the radical program of the Liberty Boys. In fact, however, there was little difference between the course proposed by the Committee of Fifty-One and that advocated by the Sons of Liberty. At most, the difference was a small one of degree only; the important fact was that the Committee's stand demonstrated the growing radicalism of the population as a whole. Actually, the call for a continental congress originated with the radicals, who obviously stood to gain from involving New York in a concerted policy of general resistance. Sears and McDougall had proposed a congress in their letter of May 15 to Samuel Adams. Any doubts about the radicals' stand on the convening of a congress must have been dispelled by Boston's reply. Adams' answer, dated May 30, ignored the Committee's letter of May 23 to respond instead to the Sears-McDougall note of the fifteenth. The Fifty-One were surprised to find Adams' praising their supporting nonimportation, and on June 6 they answered the Boston Committee of Correspondence: "we apprehend you have made a mistake—for on revising our letter to you, so far from finding a word mentioned of a 'suspension of trade,' the idea is not even conceived. That, and every other resolution, we thought it most prudent to leave for the discussion of the proposed general Congress." The Liberty Boys may have been somewhat embarrassed by the confusion over the letters, but they had made their point, and more importantly, had to a large extent succeeded in restricting future options open to their opponents. The call for a continental congress thus had the support of all factions; to everyone it was clear that a congress would adopt extreme measures to protect the liberties of the colonies.[26]

Responses to the proposal to hold a continental congress were overwhelmingly favorable, with the result that at the Committee's meeting of June 27 Alexander McDougall opened debate on the "most eligible mode of appointing Deputies to attend the ensuing general Congress." The matter was not discussed seriously, however, until June 29, when McDougall proposed that the Committee nominate five delegates to represent New York City and invite other counties to endorse the five or name their own delegates. McDougall recommended further that the names of the five nominess "be sent to the Committee of Mechanics for their concurrance." [27]

McDougall's scheme was rejected. Instead, the Fifty-One voted on July 4 to submit nominations for delegates "only to the town at large." Attention then turned to the choice of nominees. Isaac Sears and Peter Van Brugh Livingston immediately put forward the names of Isaac Low, James Duane, Philip Livingston, John Morin Scott, and Alexander McDougall. Low, Duane, and Livingston were confirmed without debate, but the choice of Scott and McDougall was questioned. After some heated discussion, "the majority of voices" elected John Alsop and John Jay. Alsop, a De Lancey supporter, was a rich merchant and a future loyalist; Jay at 21 years of age was a successful attorney and a law partner of Robert R. Livingston, Jr. Politically, Jay was something of an enigma. His conversion to the Livingstons may have been rather accidental: On April 28, 1774 he had married Sarah Van Brugh Livingston, the youngest daughter of William Livingston—having failed twice before to win the hand of two daughters of Peter De Lancey! The Committee called on the people to gather at City Hall, centrally located at the intersection of Broad and Wall Streets, on Thursday, July 7 to approve or reject the Committee's nomination.[28]

At first glance, the Committee's choice of nominees tends to support a conservative interpretation of the Fifty-One's actions. Such were the views of contemporaries. For example, Thomas Jones left this description of the five nominees:

> Livingston was a "Laidlean," and though a republican, not one of the most inflammatory kind. Low belonged to the Church of England, a person unbounded in ambition, violent and turbulent in his disposition, remarkably obstinate, with a good share of understanding, extremely opinionated, fond of being the head of a party, and never so well pleased as when chairman of a committee, or principal spokesman at a mob meeting. His principles of government rather inclined to the republican system. Duane and Jay were both gentlemen of eminence in the law, and had each a sufficiency of ambition, with a proper share of pride; were both strong Episcopalians, and almost adored the British Constitution, in church, as well as state. Alsop was an honest, upright, wealthy merchant, had knowledge enough for a man in his way, but was by no means formed for a politician. He was a steady churchman, and loved Bishops as well as Kings.[29]

More significant was the attitude of the mechanics, who on this point were for once in agreement with Jones. They responded on July 6 by naming an alternative slate of nominees: Isaac Low, Philip Livingston, John Jay, Leonard Lispenard, and Alexander McDougall. Announcement of this ticket was accompanied by a call for "every friend to the true interest of this distressed country" to assemble in the Fields the next day at six o'clock in the evening. The meeting was chaired by McDougall. At his direction nine resolutions were unanimously adopted with the aim of countering what were termed "the numerous and vile arts of the enemies of America." The first and fifth resolutions were the most important. The first asserted that "we consider our Brethren at Boston as now suffering in the common cause of these Colonies." The fifth "instructed, empowered, and directed" the New York delegation to the continental congress "to engage with a majority of the principal Colonies, to agree for this city to a non-importation from Great Britain of all goods . . . until the Act for blocking up the harbour of Boston be repealed." [30]

A measure of the radicals' success was the rejection of the Fifty-One's nominees. Records of the meeting at City Hall on July 7 have not survived, but a broadside published the day of the meeting and the minutes of the Committee of Fifty-One provide a good indication of what transpired. The radicals demanded that New Yorkers be given the opportunity to vote for the pair of either Alsop and Jay or Lispenard and McDougall. The result was that a compromise was arranged whereby the Fifty-One and the mechanics would jointly conduct a poll of the "freeholders, freemen, and such who pay taxes." [31]

But the issue was far from settled. Smarting at their defeat, the Fifty-One voted to condemn the Liberty Boys' meeting of July 6, charging that it was "evidently calculated to throw an odium on this Committee, and to create groundless jealousies and suspicions of their conduct, as well as disunion among our fellow-citizens." In addition, the Committee voted to publish its condemnation, a decision which so angered the radicals on the Committee that they "quitted the chamber in a rage." The next day, July 8, 11 members of the Committee resigned in protest. The 11—Francis Lewis, Joseph Hallett, Alexander McDougall, Peter Van Brugh Livingston, Isaac Sears, Thomas Randall, Abraham P. Lott, Leonard Lispenard, John Broome, Abraham Brasher, and Jocobus Van Zandt—asserted that "the people have an undoubted right to convene themselves, and come into whatever resolutions they shall think proper." [32]

These developments obliged the remaining members of the Committee of Fifty-One to rethink their position. The result was that the Committee moved closer to radical policy. On July 13 the Fifty-One voted ten carefully worded resolutions expressing the view that the Boston Port Act was "subversive of every Idea of British Liberty" and that "if a non-importation agreement of goods from Great Britain should be adopted by the Congress, it ought to be very general and faithfully adhered to." The Committee renominated Jay, Duane, Alsop, Livingston, and Low, and called upon the people to meet on July 19 at the Coffee House to vote on the resolutions and the nominations.[33]

Historians know little about the July 19 meeting, but it is evident that its tone was bitter. The recent conduct of the Fifty-One, and in particular the July 13 resolutions, were sharply denounced. John Morin Scott "charged the drawers of the resolves then under Consideration with a design of thereby disuniting the Colonies." This time the nominees of the Fifty-One were in fact elected, but the vote was so uncertain that three of them—Alsop, Jay, and Low— declined appointment "until the sentiments of the town are ascertained with great precision." The July 13 resolutions were defeated, and a new committee was named to draw up more acceptable motions.[34]

If the Liberty Boys or the mechanics expected the new committee to endorse their more radical program, they were to be disappointed. The resolutions passed at the July 5 meeting were rejected, and in an effort to reunite the colony a set of resolutions was adopted which closely adhered to the policies advocated by the Fifty-One. The Boston Port Act was denounced in words identical to those used by the Fifty-One as was the promise to abide by the decisions of the united colonies. In contrast to the resolutions of the Liberty Boys, no instructions were given to the congressional deputies.

Further efforts by the radicals to pursue an independent line were abandoned, and the remaining differences between the Fifty-One and the Sons of Liberty were now easily settled. July 28 was set as election day for congressional delegates. It was agreed that the election would be supervised jointly by the aldermen and Common Council of the city, the vestrymen, the Liberty Boys, and the Fifty-One, and that the poll would be open to the freeholders, freemen, and "persons who pay taxes." Any lingering possibility of further discord between the Fifty-One and the Liberty Boys was removed on July 26 with a promise by the Fifty-One to support a "general non-importation agreement" if such a policy was recommended by the continental congress. The next day the Liberty Boys unanimously endorsed the candidacy of Livingston, Low, Alsop, Duane, and Jay, thereby making their election certain.[35]

In retrospect, it is apparent that the maneuvering of the factions within and without the Committee of Fifty-One had accomplished very little, except to demonstrate that New Yorkers were agreed that the Boston Port Act must be resisted and a continental congress supported. This is the critical fact which should be stressed. The struggle which some contemporaries and later historians perceived between "conservatives" and "radicals," while not without foundation in fact, was really of little significance. None of the Fifty-One's nominees, with the possible exception of Alsop, could be regarded as a "conservative," if, in the context of the events under consideration, the term is to be understood as implying an opposition to strong resistance to Parliament. The unimportance of the dispute prompted one local wit to comment cynically: "It may indeed, give Occasion for some *Wise-acre* to obtrude this Question; 'Why then have we two Committees, and to what Purpose are they endeavouring to counteract each other?' But surely it would be very unreasonable to insinuate, that any *Harm* could arise from a Committee, in which there are more *Lambs* than *Wolves.*" [36] The truth was that New Yorkers were becoming increasingly radicalized as a result of the growing conviction that their political liberties and local institutions were under grave threat of abolition. Measures, which had only recently seemed extreme, now seemed moderate. The mood of the colony was aptly summarized in the revealing comment of the De Lancey historian and future loyalist, Thomas Jones: "Five were sent from New York. They were chosen by the people at large, with little or no opposition, *all parties, denominations and religions, apprehending at the time, that the Colonies laboured under grievances which wanted redressing.*" [37]

The radical temper evident among New Yorkers reflected a growing radical consciousness in the colonies as a whole, which was manifested in the decisions reached by the Continental Congress, which assembled at Carpenters' Hall, Philadelphia, in the first week of September 1774. According to Duane, the New York delegation believed that the "grand Object" of the Congress was the establishment of "a firm Union between the Parent State and her Colonies," but they soon discovered that, so far as the majority of delegates were concerned, the question of resistance significantly outweighed the drafting of a new imperial constitution. The tone of the proceedings was set early with the adoption of the 19 Suffolk Resolves. Clearly inflammatory, these resolutions, voted by special convention in Suffolk County, Massachusetts, boldly undertook to instruct the king in the principles of Anglo-American government by reminding him that he ruled "agreeable to compact." As well, the resolves asserted that the coercive acts were "gross infractions" of American liberty and recommended the immediate adoption of plans to defend the colonies militarily. In marked contrast was the reception accorded Joseph Galloway's Plan of Union, a scheme to establish an American governor general and parliament. This proposal, Duane noted, was "rejected and ordered to be left out of the minutes." [38]

The main business of the Congress was the drawing up of a comprehensive economic boycott of the Mother Country. Known as the Continental Association, the essential features of the agreement, passed October 18, 1774, were these: After December 1, 1774 the colonies would suspend all imports from England and her possessions; after the same date the importation of slaves and participation in the slave trade would end; after March 1, 1775 the purchase and consumption of British products would cease; American exports to England and the empire would be discontinued from September 10, 1775. Each town or locality was requested to set up a committee of inspection to enforce these measures. Goods imported "illegally" could be sold to raise money for Boston's poor.

It was the terms of enforcement that were really significant. They conferred on the Congress and its agents powers equivalent to those enjoyed by the legally established colonial governments; in effect, the Association established alternative governments. It was, in short, a revolutionary act. The enforcement procedures were set out in the eleventh article, and were as follows:

That a committee be chosen in every county, city, and town, by those who are qualified to vote for representatives in the legislature, whose business it shall be attentively to observe the conduct of all persons touching this association; and when it shall be made to appear, to the satisfaction of a majority of any committee, that any person within the limits of their appointment has violated this association, that such majority do forthwith cause the truth of the case to be published in the gazette; to the end that all such foes to the rights of British-America may be publicly known, and universally contemned as the enemies of American liberty; and thenceforth we respectively will break off all dealings with him or her.[39]

New York's delegates returned from Philadelphia apparently converted to the militant stand of the Congress and determined to persuade the Fifty-One to support the course agreed to by the Congress. Observers like Jones were stunned by their change of attitude, and even Smith, who was close to the delegates if not the Committee as a whole, was somewhat puzzled. Smith explained the changing mood within the Fifty-One in the following illuminating passage in a letter to Philip Schuyler:

> You knew what Spirit prevailed in our Committee of 51 before the Congress. . . . Their Delegates are become Converts to the prevailing Sentiments of the Congress. . . . Suppose some of them who were once opposed to the Liberty Boys should have reasoned thus at Philadelphia. The Government's favor we have already lost. And the Question is whether we shall court the Continent or some Merchants of New York, and from the last we have little to fear. There is an approaching Election and with Part of the Trade, Part of the Church, all the Non Episcopals and all the Liberty Boys we may secure Places in the Assembly and laugh at the Discontented. . . . This Plan will sacrifice the present City Members but this is Nothing. . . . Besides Necessity has no Law.[40]

If, as Smith implied, the actions of the Fifty-One were partly influenced by political considerations on the part of the majority of De Lanceys and the merchants, on the one hand, and the Livingstons, on the other, they failed to produce anything like a satisfactory result for either faction. The Fifty-One announced acceptance of congressional policy, and on November 7 recommended the election of "eight fit persons" in each ward to act as a committee of inspection. For reasons that remain unclear, the mechanics objected to this proposal. If Smith's assessment was correct, probably they wanted to block any resurgence of De Lancey influence. At any rate, the Fifty-One were obliged to acknowledge publicly that "some difficulties have arisen relative to . . . choosing a Committee of Inspection," and on November 14 they arranged to meet with the mechanics and other popular leaders to discuss alternative proposals. The two factions met on November 15 and 16. The upshot was a decision to dissolve the Fifty-One and replace it with a new general committee of inspection composed of 60 members to be chosen from two lists each of 100 names submitted by the Fifty-One and the mechanics respectively. The names of 60 nominees were published November 17 and confirmed November 22 at a large public rally. The change represented another significant step toward revolution and a sharp blow to the advocates of moderation, especially the De Lanceys, but also to a lesser degree the Livingstons. Smith's analysis is revealing:

> By the Interest of the Delegates the Committee of 51 is to be dissolved and a New Committee appointed to execute the Decrees of the Congress, which is to consist of the Delegates and such a Sett as the most active Liberty Boys approve and had, thro' the Mechanics who were consulted, chosen in Conjunction with the Committee of 51 from which a Sett who formerly dictated all their Movements have retired outwitted and disgusted and as they think betrayed.[41]

The fact that both the De Lanceys and the Livingstons were prepared to attempt the manipulation of the Committees of Fifty-One and Sixty for their own narrow purposes suggests that neither had yet grasped the significance of the revolutionary changes that were taking place in New York and the other colonies. But the sequence of events triggered by the Boston Tea Party favored the rise of radical men, radical measures, and radical ideas, with the result that the Livingston-De Lancey quarrel was rapidly becoming politically irrelevant. This is not to imply either that the radicals acted as revolutionary conspirators or that the De Lanceys or Livingstons acted as an "opposition" to the radical leaders. Quite the reverse. The Tea Party and the Boston Port Act radicalized everyone, as Thomas Jones so perceptively noted. The radicals' strength derived precisely from the fact that they were in late 1774 and early 1775 truly representative of all the people. More than anything else this radicalization of the people effectively committed New York to revolution and independence.

NOTES

1. Gage to Barrington, January 17, 1771, *Thomas Gage Correspondence, II*, p. 567.
2. Beekman to John Blackburn, November 10, 1772, White, ed., *The Beekman Mercantile Papers*, II, p. 682. In June 1773 Beekman analyzed the merchants' problems at length. He wrote to Fluyder, Marsh, and Hudson of London: "I can compute this great Stagnation in Trade entirely to the General and great Credit given to our Merchants here, for was Credit given only to men of Property, they would as formerly import largely, and that without any risque to their Creditors, or themselves, by which goods they would be able to gett a living proffitt, and consiquently make punctual payment, but now adays men of little or no property import the most goods which they must sell at any rate (to endeavour to keep up their credit) which others must do the same or keep their goods upon hand, which is the case of many, and on account of which they are obliged to Stop importing untill trade getts in its old channel. . . ." June 19, 1773, ibid., II, p. 748.
3. Livingston to Robert R. Livingston, Jr., March 5, 1772, Livingston Papers, Bancroft Collection, p. 20, New York Public Library.
4. Smith, *Historical Memoirs*, I, p. 138.
5. Ibid., p. 141.
6. Lucy S. Sutherland, *The East India Company in Eighteenth Century Politics* (Oxford, 1952), pp. 222-231; Benjamin W. Labaree, *The Boston Tea Party* (New York, 1964), pp. 58-79; Danby Pickering, ed., *The Statutes at Large from Magna Carta to the End of the Eighteenth Parliament of Great Britain*, 46 vols. (London, 1762-1807), XXX, pp. 74-77. The act regulating the affairs of the East India Company is printed in ibid., pp. 124-143. The Tea Act was first printed in New York in the *New York Gazette, and Weekly Mercury*, September 6, 1773.
7. Smith, *Historical Memoirs*, I, p. 156. See also Tryon to Dartmouth, November 3, 1773, *New York Colonial Documents*, VIII, p. 400. For a good contemporary account of the activities of the tea smugglers see

Thomas Hutchinson to Hillsborough, August 25, 1771, and same to same, September 10, 1771, *Calendar of Home Office Papers of the Reign of George III 1760-1775*, 4 vols. (London, 1878-1899), II, pp. 289-290, item 810; p. 294, item 827. An illuminating general discussion is Hoh-Cheung and Lorna H. Mui, "Smuggling and the British Tea Trade before 1784," *American Historical Review*, LXXVI (October, 1968), pp. 44-73.

8. *To the Friends of Liberty and Commerce*, November 5, 1773, Broadside Collection, New York Historical Society; *New York Gazette, and Weekly Mercury*, December 6, 1773; Leake, *Memoir of the Life and Times of General John Lamb*, p. 77; Becker, *History of Political Parties in New York*, p. 104; Labaree, *Boston Tea Party*, pp. 93-94.

9. December 1, 1773, Council Minutes, XXVI, p. 379, New York State Library; Smith, *Historical Memoirs*, I, pp. 157-158.

10. Ibid., pp. 157-158. The Boston resolutions were printed in the *New York Gazette, and Weekly Mercury*, December 13, 1773.

11. Smith, *Historical Memoirs*, I, pp. 159-160; *New York Journal*, December 23, 1773; Council Minutes, XXVI, p. 382, New York State Library.

12. *New York Journal*, December 23, 1773; *Proceedings of a Numerous Meeting of the Citizens of New York*, December 17, 1773, Broadside Collection, New York Historical Society; Smith, *Historical Memoirs*, I, p. 162; Bernard Mason, *The Road to Independence: The Revolutionary Movement in New York, 1773-1777* (Lexington, Ky., 1966), pp. 14-15.

13. Tryon to Dartmouth, January 3, 1774, *New York Colonial Documents*, VIII, pp. 407-408; Becker, *History of Political Parties in New York*, pp. 107-108.

14. *New York Gazette, and Weekly Mercury*, April 25, 1774; *American Archives*, 4th and 5th series, 9 vols. (Washington, 1837-1853), 4th series, I, pp. 249-250.

15. For a detailed account of the passage of the coercive legislation, see Bernard Donoughue, *British Politics and the American Revolution: The Path to War 1773-1775* (London, 1964), pp. 73-104. The Coercive Acts were the Boston Port Act, the Massachusetts Government Act, and the Administration of Justice Act. In addition, Parliament passed in June the Quartering Act which authorized the billeting of soldiers in public and private buildings in all the colonies. The acts are printed in *Statutes of Large*, XXX, pp. 336-341, 367-371, 381-390, 410.

16. McDougall, Political Memorandums Relative to the Conduct of the

Citizens on the Boston Port Bill Refering [sic] to the Papers indorsed—Proceedings on the Boston Port Bill in New York, McDougall Papers; Box I, New York Historical Society.

17. Ibid.; Smith, *Historical Memoirs*, I, p. 186.

18. McDougall, Political Memorandums; Champagne, "New York and the Intolerable Acts," *New York Historical Society Quarterly*, XLV (April, 1961), p. 200.

19. McDougall, Political Memorandums. The members of the Committee of Fifty were: John Alsop, William Bayard, Theophylact Bache, Peter V.B. Livingston, Philip Livingston, Isaac Sears, David Johnston, Charles McEvers, Charles Nichol, Alexander McDougall, Capt. Thomas Randall, John Moore, Isaac Low, Leonard Lispenard, Jacobus Van Zandt, James Duane, Edward Laight, Thomas Pearsall, Elias Desbrosses, William Walton, Richard Yates, John De Lancey, Miles Sherbrook, John Thurman, John Jay, Benjamin Booth, Joseph Hallet, Charles Shaw, Alexander Wallace, James Jauncey, Gabriel H. Ludlow, Nicholas Hoffman, Abraham Walton, Gerardus Duyckinck, Peter Van Schaack, Henry Remsen, Hamilton Young, George Browne, John Broome, Peter T. Curtenius, Peter Goelet, Abraham Brasher, Abraham P. Lott, David Van Horne, Gerardus W. Beekman, Abraham Duryee, Joseph Bull, William McAdam, Richard Sharpe, Thomas Marston. See Jones, *History of New York*, I, p. 442.

20. McDougall, Political Memorandums; Smith, *Historical Memoirs*, I, p. 186.

21. Ibid., 186; McDougall, Political Memorandums; The members of the Committee of Twenty-five were: John Alsop, Theophylact Bache, Peter V.B. Livingston, Isaac Sears, David Johnston, Alexander McDougall, Thomas Randall, Leonard Lispenard, Jacobus Van Zandt, Thomas Pearsall, Richard Yates, John Broome, Nicholas Hoffman, Abraham Walton, Henry Remsen, George Browne, Peter T. Curtenius, Abraham P. Lott, John Aspinwall, Gerardus W. Beekman, Abraham Duryee, Joseph Bull, Richard Sharpe, Thomas Marston, Francis Lewis. Aspinwall and Lewis were not members of the Committee of Fifty-One. Jones, *History of New York*, I, p. 441. See also Mason, *Road to Independence*, p. 27, note 66; Champagne, "Liberty Boys and Mechanics of New York City," *Labor History*, VIII (April, 1967), pp. 115-135; Staughton Lynd, "The Mechanics in New York Politics, 1774-1788," ibid., V (Fall, 1964), pp. 215-246.

22. *American Archives*, 4th series, I, pp. 293-294.

23. *Ibid., pp. 294-295; Smith, Historical Memoirs*, I, p. 187; McDougall, Political Memorandums.

24. Ibid.

25. *American Archives*, 5th series, I, 297-298. McDougall, who delivered the Committee's reply to Paul Revere May 24, noted, "I urged upon him the expedience of their Committee's appointing time & place for the Congress as we did not do it. . . ." McDougall, Political Memorandums.

26. Ibid.; *American Archives*, 4th series, I, p. 303.

27. Ibid, p. 307; McDougall, Political Memorandums.

28. *American Archives*, 4th series, I, pp. 308-309

29. Jones, *History of New York*, I, p. 35. The term "Laidlean" is a reference to the Reverend Archibald Laidly, a Scottish Presbyterian appointed to serve New York's Dutch congregation in 1763. Laidly was an ally of the Triumvirate, described by Jones as a man "of jesuitical, republican, and puritan principles," ibid., p. 21.

30. *New York Gazetteer*, July 14, 1774.

31. *American Archives*, 4th series, I, pp. 309-310. The poll was apparently never held. Nevertheless, on July 9 McDougall declined nomination on the grounds that the method of election, which did not allow the voters to select any five of seven candidates, "was an infringement of . . . Liberty." McDougall, *To Freeholders, Freemen, and Inhabitants of the City and County of New York*, Broadside Collection, New York Historical Society.

32. *American Archives*, 4th series, I, pp. 313-314.

33. Ibid., pp. 314-317.

34. Ibid., p. 317; John Jay to John Morin Scott, *John Jay, the Making of a Revolutionary: Unpublished Papers, 1745-1780*, Richard B. Morris, ed. (New York, 1975), pp. 134-135; *July 19, 1774*, Broadside Collection, New York Public Library. The members of the new committee were John Morin Scott, Isaac Low, Peter Van Brugh Livingston, Leonard Lispenard, Alexander McDougall, James van Varck, William Goforth, John Lamb, Theophilus Anthony, John Moore, Isaac Sears, Henry Remsen, Thomas Randall, John Jay, and James Duane. Low, Remsen, and Moore, declined to serve because of "a supposed Irregularity in their Appointment."

35. *American Archives*, 4th series, I, p. 319.

36. *Remarks upon the Resolves of the New Committee*, July 22, 1774, Broadside Collection, New York Public Library.

37. Jones, *History of New York*, I, pp. 34-35. The Committee of Fifty-One made the same point in a letter to Boston's Committee of Correspondence, written in August: "Permit us to add, that whatever grounds you have to question the patriotism of the order of Merchants, which is strongly implied in your letter to our Committee of Mechanics, it is

a debt of justice to affirm that the spirited and disinterested conduct of the commercial part of this city, ought to place them above the reach of suspicion, since at all times, and upon every occasion, they have proved themselves the unshaken friends of constitutional liberty, and have virtuously sacrificed the advantages of their profession to the public good." August 9, 1774, *American Archives,* 4th series, I, p. 323. Outside New York City the Committee of Fifty-One received little support. Three counties—Suffolk, Orange, and Kings—sent delegates to the Congress, and four counties—Albany, Westchester, Dutchess, and Ulster—endorsed Livingston, Duane, Alsop, Jay, and Low.

38. Duane, "Propositions Before Committee on Rights, September 7-22, 1774," *Letters of the Members of the Continental Congress,* 7 vols. (Washington, 1921-1934), I, p. 38; September 28, 1774, Duane's notes on his copy of Galloway's Plan. Duane Papers, Box III, New York Historical Society.

39. *Journals of the Continental Congress,* 34 vols. (Washington, 1904-1937), I, pp. 75-80.

40. Smith, *Historical Memoirs,* I, p. 203.

41. *Ibid.; New York Gazetteer,* November 17, 1774; *Advertisement,* November 17, 1774, Broadside Collection, New York Public Library; Colden to Dartmouth, December 7, 1774, *Colden Letter Books 1760-1775,* II, pp. 372-373. The members of the Committee of Sixty were: Isaac Low, Philip Livingston, James Duane, John Alsop, John Jay, Peter Van B. Livingston, Isaac Sears, David Johnston, Charles Nicoll, Alexander McDougall, Thomas Randall, Leonard Lispenard, Edward Laight, William Walton, John Broome, Joseph Hallet, Charles Shaw, Nicholas Hoffman, Abraham Walton, Peter Van Schaack, Henry Remsen, Peter T. Curtenius, Abraham Brasher, Abraham P. Lott, Abraham Duryee, Joseph Bull, Francis Lewis, John Lasher, John Roome, Joseph Totten, Thomas Ivers, Hercules Mulligan, John Anthony, Francis Basset, Victor Bicker, John White, Theophilus Anthony, William Goforth, William Denning, Isaac Roosevelt, Jacob van Voorhees, Jerimah Platt, William Ustick, Comfort Sands, Robert Benson, William W. Gilbert, John Berrian, Gabriel W. Ludlow, Nicholas Roosevelt, Edward Flemming, Lawrence Embree, Samuel Jones, John De Lancey, Frederick Jay, William W. Ludlow, John B. Moore, George Januwa, Rodolphus Ritzma, Lindley Murray, Lancaster Burling.

CHAPTER SIX

Between Peace and War:
Making a Revolution, 1775-1776

In analyzing the final stage of the drift toward independence two features stand out. First was the radicalization of the colonists, which was complemented by a hardening of the British attitude. Neither of these developments meant that revolution was inevitable, but it is clear that by late 1774 both sides had adopted what might be termed "non-negotiable" positions not easily susceptible of compromise. Second was the collapse of the De Lanceys, and because this story has not been well understood, it is the more interesting of the two. Though it has been suggested previously that the signs of the De Lancey collapse were evident from late 1769, it was really only during the first four months of 1775—the crucial period in the making of the decision for independence—that the De Lancey fall became apparent to everyone. Their sudden collapse was truly remarkable. As late as September 1774, so astute an observer as John Adams stated that New York public life turned on the actions of just two families: the Livingstons and the De

Lanceys. And Adams' source of information was, ironically, none other than Alexander McDougall.

What makes the De Lancey collapse interesting and important is that it allows historians to confront squarely the problem of discerning how loyalism evolved. Though loyalism is certainly no longer a neglected field of inquiry, it remains the case that historians have difficulty "explaining" loyalism. For the most part scholars have assumed that loyalists were loyal to Britain because of some natural inclination toward a type of conservatism that was fundamentally pro-British in character. For this reason historians have often detected strains of loyalism well before the Revolution had begun.

The De Lanceys present scholars, however, with a model of loyalist attitudes and behavior not found in the mainstream of loyalist historiography. For one thing, so far as we know, the De Lanceys did not subscribe to the sort of classic conservatism which William Nelson has suggested marked the American tory. Because the De Lanceys' beliefs and actions appear to be virtually identical to those of the revolutionaries, it has been suggested that the De Lanceys be viewed as "whig-loyalists," a term suggestive of the close identity between loyalist and patriot ideas. But if the De Lanceys held many of the same beliefs and attitudes as the revolutionaries, a problem arises: Why did the De Lanceys become loyalists? The argument advanced here is that the De Lanceys' loyalism was the result of the accidental interplay of events arising from the Livingston-De Lancey rivalry. To be sure, other scholars have occasionally noted the apparently "accidental" quality of the De Lanceys' loyalism, and, for that matter, the Livingstons' patriotism. The point is that these "accidents" were not merely a curiosity or a coincidence to be noted in passing; the "accidents" of the Livingston-De Lancey rivalry were vital to the making of New York's revolution.

As the new year of 1775 began, the De Lanceys' future was far from being finally determined. Their thoughts were firmly fixed on the Assembly session scheduled to commence January 10, and on how to use the session to upstage the Livingstons and their radical allies.

The new session of the New York Assembly attracted more interest than usual in New York and elsewhere. Everywhere in the colonies moderates looked to New York and its Assembly to find a way toward peaceful reconciliation with England. A typical view was that expressed by Cadwallader Colden, who assured English friends that the Assembly was effectively controlled "by the Moderate Men, who by all means avoid Disorder and Confusion." [1] It is not surprising that Colden thought in these terms, but it is surprising that other moderates also expected the New York Assembly to reverse the obvious deterioration in Anglo-American affairs.

Why moderates thought this way is far from certain, but one reason may lie in the unexpectedly strong attack launched against the First Continental Congress by New York's Anglican clergy in the late fall of 1774. The principal organizers of the attack were Samuel Seabury, Charles Inglis, and Thomas Bradbury Chandler, a New Jerseyite with close ties to the New York church. The essence of the attack was the accusation that the principal aim of the Congress was nothing less than the independence of the Thirteen Colonies from Britain and the creation of 13 American republics. Though historians with the benefit of hindsight rightly regard these clerical writings as important sources of loyalist ideology, the attack was somewhat premature, its effects unclear. Seabury and his friends have probably influenced historians more than they influenced their contemporaries. What was significant, however, for New York was that the churchmen were generally regarded as strong De Lancey supporters, and it was probably assumed, though no clear supporting evidence has come to light, that the attack was inspired by the De Lanceys.

Even so, the recent conduct of the New York Assembly offered little comfort to moderates. Actually, the record of the House of Assembly on the constitutional crisis was far from clear. At best, the Assembly's position was ambiguous; in fact, its views were unknown. The Assembly had not played a significant role in the colony's affairs since the turmoil of the 1769-1770 session. The deputies had met only briefly in 1772, 1773, and 1774. The 1773 sitting occurred early in the year well before the tea episode, and the 1774 session preceded the passage of the Coercive Acts. Moreover, the record of the House since 1764 hardly justified the moderates' hopes. Both the Livingstons and later the De Lanceys had firmly resisted British policy, and the De Lanceys had been, if anything, the more radical in their opposition.

From early November 1774 the De Lanceys had been engaged in carefully devising strategy for the approaching session of the legislature. Though the De Lancey position was far from enviable, they saw in the latest imperial crisis fresh hope for new political triumphs. Adding to their confidence was the fact that since April 1774, following Tryon's return to England, the government of New York had been in the familiar aging hands of Cadwallader Colden. The De Lanceys decided therefore that the best course of action was to force as quickly as possible a dissolution of the House. This would mean new elections and a chance for the De Lanceys to put forward an attractive scheme for constitutional reconciliation with the Mother Country. According to Smith the De Lanceys settled upon a complicated and somewhat devious two-part plan. They would vote approval of the proceedings of the Continental Congress and endorse the formation of the Committee of Sixty, moves, they calculated, which would oblige Colden to dissolve the House. They then could go to the voters legitimately posing as the friends and defenders of American liberty. It was critical, Smith thought, that the Livingstons do everything in their power to blunt the De Lancey offensive. He explained the situation to Philip Schuyler this way:

With this Hint you'll be able to predict what the Conduct of some old Politicians will be at the next Session and will perceive that the Current will set all one Way for Liberty in both Houses unless Some Persons will throw Obstacles in the Way to blow up the Powder now concealed and draw certain Leaders into Day Light who must for Fear of distant Wrath and to give the Project all the Wished for Extent of Success be unknown.[2]

Few were better placed than Smith himself to throw obstacles in the De Lanceys' way, and when the governor's Council met on January 5, 1775, he acted promptly and skillfully. The meeting began well for the De Lanceys. Colden laid before the Council his draft of the lieutenant governor's formal opening address to the

House of Assembly. The text was clearly De Lancey-inspired. In harsh and uncompromising language the speech called on the deputies to denounce the proceedings of the Continental Congress and to declare their firm attachment to the English Crown. Smith objected to the entire draft. It was, he said, a foolish and quite unnecessary attempt to provoke a confrontation with the Assembly. Moreover, it was a confrontation which the government must most certainly lose. The speech would, Smith perceptively noted, "force the House to declare their Creed. . . . That it would prevent the Moderate from any Escape; that such as wished to be silent would be obliged to speak." In short, Smith warned, the speech was politically disastrous; its author would be severely censured in New York and England. A younger, tougher Colden might well have defied public opinion—the lieutenant governor had never been the sort of man who took advice easily—but at 87 years of age Colden was at last beyond the rough and tumble of hard political combat. "Much confounded" by Smith's unexpected attack, a shaken Colden retreated, agreeing to write a new and more moderate address. At the same time the lieutenant governor inadvertently admitted the collusion between himself and the De Lanceys. According to Smith, the old man "said he was afraid of a civil War and was led to this Speech by some hint that the House were to be urged to adopt the Principles of the Congress." The De Lanceys were understandably furious at Colden's disclosure. A De Lancey ally, the merchant Henry White, told Smith that his actions "had subverted the Project of the De Lanceys, Duane and Low, who had put Colden on a violent Speech to procure a Dissolution . . . White says he knows that they had seen the draft before the Meeting." [3]

Defeated on one front, the De Lanceys abruptly changed strategy. As the faction's leaders saw matters, Assembly approval of the Continental Congress now seemed unwise and unnecessary. If, as now appeared certain, there was to be no dissolution, the De Lanceys reckoned they stood to gain little from an endorsement of Congress' decisions. On the contrary, a vote in favor of the Congress now could only add to the prestige of their opponents who would be seen clearly to have the initiative. What the De Lanceys must do, their leaders decided, was draw the attention of the colonists away from the proceedings at Philadelphia by devising and promoting an alternative scheme for securing a redress of American grievances, one quite independent of that put forward by the Congress, and one designed also to save the empire.

The De Lancey leadership met the evening of January 9 at Hull's Tavern to draw up suitable proposals. Those present included John Watts, Oliver De Lancey, Hugh Wallace, William Axtell, and John Harris Cruger, all members of the governor's Council, and James De Lancey. As the Livingston forces were sure to move a motion approving the actions of the Continental Congress, the first matter of business for the De Lanceys was the defeat of the motion. A sign of the changing times was the fact that De Lancey leaders were far from confident that the motion could be defeated. A careful head count suggested that while 11 assemblymen would vote against the Livingston motion, as many as 14 deputies would probably vote for it. The vote must be blocked. But how? Hugh Wallace, who had replaced William Walton on the council in 1769, suggested an appropriate stratagem, which he reported to Smith the next day. Smith wrote the following account of the conversation: "Wallace advised to move at the first Meeting [of the Assembly] an Address to the King as superseding any Thing else." According to Wallace, Oliver De Lancey liked the suggestion, but Watts was against it. James De Lancey favored delay, but finally, as Smith put it, "The Generality [was] for this Measure as the only Scheme to prevent voting in Favor of the Congress." In fact, of course, the stratagem was most unimpressive, especially if it was intended to be a prelude to some alternative plan to salvage England's American empire. In truth, the De Lanceys had no ideas, no master plan. In seizing upon Wallace's suggestion, the De Lancey leadership was clutching at straws, and they knew it. A discouraged and worried Wallace confided to Smith his opinion that if the Assembly approved the decisions of the Congress "Gentlemen should league and defend themselves by Force." The old colonial elite was bankrupt, its time fast running out.[4]

Not surprisingly, when the Assembly convened Tuesday, January 10, 1775, the Wallace strategy was quickly set aside, James De Lancey having decided that an address to the King should be delayed indefinitely. Instead, the Assembly appointed a committee to draft petitions to the King and Parliament and to draw up "a state of Grievances of this Colony." The committee was appointed at the end of January, but serious debate on the petitions and grievances did not begin until early March. In the intervening period the De Lanceys succeeded in close voting to block attempts by the Livingstons to secure the House's approval of the proceedings of the Continental Congress. On January 26, February 17, 21, and 23, the De Lanceys defeated by votes of 11-10, 15-9, 15-10, and 17-9 respectively a series of Livingston motions, first endorsing the proceedings of the Continental Congress; second, thanking New York's congressional delegation; third, thanking the merchants of New York City for their patriotic observance of the Continental Association; and, fourth, supporting the nomination and election of delegates to the Second Continental Congress.[5]

Fortunately, the speeches of two De Lancey allies against the motion to appoint deputies of the Second Continental Congress have survived. The speeches of Crean Brush of Cumberland County and Isaac Wilkins of the Borough of Westchester merit careful study because of the light they shed on De Lancey political ideology; viewed against the background of the De Lanceys' leadership of the Assembly since 1770 they also provide insights into a significant strain of New York loyalism. Brush began his speech by stating what would become a key loyalist argument: the fundamental illegality of the Congress. Brush asserted that "as the late Congress acted without any power or authority derived from this House, (at least as far as respected this Province), from the Laws and Constitution of our country, its Proceedings could not, with propriety, come before us for consideration." The provincial houses of assembly were the proper agencies to solicit for a redress of grievances, and to transfer the assemblies' authority to a body "unknown to the Constitution" was, Brush thought, treasonable.

More importantly, Brush was angered by the apparent failure of the Congress to pursue seriously the question of reconciliation. This failure, Brush believed, stripped the Congress of any pretended authority the delegates might claim to speak or act for the united colonies. It was obvious, Brush asserted, that the Congress in fact aimed at nothing less than a complete break with England. Why else, he asked, had the Congress listed not only "real" grievances but as well "have even industriously sought after and inserted in their catalogue what can never be esteemed as such." In short, Brush concluded, the New York Assembly could not "consent to a motion which would establish a body who have assumed the most unlimited powers, and are actuated by the most dangerous princi- ples ... and may probably involve this once happy country in all the horrours of a civil war." [6]

Wilkins began his long speech by reviewing the history of the imperial controversy since 1765. From the Stamp Act to the Boston Tea Party, he said, Americans had consistently expressed their op- position to British colonial policy "in a legal and constitutional way." They had acknowledged the supreme authority of the King and Parliament in matters pertaining to the general administration and direction of the empire, but had quite properly claimed and insisted upon the right to be taxed only by representatives of their own choosing, to which end they had petitioned Parliament and boycotted English imports which were subject to unconstitutional taxes. The colonists' aim had been limited to one fundamental ob- jective: self-taxation. Since the Boston Tea Party, however, Amer- ican objectives had changed radically, Wilkins charged. Instead of boycotting tea—"that easy and effectual method that offered itself to us"—the colonists, according to Wilkins, "flew into the most indecent rage, and hastily adopted every unwarrantable measure that could irritate and provoke the Government." As Wilkins saw matters, the new self-styled leaders of the colonies had shown themselves to be "void of common sense." Their behavior, if not stopped quickly, could only result in revolution.

Was it too late to stop the apparently steady drift toward revolu- tion, to undo the damage worked by "illegal and disorderly ... Committees, Associations, and Congresses?" Wilkins thought not. A few colonies, like Massachusetts, might well be lost to the radi- cals and revolutionaries, but New York certainly could still be saved for the empire. New York, Wilkins declared, "could instantly break loose, and, by a well-timed effort, rescue ourselves from de- struction, and endeavour to make peace for ourselves—not a shame- ful—not an ignominious peace, but such an one as will secure to us our liberties and properties, and render the union between us and our mother country permanent and lasting." In no way could such a decision be interpreted as a "base desertion of our sister Colonies," Wilkins said. Quite the reverse. "If this loyal Province will do her duty and act with wisdom and moderation in the critical juncture, she may yet save America." [7]

Both speeches, especially Wilkins', provide important clues to De Lancey political ideology. The De Lanceys remained at heart Rockingham Whigs, or more accurately, adhered to the principles of the Rockingham Whigs as they understood those principles; that is, the De Lanceys believed in a constitutionally limited imperial authority, one possessing in theory absolute sovereignty over the colonies but in practice permitting the colonies a large measure of autonomy, especially in the matter of taxation, which the De Lanceys, like all Americans, held to be a right vested exclusively in themselves. The Stamp Act crisis provided the De Lanceys with an ideal model for the solving of imperial disputes. It was ironic, but very suggestive, that they came to look upon the Stamp Act crisis— in its own way as violent and radical as any before the Battle of Lexington and Concord—as a model of "peaceable" reconciliation. The truth was that the "Stamp Act crisis" the De Lanceys remembered had never existed; it was a figment of their imagination. The "real" Stamp Act crisis was volatile and revolutionary, and it established no principle except the principle that Parliament possessed absolute sovereignty over the colonies in all matters relating to government and taxation. The full implications of the terms of the Stamp Act repeal were not immediately evident, but after 1767 most Americans came to understand Rockingham's position, and with this realization began the process of American radicalization. The De Lanceys never comprehended the change. Because their policies were based on illusion and self-deception, it was inevitable that they would fail disastrously.

The irrelevance of the De Lancey approach to the problems of the empire was evident in the reception accorded the Assembly's reconciliation proposals. These took shape during March. On March 3 the deputies debated and drew up a "state of grievances." The document was hardly controversial, though it did not follow the letter of radical policy. The grievances enumerated formed a now familiar litany: unconstitutional taxes, the Declaratory Act, the establishment of admiralty courts having concurrent jurisdiction with common law courts, the suspension of the New York legislature, Parliament's refusal to let New York issue legal tender paper money, the sending of Americans to England for trial in cases of treason, and the coercive acts. Following from the grievances the House adopted five resolutions March 8: first, allegiance to the Crown of England was acknowledged; second, all acts of Parliament "calculated for the general weal of the whole Empire" and not "inconsistant with the essential rights and liberties of Englishmen" were accepted as binding on the colony; third, the right of Americans to self-taxation was asserted; fourth, unconstitutional taxes and the "extending the Courts of Admiralty beyond their ancient limits" were declared to be destructive of liberty; fifth, it was stated that the right of Americans to "a trial by a Jury of the vicinage, in all capital cases, is the grand security of freedom, and the birthright of Englishmen." At the end of March the Assembly incorporated these resolutions into three petitions addressed to the King, the House of Lords, and the House of Commons. On March 3 the New York House of Assembly adjourned never to meet again.[8]

Although Alexander McDougall reported that the "Statement of Grievances" met with general approval, the Assembly's refusal to consider the proceedings of the First Continental Congress, as well as its decision to ignore altogether the Second Continental Congress scheduled for May, was widely and angrily condemned.[9] Patriot anger was directed principally at the De Lanceys, and it quickly took a most extreme form. Rumors spread that De Lanceyites in the New York Council and Assembly had accepted ministerial bribes; within weeks of the Assembly's adjournment New York was implicated from one end of the continent to the other in nothing less than a sinister ministerial plot to subvert the colonial cause.

By and large the charges were quite impossible to prove and in any case most remained vague and imprecise, their authors proceeding more by innuendo and suspicion than on the basis of fact. They tell very little about the conduct of New York's leaders, but a great deal about the public mood in all the colonies: the fears and uncertainties of Americans everywhere, the widespread recognition of New York's political and strategic significance.

Rumors of a ministerial conspiracy involving New York began to circulate in March. Most appear to have originated outside New

York. The following letter from the General Committee of Charleston, South Carolina, addressed to the Committee of Sixty was typical:

> We are not insensible of the consequence of your Colony in the great Chain of *American* Union.—Nor do we imagine the Ministry insensible of it; we are well aware of your unhappy situation, and of the many artful measures that have been, and now are, taking, if possible, to throw you into confusion. We are well aware of the poison that is daily distilling from some of your pensioned presses, and the hireling writers that have crept among you. We are not ignorant of that crowd of placemen, of contractors, of officers, and needy dependents upon the Crown, who are constantly employed to frustrate your measures. We know the dangerous tendency of being made the headquarters of *America* for many years.[10]

The rumors of New York's perfidy often originated in England among pro-American sources close to the parliamentary opposition and business community. A case in point was William Lee, a scion of the Virginia Lees and an English-trained lawyer resident in London since 1768. Lee moved easily among the nation's foremost policy makers, politicians, and businessmen. Along with his brother, Arthur Lee, the colonial agent for Massachusetts, he was deeply involved in local city politics as a partisan of John Wilkes, the radical writer prosecuted for seditious libel in 1763. In 1773 Lee was elected sheriff of London, and two years later was elected alderman, the only American ever to hold that post. Writing from London in September 1774, Lee warned his brother, Richard Henry Lee, that the Ministry was contemplating the use of military force to bring the colonies into line and was actively looking for support in America for such a policy. Lee wrote: "In this progress, you will no doubt find many obstructions from the slavish principles of some, and the prospects of rewards and preferments, which are liberally held out from hence, to some principal people in all the colonies, and particularly in New York." In January 1775 Lee again advised his brother that a buildup of British military forces in

America was imminent "to support the friends of government, as they are fashionably called, who conspire to destroy the Liberties of their country, viz: the Hutchinsons, Ingersolls, De Lanceys, etc." A month later Lee reported that "Colden, Watts, De Lancey, White one of the Council, McEvers, and Lott the Treasurer of New York, have written that they will support the ministerial and forming schemes to create a division among the Colonies, and plans against America." [11]

Doubts in the other colonies about New York's fidelity to the American cause were allayed temporarily by the election of the Committee of Sixty and the obvious determination of the Committee to enforce the terms of the Continental Association. In November 1774, for example, William Hooper of North Carolina observed to James Duane that "I have surprised every person with whom I have conversed with the candid representation I have made of the New Yorkers and their firm and steady resolution strictly to adhere to the proceedings of the Congress." Such sentiments were short-lived, however. The conduct of the Assembly immediately aroused all the old suspicions of ministerial treachery. By February Alexander McDougall was predicting that New York would be the last colony north of Georgia to take up arms against the king.[12]

The most remarkable, and certainly the most detailed, attack on the integrity of the New York provincial government was launched in the pages of the *Pennsylvania Journal* of February 22, 1775. The attack took the form of a description and analysis of the English interests and connections of each of the members of the New York Council and Assembly. It was a brilliant piece of propaganda, subtly evoking on the strength of very little hard evidence an atmosphere of the most terrible corruption.

If the *Journal* was to be believed, New York was in the grasp of ministerial tools and scoundrels. It appeared that only three men among the colony's political leadership were free of damaging ministerial ties: Councillor William Axtell, and Assemblymen Charles De Witt and Jacobus Myndertse, the members for Ulster county and the town of Schenectady respectively. Axtell possessed personal credentials likely to warm the heart of any true friend of liberty. According to the *Journal,* he was "descended from Colonel

Axtell, who guarded the High Court of Justice at the Trial of King Charles the First." [13] Nothing was reported of De Witt or Myndertse, who were described simply as "farmers."

As Crown appointees, all the Council stood condemned. Their terms of appointment were not, of course, remarkable, but the *Journal* nevertheless successfully conveyed the impression that in the case of New York, unlike other colonies, the appointments were of particularly sinister significance. The interests of the Council read as follows: Colden was "well known for his zeal for issuing the stamped papers in 1765"; Daniel Horsmanden, the chief justice, received £500 annually "out of the American revenue in the Boston Box"; John Watts was related by marriage to the De Lancey family; Oliver De Lancey was a "brigadier General of the Militia, and father-in-law to Sir William Draper, and brother to Lady Warren, whose daughter married Colonel Fitzroy, brother to the Duke of Grafton"; Charles Ward Apthorpe was related to Mrs. Thomas Gage and a former army contractor; Roger Morris was a retired lieutenant colonel who had married into the Philipse family "and then sold out"; William Smith had one son in the army and a brother-in-law on the personal staff of General Gage; Hugh Wallace was a merchant "greatly connected with the army"; Henry White had been an agent for the East India Company and was a navy victualler; John Harris Cruger was a De Lancey relative; and James Jauncey, Jr., the master of the rolls, was married to the daughter of Andrew Eliot, collector for the port of New York, who in turn was the brother of Sir Gilbert Eliot, "one of the Carlton House junto." [14]

Although the connections of most of the assemblymen were not as important as those of the councillors, they were in the opinion of the *Journal* equally worthy of note. Five deputies were related to members of the Council and shared their English ties: James De Lancey, Jacob Walton, John Cruger, James Jauncey, and Frederick Philipse. Three assemblymen possessed connections of special interest and concern: James De Lancey was the brother-in-law of Governor John Penn of Pennsylvania; Isaac Wilkins, a former student of Dr. Myles Cooper at King's College and "an intimate friend of Dr. Chandler of Elizabeth town," was preparing himself for "Episcopal Orders"; Peter R. Livingston was a brother-in-law of

Lord Percy, an officer attached to Gage's command. In addition, a large number of deputies held lesser posts under the crown. Fifteen were officers in the colonial militia, while 11 held minor judicial appointments "during pleasure" or acted as justices of the peace.

It was, to be sure, an intriguing catalog, but it was far from being an indictment for treason. Perceptive readers could well ask: So what? Leading men in every colony had their English connections, and most of the more successful merchants had done business at some time with the armed forces. Certainly service in the militia, required by law of all able-bodied men, or in some minor court post hardly constituted serious evidence of tory inclinations. Mindful of a skeptical public opinion, the *Journal* concluded its report by posing a question: "Whether the great number of crown officers, or their near relations in the Assembly, is not proof either of our extreme negligence of our Liberties, or of the vigilance of government for biassing our Members?" [15]

The rumor mill ground on. Considerable grist was added in May when, for the first time, specific allegations of bribery reached the colonies. Again, the source of this intelligence was William Lee. In a letter written in April, Lee asserted that the Ministry had dispatched £125,000 to General Gage to be used to buy support among colonial leaders. According to Lee, the Ministry expected most of the money to be spent in New York. "Several of the majority in the Assembly," Lee wrote, "all of whose names I have not yet learnt, had actually received a bribe, in money of £1000 sterling a man, to vote as they did in the Assembly in January last, against taking into consideration the proceedings of your Congress." The De Lanceys, Wattses, and Coldens, Lee asserted, "are to be rewarded much higher, by places of honour, profit, and pensions." As Lee understood the Ministry's intentions, John Watts was to be named lieutenant governor. Colden would retire on a comfortable pension. James McEvers, characterized by Lee as "a young Colden," and members of the Watts family were to be offered places on the governor's Council. Myles Cooper, the president of King's College, would be consecrated as the first American bishop. James Vardill, a former New Yorker long resident in London and "a ministerial writer against America, under the signature of Coriolanus," was promised a position as King's Professor at King's College at an annual salary of £200. Major Philip Skene, a retired army officer now turned New York land speculator, was to receive two appointments as commandant of Crown Point and as Surveyor of the Woods, and as well 120,000 acres of land. Other less-prominent New Yorkers, Lee added, were also scheduled to receive generous land grants.[16]

In January 1775, for example, Philip Skene was appointed governor of the forts of Crown Point and Ticonderoga, and was given the promised land grant. In April the ministry awarded Cooper and Chandler honorariums worth £200 per annum for "your merits and Services," and James Rivington, printer of the *New York Gazeteer,* a paper distinguished for its proadministration policy, was named king's printer at an annual salary of £100.[17]

The most obvious manifestation of ministerial bribery involved the disposition of land grants, and on this count the government was clearly guilty as charged. During the spring of 1775 Lord Dartmouth, the colonial secretary, began urging Governor Tryon, who returned to New York in June, to assure New Yorkers of the king's wish to indulge "every reasonable request" of "His faithful subjects in New York." In April the Ministry issued a "secret" warrant to a Colonel Allen MacLean authorizing him to raise a regiment of loyal troops from among New York's Scottish community on the understanding that each head of family recruited was to be promised a hundred acres of land. It says a good deal about attitudes in New York that the scheme failed almost completely, though MacLean later recruited about 700 men in Quebec. Other similar efforts were more successful, however. In all between April 1775 and July 1776, the most critical period for British policy makers, loyalist families received nearly 275,000 acres in New York, including the disputed New Hampshire Grants region.[18]

A fascinating insight into the techniques of ministerial bribery is contained in the unpublished autobiography of Philip Van Cortlandt. Writing after the Revolution, Van Cortlandt recalled Governor Tryon's attempts to induce his father, Pierre Van Cortlandt, to join the loyalist cause by generous offers of land. In a manner suggestive of the biblical account of the Temptation of Jesus, Van Cortlandt described how on the eve of the Revolution Tryon took his father to a high point of land and told him that all the land he could see would be his if he enlisted with the king. Van Cortlandt declined.[19]

This leaves unresolved the issue of the bribing of members of the Assembly in which the De Lanceys were directly involved. Were assemblymen bribed? The question is as important as it is controversial. Bernard Mason inclines toward the view that the bribery charges may well be true. The supporting evidence, he believes, is contained in William Smith's account, discussed above, of the January 9 meeting of De Lancey leaders at Hull's Tavern. There, it will be recalled, the De Lanceys had calculated a vote of 14-11 in favor of the Continental Congress, but in the Assembly the actual vote on the Livingston motion to endorse the proceedings at Philadelphia was 11-10 against the motion. The De Lancey eleven held firm, but how are we to explain the abstentions on the Livingston or whig side? Was pressure applied, and, if so, what sort? [20]

A definite answer cannot be given. Certainly Mason's point is a telling one. Nevertheless, within the broader context of events since 1764 the Assembly's conduct is not perhaps as sinister as might be supposed. Over a ten-year period the Assembly's record had been consistent. The House under Livingston and later De Lancey leadership had vigorously pressed the case for American rights in a manner hardly pleasing to British authorities. At the time of the Stamp Act crisis the New York Assembly led the American protest, and the House continued in its own fashion to establish a somewhat independent course. A key factor which must be borne in mind in any interpretation of the Assembly's behavior was the Colden-De Lancey deal of 1769. The radicals never forgave the De Lanceys for what they regarded as an act of the basest treachery; from that moment the radicals believed the De Lanceys were tools of the Ministry. But were they? As Whitehall recognized only too well, the De Lanceys had in fact struck a significant blow for local autonomy by inducing Colden to violate his instructions on a matter of major policy. A review of events provides no evidence whatever that before late 1774 the British ever once regarded New York or its political leaders as pillars of ministerial support.

It is also worth repeating that most of the charges of bribery originated outside New York. Within New York itself the Assembly's behavior was viewed rather differently. Despite Colden's enthusiastic assertion in February 1775 that "the loyalty and firmness of the Assembly of this Province, and of the People in general will appear in a very strong light," the Assembly's actions fell far short of the sort of behavior which might have been expected of dutiful, not to mention bribed, subjects. Many New Yorkers, including some whose sympathies were clearly radical, believed that the Assembly's resolutions were in line with the spirit if not the letter of congressional policy. William Livingston, for example, conceded that the Assembly shared the same "fundamental principles" as the Congress, differing from that body only "in modes of opposition." John Rogers, a presbyterian pastor close to the Liberty Boys, observed that, "The Assembly of this Province is the only one on the Continent that has met and not approved the measures of the Continental Congress. . . . They too determine to oppose the present measures of Administration towards us only in a different mode." Another observer, Samuel Cooper, reported that "the Assembly at New York forbade an express approbation [of the Continental Congress] but have resolved almost all the Acts complained of by the Congress to be Grievances." Two colonists rejected outright any suggestion that bribery had had any effect on the Assembly's conduct. Peter Van Schaack, a future loyalist and admittedly a man inclined toward an optimistic interpretation of the Assembly's actions, declared, "we cannot, people *will not,* receive partial favors in this time of general calamity. Our Assembly, I am confident, had no such aim, and they generously meant, by their proceedings, to subserve the *common cause.*" Another writer noted: "The ministerial influence at New York has not prevailed as was expected, to keep that colony from joining the others. Great dependence was had upon their monied men; but the cause of liberty was too popular, and the numbers that espoused it too many and too independent, either to be bribed or overawed." Finally, it should be added that these views also reflected the Ministry's opinion. It angrily rejected the Assembly's petitions and statement of grievances on the grounds that they differed little from the sentiments expressed by the Continental Congress.[21]

In the final analysis, however, the bribery question must remain unresolved. This is perhaps fitting because it symbolizes the hard fact that by the spring of 1775 the Assembly's conduct was no longer a matter of political significance. The Assembly lost its last chance to influence policy when it voted against the proceedings of the Continental Congress. The impact of that vote and its decisive results were aptly summarized by William Livingston: "The party attached to the interest of the Bostonians were greatly embarrassed. They could obtain no sanction from the powers of government and were obliged to proceed in an unconstitutional manner." [22] The Revolution had begun.

The dismantling of the old regime was already well advanced before the Assembly had ended. Since late 1774 the Committee of Sixty had exercised effective control over the city's, and to a lesser extent, the colony's economy. The Continental Association was carefully and thoroughly enforced. During December 1774 and January 1775, for example, the Committee confiscated "illegal" imports worth an auctioned value of nearly £350, which in accordance with the terms of the Association was applied to the relief of Boston's poor. The complete success of the boycott was readily acknowledged even by its most committed opponents. Cadwallader Colden, for example, noted that the boycott "is ever rigidly maintained in this Place," and he added a significant point by way of explanation: "The enemys of Government do all they can to propagate an opinion that the Ministry will yet draw back and quiet the Colonies by a Repeal, they constantly held up the case of the Stamp Act, and find this an Argument which influences many friends of the Government to lye bye; dreading the consequences of making themselves conspicuous in the Cause should the Government again yield." [23] Colden's interpretation was open to question, but his facts were essentially accurate. The radicals were succeeding not by subterfuge so much as by the fact that a large majority of the colonists, including "conservatives" who expected another "Stamp Act crisis," warmly approved of the radical program of resistance.

A good illustration of the extent of bipartisan support for rigid enforcement of the Association was provided by the events surrounding the arrival of the Glasgow-based ship, *James*, in early February. An attempt to dock and unload the *James'* cargo on

February 2 was immediately "suppressed" by an angry Sears-led "Mob." For several days the *James* lay at anchor off Sandy Hook under the watchful eye of the ever-vigilant Committee of Sixty. On Thursday, February 9, the *James* again entered the harbor, this time escorted by His Majesty's Ship *Kingfisher*. This caused, as William Smith reported, "an uproar at the Coffee House" led by none other than Oliver De Lancey. "Oliver De Lancey," Smith wrote, "came down to the Coffee House, and said to Philip Livingston and Francis Lewis pointing to the Scotch Ship, *What does that damned Rascal come up here again for? Why don't he quit the Port?* John De Lancey was also active in declaring that the Fellow was not solicited to stay. . . ." Meanwhile, the *James'* commander, a Captain Watson, was seized by angry patriots, "some of whom appeared armed," and paraded through the streets. "Urged by the Populace," Watson hastily retreated to the safety of the *Kingfisher*, whose captain had also been chased "by Sears and 20 men." The affair ended as abruptly as it had begun with the departure of the *James* on February 12.[24]

Another incident in early March attested to the continuing effectiveness of the boycott. Two merchants, the brothers John and Robert Murray, attempted for a second time to violate the terms of the Association. Fearing "great loss" financially to themselves, they secretly landed a small cargo at Elizabethtown, New Jersey, across from Staten Island. The secret was soon out. The Murrays were hauled before irate members of the Committee of Sixty and made to apologize for "the trouble and uneasiness" they had caused. Alexander McDougall reported that "our citizens were so enraged at them for the horrid deed, that it was with difficulty they were prevailed upon not to banish them." He added that this demonstration would undoubtedly "deter any man, however base, from another breach." [25]

It was only a short step from directing the colony's economy to directing its politics. In fact, it was evident that the transition had in large measure already been effected. The selection of delegates to the Second Continental Congress and the establishment of a provincial congress in late February and early March placed political control of New York firmly in the hands of the Committee of Sixty. The idea of forming a provincial congress to supersede the Assembly had clearly been canvassed for some time among leaders of the Livingston and Sons of Liberty factions. In late February three pro-Livingston leaders in the Assembly dispatched a revealing letter to Abraham Yates, Jr., chairman of Albany's Committee of Inspection. The letter, written by Philip Schuyler, Abraham Ten Broeck, and Peter R. Livingston, the representatives for Albany, and the manors of Rensselaerswyck and Livingston respectively, read in part as follows:

> You will at one glance perceive by the last decision of the house, that there is no prospect that It will recommend to this Colony the appointment of delegates to attend at the next proposed Congress. We think it therefore our duty to give you the early Intelligence, that you and the other Gentlemen who recommended to us to approve of the proceedings of the Congress may take such measures as the exigency of the case, your own good sense, and your affection for the publick welfare in this very Critical hour shall point out, prompted however by sentiments of the most cordial affection for the Interest, and honor of our Country, we venture to suggest, that we think it would be attended with Salutary Effects if our respectable County took the lead on this Occasion, and recommended to the other Counties in the Colony the appointment of delegates to meet in provincial Congress for the Purpose of the entering into such resolutions as the State of this Colony may require and for appointing delegates to it in this Continental Congress, and we have reason to Conclude, that several of the Counties wish this mode to be adopted. . . .[26]

The success of a provincial congress was closely related to and dependent upon the election of delegates to the Second Continental Congress, and it was a mark of the political sagacity of the militants on the Committee of Sixty that they were able to present these two related but independent issues to the city's voters as one package. On March 1, 1775 the Sixty posted copies of the following notice calling upon the freeholders and freemen to assemble at the Exchange Monday, March 6 to answer two questions:

> To the Freeholders and Freemen of the City and County of New York.

As the last Congress, held at Philadelphia, recommended, That another Congress should be convened at the same Place, on the 10th Day of May next; and the Election of Delegates ought not longer to be delayed, most of the other Colonies having already appointed them. And as this Committee has no Power without the Approbation of their Constitutents, to take any Measures for that Purpose: They therefore request, That the Freeholders and Freemen of the City and County of New York, will be pleased to assemble at the Exchange on Monday the 6th Instant, at 12 o'clock, to signify their Sense of the best Method of choosing such Delegates; and whether they will appoint a certain Number of Persons to meet such Deputies as the Counties may elect for that Purpose, and join with them in appointing out of their Body Delegates for the next Congress.[27]

The Sixty also announced that a convention of deputies—in fact, the nucleus of a provincial congress—would gather April 20 at New York City.

Of the two questions, the second was the more critical; an affirmative answer would have the effect of formally transfering legislative authority in the colony from the Assembly to a new congress. The course proposed was revolutionary, and not surprisingly those opposed to revolution made a determined effort to block it. The opponents, led by the De Lanceys and described as "a number of Citizens equally reputable with those of the Committee, and far superior in numbers," met on the evening of Friday, March 3 at the Broadway tavern of the Widow De La Montagnie to plan a counteroffensive.[28]

Actually, the results of the meeting were inconclusive. The De Lancey faction's chief worry was that the radicals would repeat their triumph of May 1774. A key to the radicals' success then had been their manipulation of public meetings to secure approval of measures not necessarily supported by a majority of the colonists. It was now evident, especially to those who were still serious in their desire to see a reconciliation, that by surrendering to the radicals on the issues of storing East India tea, the Boston Port Act, and the First Continental Congress, much had been lost. Perhaps it was not too late to reverse the direction of events. The De Lancey leadership consequently pressed hard for an exact polling of the city on the question of choosing delegates to the Second Continental Congress. In particular, they opposed the debating of difficult constitutional questions before huge mass audiences. "They were apprised," the meeting declared, "of the confusion, the heats, and animosity, of which such a proceeding is generally productive; that on such occasions those citizens, who alone ought to be consulted, and who alone have a right to give their voices, namely, the *Freeholders* and *Freemen*, were liable to insults and indignities." The Friends of Constitutional Liberty, as the De Lanceys and their friends now styled themselves, accordingly proposed that the election of delegates be postponed indefinitely until measures agreeable to "all parties" could be devised. News of the meeting brought a swift response from the Liberty Boys. On Saturday, March 4, they issued a statement warning that the purpose of the Friday meeting was "to defeat the design of sending Delegates to the Congress," and announcing their own determination to adhere to the Sixty's recommendations.[29]

Accounts of the freeholders meeting of March 6 vary considerably. Clearly, feelings ran high and tempers were short. Serious violence was only just avoided, while some minor fisticuffs did occur. Something of the atmosphere of the meeting is suggested by the two following reports. The first is by the De Lancey stalwart, Thomas Jones, and presents the De Lancey or, as Jones terms it, "loyalist" point of view:

Early in March, 1775, the City committee notified the inhabitants, that on such a day, the delegates for the ensuing Congress would be elected, and desired their appearance at the Exchange for that purpose. The Loyalists had already determined to oppose the election. The day came. The Loyalists assembled in the Fields, and went to the place of election in a body peaceably and quietly. They consisted of at least, four to one of all the legal voters in the City, and had a poll been taken, it would have appeared so. The republican party in order to swell their numbers, marched round all the docks and wharves, with trumpets blowing, fifes playing, drums beating, and colours flying; by this means collecting all the boys, sailors, negroes, New England and Jersey boatmen, that could be mustered. The motley assemblage marched to the place of election, where a large and select party of the most violent republican partizans (contrary to the laws and rules of elections) formed themselves into a company, armed with bludgeons and quarter-staves, under the direction of and headed by Isaac Sears, and Richard Livingston, with John Smith, Joshua Hett Smith, and Peter R. Livingston, . . . and threatened destruction to any person who should oppose the election of delegates.[30]

The second report is from the *New York Journal,* a paper friendly to the Liberty Boys:

Early on Monday Morning Preparations were made for the Meeting in the Exchange; A Union Flag with a red field was hoisted on the Liberty Pole, where at nine o'clock the Friends of Freedom assembled and having got into proper readiness, about 11 o'clock the Body began their March to the Exchange. They were attended by Music; and two Standard Bearers carried a large Union Flag, with a Blue Field on which were the following inscriptions: GEORGE 111, REX AND THE LIBERTIES OF AMERICA. NO POPERY. On the other [side] THE UNION OF THE COLONIES AND THE MEASURES OF THE CONGRESS. Sometime after they had arrived at the Exchange came also the other company who had met at the Widow De La Montagnie's, among whom were some officers of the Army and Navy, several of His Majesty's Council, and those members of the House of Representatives who had refused taking into consideration the Proceedings of the Congress, together with the officers of the Customs and other Dependants of the Court, etc. Soon after the parties met some confusion arose, but subsided without any bad consequences.[31]

Radicals easily dominated the meeting. Significantly, the questions put to the meeting were not those contained in the March 1 notice. The first question was dropped entirely in an obvious bid to force acceptance of the second. The questions put were these: (1) "Whether they will appoint and authorize a certain Number of Persons to meet such Deputies as the Counties may elect, and join with them, for the Sole Purpose of appointing out of their Body, Delegates for the next Congress?" and (2) "Whether they will authorize the Committee to nominate eleven Deputies for their Approbation?" The *New York Journal* reported that "a very great Majority" answered both questions affirmatively, but conceded that a minority demanded a poll on the first question and claimed that on the second it was impossible "to determine on which side the majority was." [32]

The important point was that once again the radicals had scored a significant victory at the moderates' expense. As in May 1774, the moderates utterly failed to influence public opinion, which was now more or less solidly committed to the radicals' program of extreme resistance. Ironically, the moderates were undone by their own genuine commitment to American liberty and undoubted sympathy for the radicals' point of view. What this meant in practical terms, however, was that no individual or group, with the exception of a few Anglican clergy, came forward to oppose the apparently inevitable drift toward revolution. Such opposition might have had enormous influence in creating a climate of opinion favorable to some form of constitutional reconciliation. If observers as different in outlook as Thomas Jones, William Smith, Alexander McDougall, and Isaac Sears are to be believed, a majority of New Yorkers were still rather moderate on the issue of reconciliation. They were rapidly being radicalized, however, pushed toward rebellion, and the apparent approval of New York's leading men insured that the radical program would succeed with little or no opposition.

Jones' description of the March 6 meeting, while colorful, was thus quite misleading. Far from demonstrating their opposition to the proceedings, the De Lanceys and their friends conveyed the impression that they supported the Committee of Sixty. Smith perceptively grasped the significance of the De Lanceys' conduct:

It was an Infatuation to have Officers of the Crown at their side in the Face of the People as the Pasquinados alleged that the Anti Delegate Men were only such as were in the Interest of Government on Ministerial Principles—Dependent Tools or expectants of Offices. This was a grand Victory to the Liberty Boys—now know their Strength, and will probably be assuming, and it was weak in the Council to shew the Instability of Government.[33]

The radicals had carried the day at the Exchange, but many moderates, including the Livingstons, had been alarmed by the threat of violence and the uncertainty of the result, the protestations of the militants notwithstanding. The questions raised at the public meeting at the Exchange were consequently carefully thrashed out again at two meetings of the Sixty on the evenings of the sixth and eighth respectively. The result was a sort of compromise, though one which in no way really harmed the militants' position. Eleven men were nominated, the five New York delegates to the First Continental Congress, and six new men: Leonard Lispenard, Abraham Walton, Francis Lewis, Isaac Roosevelt, Alexander McDougall, and Abraham Brasher. With the exceptions of Walton, who became a loyalist, and Low, who declined nomination, the loyalty of the new men to the radical program was not in doubt. At the second meeting the moderate John Jay, a man with a foot in both the Livingston and De Lancey camps, persuaded the Committee to adopt election procedures which would insure that only freeholders and freemen voted and that each voter be asked individually the same questions put at the meeting at the Exchange. The polls were to be manned by members of the Sixty and the name of each voter was to be recorded and reported to the Committee. The election was set for March 15.[34]

Campaigning during the next week was hectic. The English traveler, Dr. Robert Honyman saw the campaign this way: "Politics, Politics, Politics! There are numbers of Handbills, Advertisements, Extracts from Letters on both sides daily and hourly printed, published, pasted up, and handed out. Men, women, children, all ranks and professions mad with Politics." Honyman's view was supported by Robert R. Livingston, Jr. Politics, Livingston wrote, is "at present the only subject of the Genteeler people among us." [35]

Opponents of the convention campaigned hardest. Their policy was simple. As one of their political cards put it: "No Provincial

Convention. Let us choose for ourselves. The old Five Delegates. No Deputies." Whatever chance this campaign might have had was ruined on March 13 when Colden laid before Council a letter from Colonial Secretary Dartmouth instructing the lieutenant governor to stop the election of delegates to what Dartmouth termed the "illegal" Second Continental Congress. The Council tried to suppress the letter, fearing it would "excite the People to be more zealous for Delegates," but word of the letter, Smith reported, "was in two Hours in every Man's Mouth." Predictably, the secretary's instruction "animated many for a Congress, who were before Luke warm." [36]

The election results convincingly demonstrated the radicals' popular support. A total of 825 votes were recorded in favor of the convention, with only 163 against. Reporting the results, the Sixty asserted that a majority of those who voted against the convention "declared they were nevertheless for Delegates." [37] A few disgruntled opponents of the convention complained that the questions had been put unfairly, but these objections notwithstanding, the results made evident the radical temper of a majority of New Yorkers.[38] The Committee of Sixty immediately dispatched letters to the counties informing them of the result and urging them to support the convention "as it tends to unite the Counties, and to preserve that harmony between them so essential to the interest of our common cause." [39]

Because of inadequate or incomplete records, the extent of popular support outside New York City for the provincial convention has been a matter of serious controversy among historians. Carl Becker argued persuasively that outside the city anticonvention or "tory" sentiments prevailed, and until recently this interpretation was the predominant one. Recently, however, Bernard Mason has significantly revised traditional opinion by closely studying scattered reports of freeholders' meetings and other similar gatherings. The evidence remains inconclusive, but nevertheless it now seems reasonable to argue that supporters of the convention were probably in the majority.

In at least five counties there is little doubt that the proconvention forces were in the ascendency. Freeholders in Albany, Kings, Suffolk, Orange, and Ulster elected deputies with little or no opposition. Cadwallader Colden, Jr. attempted to organize opposition in Ulster County, claiming that the convention was "unwarranted by law, and unknown to the British Constitution," but the effort was short-lived and a failure.[40]

More serious controversy developed in Dutchess, Queens, and Westchester counties. In Dutchess both supporters and opponents of the convention claimed to be in the majority, and it is impossible to verify the claims of either with any real certainty. Fragmentary pieces of evidence shed some light on the struggle in Dutchess, however. Since January 1775 loyalists had been soliciting signatures to a petition declaring loyalty to the king and denouncing all assemblies "not warranted by the laws of the land." In March the "friends to constitutional liberty and good order" chopped down a Liberty Pole erected by the "friends to Liberty" at Poughkeepsie. Anticonvention men boasted that they could produce lists of names of freeholders opposed to the convention, but declined to do so when challenged directly by local radicals, a fact Mason believes may indicate their minority status. In Queens county pro- and anticonvention forces held separate public meetings at Jamaica and Oyster Bay respectively. The former declared their loyalty to George III and opposition to the convention, while the latter resolved to send unofficial deputies. At Hempstead a majority of voters opposed the convention, but those at Newton and Flushing supported it. In Westchester County the opponents of the convention made a serious attempt to prevent the election of deputies. At a freeholders' meeting on April 11 they appeared in force, led by Isaac Wilkins and Frederick Philipse, Westchester's representatives in the Assembly. They condemned the proceedings and departed, marching to the singing of "God Save the King." The remaining freeholders were unimpressed by this display, however, and elected six deputies to represent the county in the convention.[41]

On April 20 the convention assembled as scheduled. Little time was spent on formal preliminaries. After choosing Philip Livingston chairman, the deputies immediately got down to the business of electing delegates to the Second Continental Congress. The colony's delegation to the First Continental Congress was unanimously reelected, as well as five new men. The delegation consisted of Philip Livingston, James Duane, John Alsop, John Jay, Simon

Boerum, William Floyd, and Henry Wisner, the old delegates, and Philip Schuyler, George Clinton, Lewis Morris, Robert R. Livingston, Jr., and Francis Lewis. The delegation was authorized "to concert and determine upon such measures as shall be judged most effectual for the re-establishment of American rights and privileges, and for the restoration of harmony between Great Britain and her Colonies." [42]

But there would be no reconciliation. On April 19, 1775 British regulars sent from Boston by General Gage to seize arms and ammunition stored by the colonists at Concord, Massachusetts, clashed twice with local militia at Lexington and Concord. Resistance had become rebellion.

News of the battle reached New York City April 23. The city was stunned, especially as rumors had flooded the city for the past week that Parliament was about to grant the colonies self-taxation. The rumors had been enough to persuade a number of merchants to fill lucrative orders from the British army in Boston, a goodwill gesture that brought an instant and hostile response from the Liberty Boys. On the afternoon of April 15 the mechanics had paraded through the streets "occasioning many tumults and outrages." Isaac Sears had been arrested for disturbing the peace, but was immediately set free, whereupon he was "led in triumph through the Town." [43]

The hope of reconciliation had been shattered. As one observer put it: "Astonished by accounts of acts of hostility in the moment of the expectation of terms of reconciliation, and now filled with distrust, the inhabitants of this city burst through all restraints on the arrival of the intelligence from Boston." Another colonist wrote of New York that "all ranks of people among them are embarked in the common cause, and are sacredly resolved to preserve the cargo or perish with the ship. The few Tories among them are silent; the cry for liberty is irresistible." [44]

Two reports, written by Thomas Jones and William Smith respectively, admirably capture the atmosphere in the city on the day the news of Lexington and Concord arrived and in the weeks immediately following. Jones wrote:

On Sunday morning the 23rd of April a confused account arrived from Boston, of a skirmish at Lexington between a detachment of the Kings troops, and a party of the rebel army; the republicans instantly took the alarm; they had wished for it for a long time, they received the news with avidity. Isaac Sears, John Lamb and Donald Campbell (a half pay officer) paraded the town with drums beating and colours flying, (attended by a mob of negroes, boys, sailors, and pick-pockets) inviting all mankind to take up arms in defence of the "injured rights and liberties of America." The posts were stopped, the mails opened, and the letters read. In the afternoon, a number of the faction under their old leaders, of whom Peter R. Livingston, John Smith, Joshua Hett Smith, Leonard Lispenard, Jr., and Anthony Lispenard, were the most active, seized upon a sloop loaded with provisions for Boston, unloaded her, and cast the cargo into the dock. On the same evening the same set of fellows, under the same leaders broke open the Arsenal in the City Hall, and forcibly took away 1,000 stand of arms, belonging to the City Corporation, and delivered them out to the rabble, to be used as the demagogues of rebellion should direct. The whole city became one continued scene of riot, tumult, and confusion. Troops were enlisted for the service of rebellion, the Loyalists threatened with the gallows, and the property of the Crown plundered and seized upon wherever it could be found.[45]

On April 29 Smith recorded the following observations:

It is impossible fully to describe the agitated State of the Town since last Sunday, when the News first arrived of the Skirmish between Concord and Boston. At all corners People inquisitive for News. Tales of all kinds invented believed, denied, discredited. Sunday in the afternoon Services 2 Sloops laden by Watts for Boston with Provisions unladen. In the Night the City Armory open the Powder taken out of the Powder House. The Taverns filled with Publicans at Night. Little Business done in the Day,—few Jurors and Witnesses attend the Courts. Armed Parties summon the Town publicly to come and take Arms and learn the Manual Exercise. They are publicly delivered out and armed Individuals shew themselves at all Hours in the Streets, consternation in the Face of the Principal Inhabitants. Sears yesterday afternoon with 360 Armed Men waited on Eliot the Collector and got the Keys of the Custom House to shut up the Port. The Merchants are amazed and yet so humbled as only to sigh or complain in whispers. They now dread Sears's Train of armed Men.[46]

Well might Colden remark to a correspondent: "You will be surprised . . . to find how entirely the legal authority of Government is now superseded in this Place, where only a few Months agoe the Prospect of public affairs gave so much satisfaction to the Friends of Government." [47] Rebellion had become revolution, and the shape of the new revolutionary government was already forming.

The radicals moved swiftly to fill the vacuum vacated by government. On April 26 the Committee of Sixty resigned, calling for the election of a new and enlarged committee of 100 members to deal with the latest crisis and the convening of a provincial congress May 22, 1775. Although the mechanics objected to the size of the committee and the large number of pro-De Lancey moderates on it, the Sixty justified their recommendations on the grounds that representation of all factions would guarantee the new committee's success, and that, with regard to the De Lanceys and their friends, "it surely never can be good policy to put it out of their power to join us heartily; it is time enough to reject them when they refuse our aid." The mechanics, however, drew up their own list of 100 names. The elections took place during three days from April 28 to May 1, and although Sears, "with the Pride of a Dictator," attempted to intimidate voters to approve the mechanics' candidates, the Sixty's nominees were confirmed. Accurate analysis of the affiliations of individual members on the new committee is no easy task given the absence of formal party ties, but the careful researches of Becker and Mason, suggest that about 45 of the One Hundred were connected directly or indirectly to the De Lancey interest, 36 to the Livingston-mechanics faction. The ties of 19 members are unknown.[48]

Meanwhile an impotent administration wrestled with the problem of postponing its own imminent demise. Colden organized a summit conference on April 24 of members of the governor's Council, Judge Thomas Jones, Mayor Whitehead Hicks, and Leonard Lispenard, colonel and commander of the city militia. What was to be done, Colden asked? The answers made it clear that the government's prospects were gloomy indeed. Jones advised ordering out the militia to restore order, but Lispenard demurred, bluntly pointing out that the militia's loyalty no longer lay with the government as they "were all Liberty Boys." Hicks stated that "the Magistratic Authority was gone." According to Jones, not, to be sure, the best of witnesses, Smith argued that as "the ferment which then raged in the city was general and not confined to a few" the government ought "to let the populace act as they pleased." Smith himself confided to his diary: "We were thus unanimously of Opinion that we had no Power to do anything and the best mode of proceeding for private Safety and general Peace was to use Diswasion from Violence." The administration formally acknowledged its inability to meet the crisis on May 1 by proroguing the Assembly, scheduled to meet May 3, to early June.[49]

Though it is tempting to see in the comments of observers like Jones, and to a lesser extent Smith, evidence of sharp divisions between patriots and loyalists, radicals and moderates, privileged and unprivileged, there remained a strong undercurrent of fundamental unity, which would be finally broken only with the decision for independence. This basic unity had been of enormous significance since 1764, and it had determined much of the course of the resistance movement. From the beginning of the protest against England's imperial policies following the end of the great war for empire, New Yorkers had acted together, the De Lancey-Livingston split notwithstanding, and had become radicalized together, ever more receptive to extreme measures of resistance. It was this factor more than anything else which tended to make revolution inevitable, and its influence was never more significant than in the months between April 1775 and July 1776. Judge Robert R. Livingston caught the importance of this sense of unity in a remark made to his wife in April: "People here," he wrote, "are perfectly Fearless I mean the Wigs and the Tories born Wigg [sic] so fast that they will soon be as much united as they are in the Massachusetts Bay." [50]

Staying united was no easy thing, however. The arrival on April 29 of the latest issue of the *Pennsylvania Journal* rocked the city with fresh allegations of bribery and corruption against prominent leaders of the De Lancey faction. Preparations were well under-way, the *Journal* asserted, to dispatch troops to New York "where they have, it is said, been requested to be sent by De Lancey, and his band of traitors, Cooper, White, Colden, and Watts, to aid them in securing New York for the Ministry." The report triggered an immediate outburst of furious indignation against the De Lanceys. "The Populace rage," Smith wrote, and Judge Robert Livingston went so far as to state that a few hotheads "actually charged their pieces in order to shoot them." De Lancey leaders did what they could to calm the fury. Oliver De Lancey and John Watts signed affidavits denying the story, and both attended a public meeting in the Fields in the afternoon. Smith noted that De Lancey moved busily among the large crowd "to asswage the Multitude." [51] Pub-lication on the morning of the twenty-ninth of a document entitled, the *Association,* went a long way toward cooling radical tempers. The *Association* was the work of three moderates, James Duane, John Jay, and Peter Van Schaack. Duane and Jay had for years kept up close connections with both the De Lancey and Livingston camps, though both were now moving steadily toward the coalition of the Livingstons and the mechanics. Van Schaack was a commit-ted De Lanceyite and a future loyalist. Despite its authorship, the document was far from being moderate in either tone or purpose. It bound its signatories to adhere strictly to the decisions of the Conti-nental Congress and to "follow the advice of our General Commit-tee, respecting . . . the preservation of peace, and good order, and the safety of individual and private property." The *Association* was posted at the Coffee House where it was greeted by general enthu-siasm. Smith stated that "all Parties ran this Morning to sign the Association at the Coffee House." The De Lanceys led the way, making themselves conspicuous at a large gathering at the Liberty Pole called to approve the *Association.* The *New York Gazetteer* reported that the *Association* drew the signatures of "one thousand of the principal inhabitants." For a brief moment, the *Association* "seemed to give Peace." [52]

Acclaim for the *Association* and the election of the Committee of One Hundred obscured briefly an issue of great and fundamental importance. The outbreak of organized warfare between British regulars and American patriots, as opposed to protest rallies, riots, sporadic violence, or other forms of minor public disorder, gave for the first time since 1764 significant meaning to terms like "tory" and "patriot." Before Lexington and Concord there were, properly speaking, no "loyalists," though men of the stripe of Colden or Seabury were known to have "ministerial" sympathies. Nor, Thomas Jones notwithstanding, were there any "republicans" or "independents." These words no longer were merely derisive. As they took on discrete and definite meaning, Americans struggled to define themselves, to choose sides as either "rebels" or "loyalists."

Radical bombast aside, the choice was an extremely difficult one to make. The natural inclination was to postpone it, and New Yorkers did this in the months following Lexington and Concord by seeing themselves as loyal rebels: people loyal to their King and the institutions of royal authority, but rebels against the king's unjust laws and bad ministers. It was a hard and awkward role to play, to prepare for peaceful reconciliation and war at the same time, but New York made the effort. For example, in May 1775 the Committee of One Hundred assured Colden "that though they are arming with the greatest diligence and industry; it is not with design to oppose, but to strengthen Government in the due exercise of constitutional authority. It is to be in a state of readiness to repel every lawless attack by our superiors and to prevent the anarchy and confusion to which ministerial misconduct has paved the way." [53]

It is a matter of some controversy how hard New York pressed for reconciliation, resisting the drift toward independence in the spring of 1775 and later. Those historians who follow Becker's thesis have tended to emphasize New York's conservative reluctance to abandon the old empire. Certainly some of the actions of the New York provincial congress, which met in the last week of May, suggest an unwillingness to enter fully into extreme measures of resistance. For one thing, the congress was very reluctant to assume formally the responsibilities of a properly elected legislature. For example, it deferred indefinitely consideration of a motion which declared "that this Congress is competent to, and ought freely to deliberate and determine on all matters relative to the internal police of this Colony." In most other respects, however, the congress was far from conciliatory. A case in point was the congress' "Plan of Accommodation" drawn up at the end of June. The Plan demanded from English authorities a repeal of all unconstitutional acts affecting the American colonies and a firm acknowledgement and guarantee of the right of Americans to self-taxation and "a free and exclusive power of legislation within themselves . . . in all cases whatsoever." In return, New York promised to contribute to the costs of defense and the maintenance of civil government and to recognize England's right to regulate imperial trade.[54]

An even better indication of the provincial congress' fundamental commitment to extreme resistance was the rapid buildup of New York's defenses. Haste was vital as the strategic importance of New York was acknowledged by military leaders on both the American and British sides: The colony would be either a link between New England and Virginia, the principal centers of revolutionary sentiment, or a wedge dividing the rebellious provinces. During May and June the provincial congress, acting in response to appeals from Philadelphia, undertook the removal of cannon and stores from the British forts at Crown Point and Ticonderoga, which had fallen to Ethan Allen's Green Mountain Boys on May 10, and began to prepare plans for the erecting of fortifications and gun batteries along the approaches to Manhattan Island. At the same time the congress urged New Yorkers to take up arms and "to perfect themselves in the military art, and, if necessary, to form themselves into Companies." On June 27 the deputies issued detailed instructions for the recruitment of soldiers. Finally, the congress debated the practicability of issuing paper money to finance the local war effort.

There was, however, no stronger evidence of the triumph of radical policies than that reflected in popular attitudes toward the loyalists. With the outbreak of fighting the question of loyalty to the new regime was of the utmost significance, and the leaders of both the Committee of One Hundred and the provincial congress were fully aware of its critical importance. Quite simply, dissenting opinions could not be tolerated. The matter of loyalty was taken up at the first session of the One Hundred at the beginning of May. The

Committee adopted a suggestion put forward by John Morin Scott and Alexander McDougall "to offer the Association without delay to the inhabitants of this City and County." The *Association* was the April 29 document drafted by Duane, Jay, and Van Schaack; it was to be offered to everyone except Cadwallader Colden—a lost soul in the eyes of the revolutionaries! Anyone who refused to sign was to be reported, though such persons were not to be designated enemies to their country "but by the determination of the Continental or Provincial Congress, or by this Committee." Despite the obvious warnings of proscription, the response to the *Association* was somewhat disappointing. By early June Colden, not, to be sure, a disinterested observer, reported that only 1800 people had signed, although "there must be at least three times that number who have an equal Right to sign." [55]

A large number of signatures might have high propaganda value, but they were really quite irrelevant as a serious measure of the stability of the new regime, which continued to move ahead without setback from strength to strength. On May 8 the One Hundred disarmed all loyalists under its jurisdiction. The Committee resolved that any citizen "who shall, during the unhappy contest with our Parent State, dispose of any Arms, Ammunition . . . to any person, knowing or have reason to believe such person to be inimical to the liberties of America, or shall put those articles in the hands of any such person, or any other person, knowing or have reason to believe that they are to be used against these liberties, he shall be held up as an enemy to this Country." By the end of May, the One Hundred's policies for New York City had been applied to the colony as a whole by the provincial congress.[56]

Though it has often been said that the American Revolution lacked much of the internal social upheaval and violence of other allegedly more bloody and chaotic revolutions, pronouncements like the one quoted above, especially the arbitrary designation of "enemies to this country" had the sort of ominous and tyrannical ring which has been characteristic of revolutionary movements in general. The parallels between the American and other revolutions are most noticeable perhaps with respect to the patriots' treatment of the loyalists, and they deserve attention, especially as they have been rather glossed over by historians. Documents like the one quoted above for disarming the loyalists make one thing very clear: More was going on in the colonies during 1774 and 1775 than merely political debates about ideology, political rights, or constitutions. The tough proscriptions against loyalists and their sympathizers, impersonalized as "enemies to this country," illustrated a fundamental point which cannot be stressed too much: The American Revolution began with an illegal seizure of power by revolutionary regimes in the different colonies *cum* states, which proceeded ruthlessly to crush all opposition. Like revolutionaries at other times and in other places, the American revolutionaries spoke in the name of the "people" and acted through the agencies of various "people's" committees of one kind or another. That they did not resort to the guillotine or its equivalent was not perhaps because this revolution was "different," but because such actions were quite unnecessary. Loyalists were silenced by effective but less spectacular means. The result was decisive. By the end of the Revolutionary War loyalism as a political force and an ideology had ceased to exist.

NOTES

1. Colden to Admiral Samuel Graves, February 20, 1775, *Colden Letter Books, 1760-1775,* II, pp. 387-388.
2. Smith, *Historical Memoirs,* I, p. 203.
3. Ibid., pp. 206-207.
4. Ibid., p. 208.
5. *New York Assembly Journal,* January 28, March, 1, 2, 3, 8, 1775.
6. *American Archives,* 4th series, I, pp. 1290-1293. Brush's constituency, Cumberland county, lay within the disputed New Hampshire Grants region between New Hampshire and New York. The district declared its independence as the State of Vermont in 1777; New York relinquished claims to Vermont in 1790.
7. Ibid., pp. 1293-1297.
8. *New York Assembly Journal,* March, 3, 8, 25, 1775.
9. McDougall to Josiah Quincy, Jr., April 6, 1775, *American Archives,* 4th series, II, pp. 283-284.
10. General Committee of Charleston to Committee of Sixty, March 1, 1775, ibid., pp. 1-2.
11. Lee to Richard Henry Lee, Spetember 19, 1774, January 10, 1775, February 25, 1775, *Letters of William Lee,* 3 vols., Worthington C.

Ford, ed. (New York, 1891), I, pp. 90, 96, 119-120, 127-129. See also Arthur Lee to Samuel Adams, February 24, 1775, Samuel Adams Papers, 1775-1776, New York Public Library.

12. Hooper to Duane, November 22, 1774, Duane Papers, Box III, New York Historical Society; McDougall to William Cooper, February 9, 1775, McDougall Papers, Box I, New York Historical Society.

13. Colonel Daniel Axtell commanded the guards at Westminster Hall during Charles' trial. See C.V. Wedgewood, *The Trial of Charles I* (London, 1964), p. 216.

14. George O. Trevelyan described Sir Gilbert Eliot as "the famous King's Friend in the House of Commons." Trevelyan, *George the Third and Charles Fox*, 2 vols. (London, 1912-1914), II, p. 196. Carlton House was one of the homes of George III's mother, the Princess Dowager.

15. *Pennsylvania Journal*, February 22, 1775.

16. William Lee to Samuel Adams, April 10, 1775, Samuel Adams, Papers, 1775-1776, New York Public Library.

17. John Pownell to James Rivington, April 5, 1775, and Pownell to Cooper and Chandler, April 5, 1775, *New York Colonial Documents*, VIII, pp. 568-569; Mason, *Road to Independence*, p. 52.

18. Dartmouth to Tryon, April 21 and May 4, 1775, *New York Colonial Documents*, VIII, pp. 569-573; Warrant to McLean, April 3, 1775, ibid., pp. 562-564; Mason, *Road to Independence*, pp. 90-91.

19. Philip Van Cortlandt, MSS Autobiography, 1, reverse side, Van Cortlandt Wills and Miscellaneous Box, New York Public Library.

20. Mason, *Road to Independence*, p. 52; Smith, *Historical Memoirs*, p. 208.

21. Colden to Dartmouth, February, 1775, *The Colden Letter Books 1760-1775*, II, p. 383; William Livingston, History of the Revolution, Chapter IV, pp. 52, 59, John Jay Papers, Box I, New York Historical Society; John Rogers to T.J. Esq., February 1775, *Historical Manuscripts Commission, Report Eleven: The Manuscripts of the Earl of Dartmouth* (London, 1887), p. 374; Cooper to Benjamin Franklin, April 1, 1775, Bancroft Transcripts, p. 79, New York Public Library; William Gordon, *The History of the Rise, Progress, and Establishment, of the the Independence of the United States of America: Including an Account of the late War; and of the Thirteen Colonies, from their Origin to that Period*, 4 vols. (London, 1788), I, p. 394. For British reaction, see Dartmouth to Tryon, May 23, 1775, *Cadwallader Colden Papers*, VII, pp. 295-296. See also Peter Van Schaack to John

Maunsell, May 7, 1775, Henry C. Van Schaack, *Life of Peter Van Schaack*, p. 39.

22. Livingston, History of the Revolution, Chapter II, pp. 72-73, John Jay Papers, Box I, New York Historical Society.

23. McDougall, "Notes on the Committee of Sixty, January-April 1775," McDougall Papers, Box I, New York Historical Society; *American Archives*, 4th series, II, pp. 342-343; Colden to Dartmouth, March 1, 1775, *New York Colonial Documents*, VIII, p. 543.

24. *New York Journal*, February 16, 1775; Smith, *Historical Memoirs*, I, p. 210; Colden to Captain Montague of the *Kingfisher*, February 9, 1775, *Colden Letter Books 1760-1775*, II, pp. 384-385; Arthur M. Schlesinger, *The Colonial Merchants and the American Revolution* (New York, 1918), pp. 490-491.

25. *American Archives*, 4th series, II, pp. 144-148; McDougall to Josiah Quincy, Jr., April 6, 1775, ibid., pp. 283-284.

26. Schuyler, Ten Broeck, and Livingston to Yates, February 25, 1775, Abraham Yates, Jr. Papers, New York Public Library.

27. Jones, *History of New York*, I, p. 480.

28. "Impartial" to the Freeholders and Freemen, March 8, 1775; "A Freeman" to the Inhabitants of New York, March 6, 1775; "A Burgher" to the Freeman, March 6, 1775; Advertisement, March 8, 1775, *American Archives*, 4th series, II, pp. 44, 49-50.

29. Ibid., pp. 48-49; Smith, *Historical Memoirs*, I, p. 211.

30. Jones, *History of New York*, I, pp. 37-38.

31. *New York Journal*, March 9, 1775.

32. Ibid. See also Jones, *History of New York*, pp. 483.

33. Smith, *Historical Memoirs*, I, p. 211. Other observers made the same point. For example, a broadside published March 8 by "Another Citizen" asserted that the Assembly had refused to consider the proceedings of the Continental Congress in order that the issues could be more easily referred to the body of colonists generally. "This seems to me," the writer stated, "the most natural construction of the conduct of the Honourable House; and that of some of the Members yesterday appears to justify this construction, for a number of them attending the meeting at the Exchange." *American Archives*, 4th series, II, p. 47.

34. Minutes of Committee of Sixty, March 6, 8, 1775 printed in Jones, *History of New York*, I, p. 482-484.

35. *Colonial Panorama: Dr. Robert Honyman's Journal for March and April 1775*, Philip Padelford, ed. (San Marino, Cal., 1939), p. 31;

Livingston to "Caty" Livingston, March 26, 1775, Livingston Family Papers, New York Public Library.

36. A Collection of Political Cards circulated in New York in 1768 and 1769 with one of 1775, Broadside Collection, New York Public Library; Dartmouth to Colden, January 4, 1775, *Cadwallader Colden Papers*, VII, p. 259; Dartmouth to American Governors, January 4, 1775, *New York Colonial Documents*, VIII, pp. 527-528; Smith, *Historical Memoirs*, I, pp. 212-213.

37. Committee Meeting, March 15, 1775. *American Archives*, 4th series, II, 187-189. The Results were as follows:

	For the Deputies	Against the Deputies
Out Ward	66	-
North Ward	99	36
East Ward	125	22
South Ward	42	23
West Ward	213	23
Dock Ward	52	32
Montgomerie Ward	228	27
Totals	825	163

38. For example, one colonist complained: "Of those who voted for this measure, it may with truth be affirmed, there was a great proportion who did it because there was no alternative. . . . Sensible that the people were determined to send Delegates, it was the art of those who framed the question, upon which the poll was taken, to state it in such a manner that the electors might be led to think that they would be deprived of Delegates unless they pursued the mode pointed out to them, for when numbers of voters demanded that their votes might be taken for the five Delegates, it was absolutely refused. Had a poll been opened upon fair principles, stating the alternative, concerning which the division of sentiments arose, there is no doubt but the old five Delegates would have been elected unanimously." "A Citizen," March 16, 1775, *American Archives*, 4th series, II, p. 139. Supporters of the convention asserted that the poll was necessary to guarantee the unity of the province. See "A Friend to the Congress," *To the Freeholders and Freemen of the City and County of New York*, March 14, 1775, Broadside Collection, New York Public Library.

39. Circular to the counties, March 16, 1775, *American Archives*, 4th series, II, p. 138.

40. Becker, *History of Political Parties in the Province of New York*, pp. 187-189; *Calendar of Historical Manuscripts Relating to the War of the Revolution in the Office of the Secretary of State, Albany, N.Y.*, 2 vols. (Albany, 1868), I, pp. 22-23.

41. American Archives, 4th series, I, p. 1164; ibid., II, p. 76; Mason, *Road to Independence*, pp. 85, 87-88; Becker, *History of Political Parties in the Province of New York*, pp. 189-190; *American Archives*, 4th series, II, p. 282; *Calendar of Historical Manuscripts Relating to the War of the Revolution*, I, pp. 20-21; *New York Gazette, and Weekly Mercury*, April 17, 1775; *New York Gazetteer*, April 20, 1775.

42. *American Archives*, 4th series, II, pp. 351-358.

43. Smith, *Historical Memoirs*, I, p. 219; *New York Journal*, December 14 and 20, 1775; *Honyman Journal*, pp. 67-70; *New York Gazetteer*, April 20, 1775.

44. Council Minutes, May 1, 1775, *Cadwallader Colden Papers*, VII, p. 288; William Hooper to Samuel Johnson, May 23, 1775, *Letters of the Members of the Continental Congress*, I, p. 96; Smith, *Historical Memoirs*, I, p. 222.

45. Jones, *History of New York*, pp. 39-40.

46. Smith, *Historical Memoirs*, I, pp. 222-223.

47. Colden to Captain George Vandeput, May 27, 1775, *Colden Letter Books 1760-1775*, II, p. 413.

48. *Calendar of Historical Manuscripts Relating to the War of the Revolution*, I, pp. 3-4; *American Archives*, 4th series, II, p. 459; Mason, *Road to Independence*, p. 74, notes 25 and 26. The members of the Committee of One Hundred were: Isaac Low, Philip Livingston, James Duane, John Alsop, John Jay, Peter V.B. Livingston, Isaac Sears, David Johnson, Alexander McDougall, Thomas Randall, Leonard Lispenard, William Walton, John Broome, Joseph Hallett, Gabriel H. Ludlow, Nicholas Hoffman, Abraham Walton, Peter Van Schaack, Henry Remsen, Peter Curtenius, Abraham Brasher, Abraham Lott, Abraham Duryee, Joseph Bull, Francis Lewis, Joseph Totten, Thomas Ivers, Hercules Mulligan, John Anthony, Francis Bassett, Victor Bicker, John White, Theophilus Anthony, William Goforth, William Denning, Isaac Roosevelt, Jacob Van Voorhees, Jeremiah Platt, Comfort Sands, Robert Benson, William Gilbert, John Berrian, Gabriel W. Ludlow, Nicholas Roosevelt, Edward Fleming, Lawrence Embree, Samuel Jones, John De Lancey, Frederick Jay, William W. Ludlow, John Moore, Rudolphus Ritzema, Lindley Murray, Lancaster Burling, John Lasher, George Janeway, James Beckman, Samuel Verplanck, Richard Yates, David Clarkson, Thomas Smith, James Desbrosses, Au-

gustus Van Horne, Gerrit Keteltas, Stephen De Lancey, Benjamin Kissam, John Morin Scott, Cornelius Clopper, John Reade, John Van Cortlandt, Jacobus Van Zandt, Gerardus Duyckinck, Peter Goelet, John Marston, John Morton, George Foliot, Jacobus Lefferts, Richard Sharpe, Hamilton Young, Abraham Brinckerhoff, Thomas Ellison, Walter Franklin, David Beckman, William Seton, Evert Banker, Robert Ray, Nicholas Bogert, William Laight, John Thurman, John Lamb, Daniel Phoenix, Anthony Van Dam, Daniel Dunscomb, James Wells, Oliver Templeton, Lewis Pintard, Cornelius P. Low, Thomas Buchanan, Petrus Byvanck.

49. Smith, *Historical Memoirs*, I, p. 221; Jones, *History of New York*, I, p. 41.
50. Livingston to his wife, April 27, 1775, Livingston Family Papers, New York Public Library.
51. *Pennsylvania Journal*, April 26, 1775; Smith, *Historical Memoirs*, I, p. 222; Livingston to his wife, May 3, 1775, Livingston Family Papers, New York Public Library.
52. Jones, *History of New York*, I, pp. 505-506; Smith, *Historical Memoirs*, I, p. 223; *New York Gazetteer*, May 4, 1775.
53. *American Archives*, 4th series, II, p. 534.
54. Ibid., pp. 1244, 1257, 1274, 1285-1286, 1326-1327, 1786, Becker, *History of Political Parties in the Province of New York*, p. 155.
55. *American Archives*, 4th series, II, pp. 468, 605; Colden to Dartmouth, June 7, 1775, *New York Colonial Documents*, VIII, p. 582.
56. *American Archives*, 4th series, II, p. 530.

CHAPTER SEVEN

Conclusion.
The World Turned Upside Down:
The De Lanceys, The Livingstons, and
the Making of New York's Revolution

In her excellent study of the development of radical American opposition to Britain, *From Resistance to Revolution,* Pauline Maier suggested that possibly the most fruitful way to distinguish the differences between loyalists and revolutionaries was through comparative biography.[1] The proceeding chapters, which have sought to set out the process by which a revolution was made in New York, have hopefully established a framework for such a comparative analysis.

New York lends itself more easily than other colonies to a comparative analysis of tory and whig forces because of the predominance of the De Lanceys and Livingstons in the colony's political life. These families were clearly alike in many ways, but there was one crucial distinction between them: The De Lanceys were loyalists, the Livingstons patriots, and if we are to understand the Revolution in New York we must attempt to understand this distinction.

169

Unfortunately, understanding this one important difference between the De Lanceys and the Livingstons is a far from easy task.
From the historical perspective both families appear to be virtually
identical in interests and outlook. Their rivalry appears to be little
more than a competitive scramble for the riches of land, commerce, political power, or imperial favor. Through the 1750s and
1760s both families changed political allegiances or shifted their
political interests with such frequency that it is difficult to discern
either firm policy or principle. The Livingstons, for example, supported the royal governors and a strong imperial tie as a counterweight to the ascendancy of James De Lancey within provincial
affairs, but when De Lancey assumed the mantle of lieutenant governor the Livingstons developed a quite radical opposition to the
formalities of the governing establishment. The De Lanceys meanwhile played a somewhat different role, one apparently equally
devoid of policy or principle. Secure in his position with the home
authorities, unconcerned by criticism from the governor, James De
Lancey appeared to be interested only in preserving the political
ascendancy of himself, his family, and his friends. When the revolutionary crisis broke out after 1763, it is clear that initially both the
De Lanceys and the Livingstons were equally opposed to British
policy for taxing and reorganizing the colonies. As was the case
before 1763, it again appeared that the two rivals were merely
scrambling for short-term advantage in a novel situation neither
was quite able to master. And it is no doubt true that in part this is
exactly what each was trying to do. But they were also trying to do
more. The revolutionary crisis, including the apparently accidental
loyalism of the De Lanceys and patriotism of the Livingstons, revealed fundamental divisions over personality, principle and interests between these two great rivals.

Historians of colonial New York have placed too much emphasis
on what should probably be regarded as the more superficial aspects of the De Lancey-Livingston rivalry and missed its more fundamental and important significance. When New Yorkers (or for
that matter outsiders such as John Adams) said that New York politics revolved around the struggle between the De Lanceys and the
Livingstons, what precisely did they mean? They did not mean
merely the struggle for office, for land, for influence with the gover-

nor or British authorities. This sort of conflict was taken for granted and was characteristic of politics in all the other colonies, as well as England. Similarly, the wielding of political power and influence—often in a manner that nowadays would be regarded as criminally corrupt—was taken for granted, and was characteristic of eighteenth-century politics generally. These were not the features of New York political life that led Americans to regard the De Lancey-Livingston rivalry as something unique. What, then, were the unique features of the De Lancey-Livingston conflict? Why was this rivalry so important to the making of the Revolution in New York?

The first thing that strikes the observer is personality. Lieutenant Governor James De Lancey was undoubtedly a uniquely gifted politician. William Pitt is supposed to have told De Lancey's widow that had her husband been born and raised in England he might have been prime minister, and whether this story is true or not, it is certainly arguable that no single man so successfully dominated the public life of his colony as did De Lancey dominate the public life of New York. As we have seen, De Lancey's English connections were of the highest quality, but they might well have counted for less than they did had not De Lancey also mastered local politics. If eighteenth-century New York was no democracy, neither was it a dictatorship. De Lancey was not a hereditary aristocrat; he ruled New York by persuasion not right. In short, in eighteenth-century terms, James De Lancey was a popular ruler.

Contemporary comment on De Lancey's magnetic personality and his almost magical—as his enemies saw matters—sway over men has tended to obscure the personalities of the Livingstons. Indeed, it is from the Livingstons and their friends that we have our best portraits of De Lancey. But the Livingstons were worthy opponents, whose personalities were also very formidable. Like the De Lanceys, the Livingstons were toughminded lawyer-businessmen possessed of the wit and determination to succeed in the rough and tumble frontier environment of New York's Hudson Valley. And succeed they surely did. In Livingston Manor they built one of the largest real estate empires in colonial America, and as merchants with bases at Albany and New York they were every bit as successful as their famous rivals. They lacked the English connections of the De Lanceys, but as Stanley Katz has perceptively noted, this was in the long run really an advantage. It may well have been a key factor in the final identification of the Livingstons with the patriot cause.[2]

During the prerevolutionary era the shape and direction of the Livingston political interest was largely the responsibility of the Triumvirate of William Livingston, William Smith, Jr., and John Morin Scott. Of the three, Livingston was the most interesting, Smith the most complicated.

William Livingston was no radical; his later career as governor of New Jersey was marked by honesty, pragmatism, and conservatism. Of his later career Carl E. Prince has written that while Livingston "was capable in the abstract of comprehending the deep-seated meaning of the democratic revolution of which he was an important part, he was still inheritor of an aristocratic tradition and endowed with a clear sense of his own superiority based on birth, class, education and fellowship with influential men." [3] A frustrated painter whose father made him go to college and undertake legal studies, there remained in Livingston a rebellious streak. The whig ideology he and his friends fashioned reflected this rebelliousness. If it was in the main a conventional ideology, it nevertheless contained a radical, iconoclastic undercurrent that was potentially revolutionary. If, in the short run, Livingston's ideology was no more than a rationale for ridding New York of De Lancey's influence, it was in the longer run a rationale for overthrowing a government and a harbinger of what Robert R. Palmer has aptly named the Age of the Democratic Revolution.

Two surviving images of William Smith, Jr. are suggestive of the man's complexity. When John Adams passed through New York in September 1774 on his way to the First Continental Congress at Philadelphia, he reported that Smith always had his face buried in a book; Thomas Jones, the loyalist historian, said that Smith acted always "with as much cunning, art, hypocracy, and dissimulation as possible." [4] There was truth in both images. Smith was an intellectual and something of a schemer. A relative of the Livingstons, Smith enjoyed the company of aristocrats. He believed in government by the better sort, but like many men whose position in society is assured, he enjoyed dabbling in popular politics and popular causes. But he was no revolutionary. His detailed memoirs make it perfectly clear that his only political concern was the destruction of the De Lancey influence. His record for duplicity was, if we may so put it, honestly gained. As a politician Smith was a behind-the-scenes operator, a wheeler-dealer par excellence. If we are to believe Smith's memoirs, and in this respect there is no reason to doubt them, everyone—even, on occasion, the De Lanceys—seems to have consulted Smith. He, in turn, never hesitated to offer advice to the royal governor, the Livingstons, the De Lanceys, the radicals, and later the revolutionaries and the loyalists. If Smith's integrity and his ideas were compromised, it was because, as Jones rightly suspected, no one in the New York knew more about what was going on than William Smith.

Nevertheless, Smith was a man of principle. He was a whig aristocrat and a loyal empire man. He opposed taxes he believed were unconstitutional, as did all Americans whatever their political stripe. He supported radical policies aimed at the repeal of obnoxious taxes or the defeat of the De Lanceys, not realizing that radicalism could also lead to revolution. But Smith never questioned Britain's fundamental authority over the colonies. In declaring his loyalty, Smith declared his lifelong commitment to elitism, conservatism, and imperialism. Later, in Canada, as chief justice of Quebec from 1786 to his death in 1793, Smith opposed the introduction of a popular assembly advocating instead the establishment of an aristocratic hierarchy that would prevent future revolutions in Britain's remaining American possessions.[5]

If it is difficult to grasp the conflicting ideologies and temperaments within the Livingston faction, it is much more difficult to come to grips with the ideology and personality of the De Lancey party. The problem stems from an almost total lack of sources. Commentary on the De Lanceys is based inevitably on inference, a procedure which admittedly is far from satisfactory. This circumstance no doubt explains why there are no full-length studies of the De Lanceys in the revolutionary era. Until recently the De Lanceys' role in the decade preceeding independence was generally misunderstood. Historians, following Carl Becker's lead, for the most part associated the De Lanceys with the "court" or high tory party and argued that the De Lanceys were steady opponents of

American rights. Of course, the problem of interpreting the De Lanceys was part of the larger problem of interpreting loyalism generally, and it is only recently that historians have begun to view loyalism as something other than a form of fairly extreme conservatism. Thanks to the work of Wallace Brown, Robert M. Calhoon, and William A. Benton a different and more rounded picture of loyalism is now emerging. Ironically, some of the best scholarship produced by the two-hundredth birthday of the United States has been in the field of loyalist historiography.

Benton's work on "whig-loyalism" is particularly important. By "whig-loyalism" Benton means to identify those loyalists whose political and social philosophies were virtually identical to the political and social philosophies of the revolutionaries. Whig-loyalists generally supported the patriot position on the issue of taxation and favored more decentralization in the running of the empire. Unlike the revolutionaries, however, whig-loyalists opposed American independence. If there is one weakness with Benton's thesis, it is that he confines his whig-loyalists to a very small group of nine men in six colonies.[6] In fact, it is clear that the concept of whig-loyalism applied equally well to many other loyalists. "Tory" was a word of patriotic abuse; it defined the political position of only a very few loyalists.

Benton's whig-loyalists were all intellectuals, men who committed their thoughts to paper. But many whig-loyalists did not take up the pen to defend their position, and foremost among these were the De Lanceys. The De Lanceys defined their whig-loyalism by actions, by a consistent pattern of behavior over many years. Lieutenant Governor James De Lancey was no royalist defender of the Crown's prerogatives. The Livingstons called De Lancey an American Stuart, but if he had any English counterpart, it was Robert Walpole; De Lancey aimed to control the House of Assembly and through it New York. His son, the Captain, followed his father's lead. Like his father, he aspired to control the Assembly. Faced with the imperial crisis after 1763, the younger De Lancey's loyalties were strictly local. At no time did he show any sympathy for any of Britain's American policies. That De Lancey and his party were driven after 1770 into the position of being "friends to government" was due primarily to an accidental miscalculation on De Lancey's part and the political brilliance of Alexander McDougall.

The career and personality of Alexander McDougall confronts us with what might be termed the "underside" of the history of the Livingston-De Lancey rivalry. In a number of important respects it was men such as McDougall—men, that is, on the fringes of the Livingston-De Lancey rivalry—who determined its development and final outcome. On the Livingston side these men included McDougall, Isaac Sears, and John Lamb and other less-prominent radicals. On the De Lancey side were included men like Thomas Jones and some of New York's leading Anglican clergy, among whom were a number of genuine tories. An understanding of this "underside" is crucial to an understanding of the Livingstons' patriotism and the De Lancey's whig-loyalism.

It has been the argument of the preceeding chapters that McDougall was the man primarily responsible for the De Lancey's downfall and by extension for the making of the Revolution in New York. McDougall was the outsider who became the insider. But it is, however, impossible to imagine McDougall's career without the Livingston-De Lancey rivalry. It was that rivalry that nurtured McDougall's political ideas and shaped his political world view. Put another way, McDougall was a product of New York's aristocratic political system. It is unlikely that McDougall could have had the influence in New England that he had in New York. In New England his famous broadside would have made no sense. It made sense in New York. New York politics was essentially aristocratic in character. The colony was governed by men who styled themselves manor lords, and even if the recent argument of Sung Bok Kim concerning the democratic nature of manorial politics and economics is accepted as correct, the image of a fundamentally aristocratic colony remains intact.[7] New York possessed the strongest aristocratic traditions of any of the American colonies. A handful of great families, most of whom were related to one another, governed the province. The De Lanceys and the Livingstons were preeminent among this group, and in terms of attitudes and interests both shared a common aristocratic outlook. William Livingston may have ranted against James De Lancey, but at least he recognized a social equal and a worthy opponent. McDougall also recognized the common class interest of the De Lanceys and the Livingstons and his attack was aimed not merely at the De Lanceys, but by implication at the whole of New York's governing class.

Historians of revolutionary New York have usually regarded Isaac Sears as being more "radical" than McDougall. McDougall, it is argued, was by virtue of his close association with the Livingstons the more moderate. Actually, it was Sears who was possibly the more moderate, McDougall the more radical. Sears' reputation as the "king" of the waterfront mob is in a number of respects misleading. As Pauline Maier has shown, mob action in eighteenth-century America was not necessarily an indication of class conflict, economic discontent, or, most importantly, "radical" politics. Until 1770 Isaac Sears was quite happy to be an ally—albeit a secret one—of Captain James De Lancey. That the alliance was secret suggests that he regarded it as something of which his supporters would disapprove. Certainly after the De Lancey debacle of 1769 Sears was caused great embarrassment by the public disclosure of his association with the De Lanceys. Nevertheless, the alliance survived for five years and was crucial in the electoral success of De Lancey candidates in 1768 and 1769. What brought these seemingly unlikely allies together? According to contemporaries, Sears joined the De Lanceys in the expectation that they would secure New York's colonial agency for Sears' friend, Stephen Sayre, an important member of London's American community with good contacts in business and government circles. Sears' hopes for Sayre were unfulfilled, but even so there is no evidence that he would have abandoned the De Lanceys had he not felt obliged to by the revelation of their partnership. Belatedly, Sears took up McDougall's cry that De Lancey had betrayed the cause of liberty. However the Sears-De Lancey alliance is finally interpreted, there is no question that it obliges us to rethink our views about relations in prerevolutionary New York between the great families and the so-called radicals. If the view of Sears' actions need revision, so too do the views of the actions of the De Lanceys.

Throughout this book the point has been made that few De Lancey sources are extant. There survives, however, one clear statement of political principle by James De Lancey which may serve to define the essence of whig-loyalism. In a letter to the Marquis of Rockingham, written in early 1771 shortly after the House of Assembly voted to appoint Edmund Burke New York Colonial Agent, De Lancey wrote:

> My Friends and I would receive great Pleasure in having one of your Lordship's Party for their Agent as I consider You as the only real Friends of the Colonies and know that while in Opposition You have always shewn yourselves our Friends and when in Administration rendered us real Service in the Repeal of the Stamp Act.[8]

From 1764 to 1776 the De Lanceys acted in a manner consistent with the sentiments expressed in the letter quoted above. They opposed the taxation policies of George Grenville and later of Charles Townshend. And if their condoning of violence seemed to go beyond the sort of behavior that Rockingham would have approved, the De Lanceys were only following recent family tradition. Oliver De Lancey, younger brother of the lieutenant governor, had an especially dubious reputation for troublemaking. Governor George Clinton thought that De Lancey would have found himself in jail on more than one occasion were it not for his name and his friends. Among young De Lancey's more notable exploits was a riot which he organized to celebrate the fall of the French fortress at Louisbourg. If this was perhaps excusable, his attack on the home of a Jewish merchant in 1750 was not. "Oliver and his party," Clinton reported in February 1750, "have last fryday night riotously attacked the House of a Jew, Broke open the Door and almost all the Windows using the most scandalous expressions." [9] Violence, along with magnetism and charm, was part of the De Lancey mystique.

The De Lanceys were men of action, and they responded well in situations where decisive action was called for. It was no surprise therefore that they emerged as popular leaders in the Stamp Act crisis. It was precisely the sort of episode for which their talents were best suited. Again, the protest against the Townshend policies favored the De Lancey ascendancy. But after 1767 and until 1774 a more sensitive and subtle approach to New York's political problems was required. In the absence of some dramatic development in England or America against which a mob could be rallied, De Lancey leadership faltered. The De Lanceys lacked subtlety. Captain James De Lancey simply did not possess his father's ability. Oliver De Lancey, the only other serious candidate for family or faction leadership, was inadequate to the faction's needs. Neither the Captain nor his uncle possessed the finesse to handle the delicate and conflicting demands of either the merchants, the more militant Sons of Liberty, or Cadwallader Colden. The Captain's one attempt at devising a grand strategy for the settlement of New York's economic and political problems—the currency deal with Colden—ended in ignominious failure, a failure which cost the De Lanceys not only the political leadership of New York but also their place in American society.

Not surprisingly, with the return to street politics in 1774, the De Lanceys' fortunes briefly revived. De Lancey men joined in the many popular and often violent demonstrations against the Boston Port Act and applauded the formation of popular committees to oversee and organize the protest. By now, however, too much bad blood had flowed between the De Lanceys and their erstwhile radical supporters to reunite the old alliance. Even the De Lancey-led coalition of merchants was breaking down as individual traders took up opposite positions. Finally the retirement of Cadwallader Colden in 1775 and his death within the year completed the almost total isolation of the De Lanceys.

But the De Lanceys still had a few friends, and principal among these were New York's Anglican clergy. The Church of England remained throughout the colonial period an important base of De Lancey support. The clergy were important now as the leading spokesmen of the De Lancey loyalist ideology. The religious influence was especially important in the history of colonial New York. The partial establishment of Anglicanism in the southern portion of the colony, and the persistent efforts of churchmen to secure the appointment of an American bishop, while at the same time using their influence at Canterbury and Whitehall to block the advance of the Presbyterians and the Congregationalists, the principal dissenter groups, were sources of endless dispute. The climax was the setting up of King's College under Church authority. The college issue cemented the De Lancey-Anglican alliance. Without Lieutenant Governor De Lancey's influence and support the project would have foundered; on the dissenter side, it was the college dispute that brought the Livingston Triumvirate to prominence. Thus by the middle years of the century religious division defined the shape of New York politics. Contemporaries commonly referred to the De Lanceys as "the Anglican Party," while the Livingstons were generally known as "the Presbyterian Party."

As the intellectual wing of the De Lancey faction, the clergy played a significant role as interpreters of De Lancey loyalist ideology, not least because of the paucity of other statements concerning the De Lanceys. The clergy's political writings can help us define De Lancey-Anglican loyalism by exposing the whiggish and tory strains within New York loyalism, the tensions, if we may so put it, between the loyalists' American whig intellect and their English tory heart. The clergy were essentially whig intellectuals, but there emerged as well in their writing a deep commitment to and love for England. It has sometimes been argued that American loyalists became pro-British rather accidentally, through necessity rather than conviction. This may well have been true for many loyalists, but it is doubtful if this can be said of either New York's Anglican clergy or the De Lanceys. In the clergy's writings and the De Lanceys' conduct we see revealed in the final crisis for the empire a fundamental attachment to England which whiggish ideology and radical protest had not shaken.

The three leading New York Anglican loyalist writers were Samuel Seabury, Thomas Bradbury Chandler, and Charles Inglis. Little need be said about Inglis, the rector of Trinity Church from 1777 to 1783 and bishop of Nova Scotia from 1787 to his death in 1816. Inglis' pamphlet, *The True Interest of America Impartially Stated,* written in 1776 in answer to Paine's *Common Sense,* is regarded by historians as a good statement of loyalist principles, but as virtually all printed copies were destroyed by the patriots before distribution, Inglis' influence was minimal. Chandler and Seabury are especially interesting in the study of loyalism because each in different ways made his own peace with the rebels after the revolution. Chandler, a New Jersey cleric closely associated with the New

York clergy in their long battle against the spread of religious dissent, was well known—if not notorious—as the author of the best of many tracts written in support of the establishment of an American bishopric, *An Appeal to the Public in Behalf of the Church of England in America,* published in 1767. For ten years from 1775 to 1785 Chandler was a loyalist exile in England. In 1785 he returned to his parish at Elizabethtown where he died in 1790. Seabury remained in New York throughout the Revolutionary War serving, except for a brief imprisonment in Connecticut, as a chaplain to British forces based at New York. In June 1783 Seabury sailed for England, not as a loyalist refugee, but as the American churchman chosen to be the first bishop of the Protestant Episcopal Church of the United States.

The clergy emerged as important loyalist spokesmen in late 1774 and early 1775, the crucial time between the dissolution of the First Continental Congress and the Battle of Lexington. They were worried essentially about two things. First, and certainly foremost, they were concerned with Congress' apparent disinterest in the question of reconciliation with Britain, which both Chandler and Seabury took as proof of the colonists' desire for independence. Second, they were worried about the vexatious tendency of Americans to defend their common liberty while destroying the liberty of those individuals who dissented from the majority opinion.

Behind the concern about the drift toward independence lay a fundamental conviction that Parliament must remain supreme in all matters relating to the empire. "It is," Chandler declared in *A Friendly Address to all Reasonable Americans,* "a contradiction in the nature of things, and as absurd as that a part should be greater than the whole, to suppose that the supreme legislature of any Kingdom does not extend to the utmost bounds of the kingdom." [10] Unlike Chandler, Seabury was prepared to acknowledge that the colonies had some legitimate grievances and were entitled to "a fixed determinate constitution of their own," but he too shared Chandler's views about Parliamentary supremacy. "Did you expect," he asked, "that Congress would throw all into confusion,— revile and trample on the authority of Parliament and make our breach with the parent state a thousand times more irreparable than it was before?" [11]

As the clergy saw matters, the breakdown of individual liberty was symptomatic of the more general breakdown of legitimate government. Organized merely as a deliberative body, the Continental Congress now wielded through its Association not only the powers of government but also, and more importantly, unprecedented direct control over the lives of individuals. Did Parliament or the Congress, then, pose the greater threat to liberty? Seabury warned with characteristic bluntness: "choose your Committee, or suffer it be chosen by a half dozen Fools in your neighbourhood,—open your doors to them,—let them examine your tea-cannisters, and molasses-jugs, and your wives and daughters petti-coats,—bow, and cringe, and tremble, and quake,—fall down and worship our sovereign Lord the Mob." [12] The more temperate Chandler made the same point. In the *American Querist* he asked, "Whether the *Sons of Liberty* have ever willingly allowed to others the liberty of thinking and acting for themselves; and whether any other liberty than that of doing as *they* shall direct is to be expected during their administration?" Would it not be better, Chandler continued, "both to our liberty and property, to be under the authority of the British parliament, and subject to those duties and taxes which they might think fit to impose, than to be under the government of the *American Sons of Liberty*, without paying any duties at all?" [13] Obviously most Americans thought not, but that was beside the point, which was that beneath these propagandistic attacks on the patriots' cause lay a more fundamental concern, an understanding of which illuminates not only much about what was central to loyalist thinking but also provides a perspective to view the whole revolutionary process in New York.

Not so many years ago, a new generation of historians, led by such men and women as Bernard Bailyn, Edmund Morgan, Gordon Wood, and Pauline Maier, inaugurated a fresh approach to the historiography of the American Revolution by effectively demonstrating that in their writings and speeches the patriots meant what they said. The revolutionaries were propagandists—that is, they wanted to persuade people of the essential rightness of their cause—but, argued these scholars, they were also enunciating fears and principles in which they believed deeply. So it was with the loyalists. They too were propagandists, but like the revolutionaries they were also men and women who believed sincerely in certain basic principles. The political writings of Seabury and Chandler suggest that New York's loyalists, for whom Seabury and Chandler were the principal spokesmen, were agreed on one fundamental principle which took precedence over any other concern. This fundamental principle was the fear and hatred of republicanism.

In loyalist historiography generally, the loyalist opposition to republican government has curiously been ignored. More accurately, perhaps, the opposition to republicanism has been obscured by the attempt to identify such other loyalist concerns as the salvation of the empire, the rights of Parliament, and the preservation of the practices and traditions of America's British heritage. Too much attention has been focused on a broad range of loyalist conservative attitudes, and not enough attention has been given to the specific problem of republicanism.

To set this issue in perspective, it is not irrelevant to note in passing the strong antirepublican character of Canada's nineteenth-century loyalist tradition. The loyalists who laid the political groundwork for the modern Canadian nation in the late eighteenth and early nineteenth centuries specifically rejected the American republican example which lay to the south. Canadians came to believe during the course of the century that their antirepublicanism was the principle which more than anything else distinguished them from the citizens of the United States. It was equally true, of course, that those Canadian "radicals" who were dissatisfied with their country's political life tended often to be enthusiastic admirers of the American republican example. It is therefore important to consider carefully what New York loyalists thought about the concept of republicanism.

The loyalist animus against republicanism emerged with varying degrees of clarity and in different ways in the writings of New York's three major loyalist writers: Thomas Jones, William Smith, and Samuel Seabury. At first glance, perhaps, one is inclined to underrate Jones' importance. His denunciations of revolutionaries and republican fanatics were obviously extreme and inflammatory, as was his conviction that a republican cabal had plotted the overthrow of the established order at least as early as the 1750s. This is Jones' description of the activities of the Whig Club, formed by the Livingstons and their friends in 1752:

In this club matters were settled, plans laid, schemes devised, and resolutions formed, for carrying the grand project into execution, of pulling down the Church, ruining the constitution, or heaving the whole province into confusion. Everything being now agreed upon, fixed and settled, the proper plans formed and digested, their batteries opened with the publication of a weekly political paper under the appellation of the *"Independent Reflector,"* and shortly after with another under that of the *"Watch Tower."* The siege thus begun, the assailants carried it on with a rancor, a malevolence, and an acrimony, not to be equalled but by the descendants of those presbyterian and republican fanatics, whose ancestors had in the preceding century brought their Sovereign to the block, subverted the best constitution in the world, and upon its ruins erected presbyterianism, republicanism, and hypocrisy. In these publications the established Church was abused, Monarchy derided, Episcopacy reprobated, and republicanism held up, as the best existing form of government in the known world.[14]

Jones was indeed extreme, but his extremism curiously paralleled the extremism of those patriots who came to believe that the king's ministers had determined upon a settled plan to destroy their liberties and the British constitution. In his single-minded, and admittedly simplistic, attack on republican ideas and republican conspirators, Jones brought into sharp focus the chief fear of New York's loyalist minority.

William Smith's views on republicanism are more difficult to define. To some contemporaries, of course, Smith's beliefs presented no problem of interpretation. Smith, said Thomas Jones, possessed a "well-known and established character, as a *rigid republican."* The following is Jones' version of Smith's explanation for his refusal to sign the *Association* drawn up in April 1775, an instrument, Jones believed, designed to deliver New York city over to the republicans:

You know (says he) that I am as good and steady a friend to the cause as any man in America; that I have advised, promoted, and encouraged the present measure from its origin;

nourished and cherished it through all its different stages to the present time. But the crisis now approaches. Great Britain has commenced hostilities, America must and will have recourse to arms; this the King, the Ministry, the Parliament, and the courts of law, *will term treason and rebellion, and the actors, traitors and rebels.* The events of war are uncertain, our army may be defeated, our friends taken prisoners, tried and convicted. A Staunch friend at the Council Board will be then necessary, whose influence can be used in favor of such unhappy persons. I am now there, and in the good graces of his Excellency the Governor. Should I sign the "Association," I may lose that favor, and perhaps my seat in Council, a risk in the present times, and under our particular circumstances by no means to be hazarded.[15]

The speech was fiction, but revealing fiction. Jones' assessment of Smith's character was not without foundation in fact; Smith was a schemer and at times a dissembler. A whig aristocrat who had obvious disdain for what he termed more than once the "rabble," Smith was nonetheless attracted to radical ideas and popular causes in the abstract. Certainly Smith had no love for the Church of England; it is significant that the clearest manifestation of his "radicalism" arose in connection with Church-related issues. Politically Smith was much more conservative. In the 1750s the Livingston faction came to look to the imperial connection as a bulwark against the De Lancey ascendency, and Smith never deviated from his fundamental allegiance to the empire. Early in the imperial crisis sometime during 1765 and 1767 Smith proposed the creation of an American parliament, but it was only a month before Congress adopted the Declaration of Independence that Smith undertook to set down fully "My Thoughts as a Rule for my own Conduct, at this melancholy Hour of approaching Distress." Smith premised his argument on a number of considerations, all of which revealed his fundamental antirepublicanism. A key point in Smith's mind was his assertion that the American colonies were not "meerly royal and crown-created, but National and parliamentary Establishments." By exposing themselves to "hazardous and expensive Undertakings," Smith said, the colonists had earned a number of rights and accepted a number of obligations. Britain also possessed rights and obligations, so that between the Mother Country and the colonies "a great National Covenant" existed which obliged Britain, on the one hand, to protect and promote the colonies, and the colonies, on the other hand, to submit to England's authority. A significant point in Smith's thinking was his belief that "neither of the contracting Parties may dissolve this Compact, as long as their joint Aim in the union, to wit their mutual Prosperity, can be attained by it." This point was the crux of Smith's argument, for though he discussed at length the arrogance of the British and the stubborn unreasonableness of the Americans, Smith maintained that there was no legitimate grounds for dissolving the imperial compact since the common purpose of the contracting parties remained unchanged. Calling for a "Return to their ancient Union, according to that Compact," Smith concluded:

That when Terms are proposed, consistant with the original Compact, neither Party can reject them and be innocent; tho' they offer no Reimbursement for the Charges of the War, not any Hostages or Surrenders for Security agt a future Apostacy; because the Controversy sprang from the Neglect of both Countries in early Days, to concert such specific Stipulations, as were necessary to prevent Strife, and reconcile their Safety with the general Supremacy of Parliament; & because the Exaction of Hostages or Surrenders, or any Thing beyond an explicit and definitive Treaty, will partake, as I conceive, of the Nature of a Cession of Rights, contrary to the Design of a Restitution to their primitive Condition—A Condition—A Condition to America after another prosperous half Century, perfectly safe, from her inevitable Growth—And to Great Britain least dangerous because from the Predispositions of God's Providence, she seems to have no other Choice than of a Civil War, which will quicken her Fall, or the Resort to a wise and liberal System of Administration for retarding that Catastrophe until the gradual Transfer of her Wealth & Inhabitants has reared an Empire for her in the Western Hemisphere superior to what she enjoys in the East, and that to such a distant Aera, as tho' offensive to her Pride, may not be really injurious to the *present* Possessors of the ancient Emporium nor even to their Posterity within the Sphere of human and rational Attachment.[16]

Seabury's writings were perhaps of more importance than the work of either Jones or Smith. This was partly the result of Seabury's position, and partly because of what he said. The Anglican clergy were the most consistant loyalists of any group in American society; of all the institutions of the old colonial order the Church of England was the most vulnerable, the pretensions of the clergy notwithstanding. For the Church and churchmen the Revolution had a special and poignant significance: Independence threatened not merely the political stability of the imperial order, but also Anglican religious ideas and faith. It was not surprising therefore that the clergy were among the first to sound the warning against independence and in every colony were among the most vociferous and articulate loyalist spokesmen. For the clergy the crisis of the Revolution involved the survival or destruction of a world view that rested on the continuation of the established political and social order.

For some time New York's Anglican clergy had suspected local Presbyterians of harboring republican sentiments and fomenting rebellion against the Monarchy, the State, and the Church. The evidence for this alleged behavior was pretty thin—Presbyterian agitation against King's College and the demand by Presbyterians for a charter of incorporation for their kirk—but it must be conceded that the turn of events after 1773, and especially the prominence of dissenters among the so-called radicals, appeared to give the clergy's charges some validity. Nothing alarmed the clergy more than the proceedings of the First Continental Congress.

Shortly after the Congress adjourned the first of Seabury's four "Letters of a Westchester Farmer" made its appearance in New York. The "Letters" stressed essentially two arguments. First, the tactics of economic boycott were criticized as unwise policy economically and as a dangerous attack on British sovereignty. Second, and more importantly, Seabury warned that the Congress was led by men who harbored republican sentiments which they were determined to force on an America they intended soon to make independent. Directing his fire at those whom he described as "the more sly favourers of an American republic," Seabury warned that the proceedings of the Congress were part of an "ill-projected, ill-conducted, abominable scheme of some of the colonists, to form a republican government independent of Great Britain." The foundations of a "grand American Republic" were Seabury thought already evident:

> To me the danger appears more than possible. The out-lines of it seem already to be drawn. . . . You may think this is a chimera, a creature of my own brain, and may laugh at it. But when you consider circumstances with a more minute attention, possibly some foundation for my suspicions may appear. That a majority of the people of the Massachusetts-Bay have it in meditation to throw off their subjection to Great Britain, as soon as a favourable season presents, can scarce admit of a doubt. The independency of that province on the British Parliament, has been declared in express terms.[17]

It is only when the clash of republican versus antirepublican is fully taken into account that the truly revolutionary character of the American rebellion can be appreciated. It is true enough, as the neo-whig historians have argued, that the American Revolution was in many respects essentially conservative. It was fought to preserve an older, familiar way of life and to preserve social and political institutions, which, if they were not egalitarian and democratic, were at least sufficiently open and representative to provide opportunities for advancement to the more enterprising. At the same time, however, the change from an imperial and monarchical form of government to one that was independent, republican, and federal was profound. As the defeated Cornwallis and his men marched out of Yorktown in 1783, a British army band struck up a popular tune, "The World Turned Upside Down." It was very appropriate and for none more than the Americans themselves. The world of the colonists have been shaken, their world view all but destroyed.

The fundamental conflict between the old colonial regime and the new republican order was vividly dramatized in the revolutionary experience of New York's elite. For this elite the American Revolution was a challenge of special significance, regardless of which side—patriot or loyalist—its members finally chose. Basically, the Revolution struck at the power and foundations of the whole elite, patriot and loyalist alike, by destroying the British, imperial, and colonial substructure on which the power and the pretensions of the aristocracy had rested. In the new republic a William Livingston might become the governor of New Jersey, but gubernatorial power rested on foundations quite different and quite new from those that maintained the power and the pretensions of New York's manors and manor lords.

The New York elite perceived the revolutionary challenge to their position only slowly and in some cases not at all. As with so much New York history during the years between 1760 and 1776 the public careers and private lives of the De Lanceys and the Livingstons incorporated the hopes, the failures, the choices, and the responses of the New York elite to the challenge of revolution. It is therefore useful to review briefly the history of the Livingston-De Lancey rivalry in terms of the development of a revolutionary challenge to the elite.

In the beginning there was no challenge to the elite. Between the early 1740s, when the De Lancey-Livingston quarrel emerged for the first time as the dominant theme of New York politics and the beginning of the imperial controversy in 1764 the De Lancey-Livingston conflict was little more than what superficially it appeared to be. That is, it was essentially simply a political power struggle between two nearly matched competitors, one group the "ins" the other the "outs." This is not to suggest that the combatants were without political principles or a political and social world view. The philosophical outlook of both was essentially identical. Both were inheritors of the whig tradition as it had evolved during the eighteenth century. Historians have rightly made much of the "radical" or "commonwealth" ideology articulated by the Triumvirate, but its influence in the short run must not be overestimated. In a very real sense the Livingston ideology was pointless and meaningless in the context of New York politics. De Lancey, the American Stuart, was a figment of their imagination; he simply did not exist. No doubt this is why the Livingston attack on De

Lancey was so singularly unsuccessful. It was only when the Livingstons were able to add to their attack a broader imperial dimension that their rhetoric began to jell into the stuff of which revolutions are made.

The effect of the injection of the imperial issue into the De Lancey-Livingston quarrel was immediate, revealing forcefully the revolutionary potential of the Livingstons' rhetoric. The Livingstons drafted in the form of an Assembly petition a brilliant defense of the American position on the question of taxation and personal liberty that summed up all the essential points about taxes, liberty, and the rights of citizens which Americans would defend and put into practice for the next 25 years.

It was characteristic of the Livingstons' elitist style that, though they had formulated what almost amounted to a revolutionary program of action, they were quite unable to put their program into action or convey its essential features to the mass of the colonists. Ironically, it was the De Lanceys who showed how the Livingston program could be put into action, though at the price ultimately of destroying themselves.

As Isaac Sears was later to acknowledge, De Lancey's leadership during the Stamp Act crisis was of crucial significance in the development of what Professor Bernard Friedman has called a "radical consciousness" in New York.[18] The De Lanceys were always at their best in situations where some decisive act, some flamboyant gesture was needed. The Stamp Act riot was admirably suited to the talents of the De Lancey family, and there is certainly no reason to think that commentators like William Smith were exaggerating when they said that the De Lanceys made the most of the opportunity. The De Lancey ascendancy from 1765 to 1770 was proof of their success.

The De Lanceys' troubles arose after 1765 from the fact that they had nothing to offer New Yorkers except the flamboyant gesture. The more subtle, intellectual Livingstons were the more resilient, the more adaptable. Though badly mauled in the Stamp Act crisis, they possessed the personal resources to recover.

For nearly five years the De Lanceys survived solely on the strength of the Stamp Act success. Though they took advantage of the popular furor over the Circular Letter, they really had little to offer in regard to the Townshend program, despite the fact that some of the more obnoxious aspects of that program were aimed directly at New York. It was not accidental that in the two election campaigns fought in 1768 and 1769, the De Lanceys dwelt almost exclusively on their successes in the Stamp Act controversy.

In contrast to the obvious expertise and flair which the De Lanceys displayed in the Stamp Act crisis was their dismal performance in the currency-troop supply controversy of December 1769. Since it has been argued that it was this crisis that more than any other event created in New York a genuinely revolutionary demand for change, it is worth reconsidering in some detail the contrast between the De Lanceys' earlier success and their later failure.

To begin, it is necessary to put aside what may be termed the Livingston-radical view of this episode, that is, the view that the De Lanceys were simply revealing their true "tory" colors by enlisting firmly on the side of the lieutenant governor and the imperial authorities. In fact, even from a radical perspective, the Colden-De Lancey deal was far from being a bad one. It could not really be argued that it was against the interests of New Yorkers. The need for currency was absolutely vital; in no way could this aspect of the Colden-De Lancey bargain be considered as an attack on popular rights. As for supporting the troops, it is undoubtedly true that the army was unpopular and regarded in some quarters as an instrument of imperial oppression. Rhetoric notwithstanding, however, the army had never been popular in New York or any other colony for that matter, yet New York's Assemblies had always, if sometimes grudgingly, found money to maintain local garrisons. But even more important was the fact that the actual terms of the deal struck directly at the powers of the governor or the home authorities to regulate New York's economic or political affairs.

The De Lancey's problem, then, derived not in the narrow sense chiefly from the deal itself. Their principal problem was one having to do with political management and organization and with the formulation and explanation of political policy. The Colden-De Lancey deal revealed in striking fashion a central weakness that characterized the De Lanceys during the entire imperial and revolutionary crisis, namely, their failure—and it may have in fact been an inability—to explain themselves or their policies. It may be that the De Lanceys had nothing to say. The difference between the De Lanceys' success and failure was the difference between action and thought. Put another way, in terms of this study, it was the crucial difference btween the De Lanceys and the Livingstons.

In her analysis of "popular uprising and civil authority in eighteenth-century America," Pauline Maier has noted the marked contrast between the boisterous and riotous behavior of American colonials and the concern for law and order and public tranquility in the new republic.[19] In a number of respects the De Lanceys and the Livingstons epitomize this important distinction. If the De Lanceys do not emerge from the extant evidence with the image of barroom brawlers—and in the case of Oliver De Lancey this characterization may not be too far off the mark—they nevertheless emerge as men most at ease in the boisterous atmosphere of the tavern, the docks, and the street corners. There was no problem, it was said, that the De Lanceys could not solve with a smile or a bottle. In terms of the Maier thesis, it seems clear that the De Lanceys were preeminantly men of the colonial era. The Livingstons, in contrast, were clearly men more in tune with the newer concern for law and order. The Livingstons were, in short, men of the republic, one virtue of which was held to be law and order.

The establishment of a new American republic was, among other things, the result of profound intellectual ferment that reached its full fruition in the years from 1770 to 1776. Though the extant record remains blurred, the evidence obliges us to conclude that the De Lanceys took no part in this movement. Significantly, the one wing of the De Lancey faction that was intellectually inclined—the Anglican clergy—was bitterly opposed to the political and religious tendencies of America's intellectual leaders. The result was that by temperament, ability, and inclination the De Lanceys excluded themselves and were excluded by others from the most profound and important changes that were taking place in the late colonial period.

It was very different in the case of the Livingstons. Historians have devoted considerable energy to demonstrating the fact that the Livingstons were conservative whigs and reluctant revolutionaries. This is true enough, but it misses the important point. Revolution is a serious step, and any thoughtful person would hesitate before entering into such a momentous change. The important fact is that the Livingstons did join the revolutionary movement. And it is not surprising that they did so. No family or group anywhere in the colonies was more keenly aware than the Livingstons of the dominant intellectual currents of their era. Within New York no one had done more than the Livingstons to bring those ideas to the attention of a broad public. Indeed, none had done more than they to lay the foundations for a republican New York.

All this is more clear with hindsight than it was to contemporaries. Whereas the De Lanceys excelled in the rough-and-tumble world of street corner politics, the Livingstons failed utterly to generate crowd enthusiasm or a popular following. Consequently the Livingstons made some terrible tactical blunders, as when, for example, they assumed that the Massachusetts Circular Letter was unimportant. Fortunately for them, however, they lived in an era, as scholars such as Bailyn and Palmer have so ably demonstrated, in which political ideas were more important than political actions. In the final analysis, the Livingstons became revolutionaries because they believed that constitutional balance and public virtue could flourish only in a republic.

If the De Lanceys and the Livingstons each in their own way initially determined how New York's Revolution would begin, they were not alone in determining either its course or its results. The latter were decided largely by minor leaders such as Alexander McDougall and Isaac Sears, men drawn from the middle ranks of society who commanded a large popular following among the people as a whole. Ever since Carl Becker and the progressive historians introduced the theme of class conflict to New York colonial history, scholars have wrestled inconclusively with the problem of class and economic discontent in the revolutionary era. In contrast to Becker's notion of a revolution to determine who should rule at home, neo-whig historians such as Robert Brown and most recently Sung Bok Kim have drawn a portrait of a democratic and egalitarian New York where even tenants enjoyed all the essential liberties of freeman. Deciding where the truth may lie is certainly no easy task, especially as the sources themselves are often both am-

biguous and contradictory. In the case of New York perhaps agreement can be reached on a few points, however. New Yorkers
recognized the existence of classes or ranks of society. It was taken
for granted as part of the world view of colonial Americans that
some men were "better" than other men, and a person was expected to defer to his betters. The controversial question is: Did
this social system cause discontent? Any answer must be qualified,
but most of the evidence so far as New York is concerned suggests
that for the most part it did not, until after 1770. But even after
that date the discontent was concerned essentially with only certain kinds of political privilege. To be precise, this discontent was
concerned with the sort of power and privilege enjoyed by the De
Lanceys, but it was not concerned either with the problem of political elitism or with economic questions, about which the average
New Yorker appears to have been quite satisfied.

To say this is, of course, merely to state that contemporary mainstream opinion agreed with whig ideas about political and economic values. But the American Revolution did bring significant
changes to the American polity. It was a genuine revolution, and it
was made possible by a revolution in ideas, ideas that were implicitly, if not always explicitly, radical.

What were the sources of the radical political tradition in New
York? If we focus our attention primarily on developments within
New York, there were essentially two sources. These were the writ-
ings of the Triumvirate and the writings of Alexander McDougall.

To deal with the Triumvirate first. At first glance it seems ironic
that a radical tradition should have emerged from such a select
group of elitists. And they were elitists in several senses. The
Livingstons were the second wealthiest family in New York, rank-
ing behind only the De Lanceys. As great landholders, the Livingstons enjoyed the privilege of being among the select few whose
estates were recognized a manors and whose owners were styled
manor lords. The Triumvirate enjoyed a college education, a privilege denied the majority of colonials; all three were lawyers, the
most prestigious calling in the colonies. Yet the Triumvirate developed a genuinely radical perspective on their society, which was
recognized as such by friend and foe alike.

Significantly the Triumvirate's radical critique was directed against certain sorts of authority symbols, which, as it turned out, rendered their ideas particularly useful to the American revolutionaries. Not surprisingly, it was not a radicalism aimed at wealth, or social, or political privilege in general. Instead, it was a radicalism aimed at particular figures who wielded apparently arbitrary power within the imperial franework of which New York was a part. For example, they worried a good deal about the authority of the arbitrary magistrate, and they attacked with special vehemence the powers of high Church officials, especially bishops.

The attack on the bishops is important to our understanding because the American radical tradition was powerfully influenced by religious dissent. A key aspect of social deference outside New England was membership in the Church of England, and even though the Church was everywhere in the colonies weak, Church membership, because of the imperial tie, carried with it prestige and social privilege. This was especially true in New York where religious disputes had often been sharp and bitter, with the result that religious affiliation was a source of social division, much more important to contemporaries than either class or economics.

Alexander McDougall was the intellectual heir to the political values of the Triumvirate. Like the Livingston trio, religious dissent played a critical role in shaping his radicalism, a fact which explains his attachment to the Livingstons through the 1760s when other popular leaders were allied to the De Lancey interest. Yet McDougall was not merely a follower of the Livingstons. What made McDougall unique and important was the fact that he brought to New York politics a fresh and genuinely radical perspective that was unquestionably his own.

McDougall's importance in the history of New York rests not so much on his famous trial of libel—on which contemporaries and some later historians have concentrated too much—but on the contents of the broadside, *To the Betrayed Inhabitants of the City and Colony of New York.* This was a single, creative burst of brilliance as important in the context of New York history as Paine's *Common Sense* was in the context of the movement for American independence.

If we are, therefore, to understand what New York's revolution was all about we must give McDougall a very careful reading. Two features of the McDougall broadside are particularly striking. First, it was without precedent. Never before had New Yorkers witnessed in print so devastating and penetrating a critique of their social system, nor such an explicit demand for change. Second, though the document was at least in part a product of the ferment initiated by the imperial crisis, it said in fact very little about the specific issues usually included among the colonists' grievances. In other words, granting some qualifications, the broadside had a purpose all its own which was not dependent solely on the gradually escalating revolutionary sentiment.

What McDougall demanded was a change to the system which allowed a small elite to govern New York with little reference to the interests or wishes of the people. The broadside took the form of an attack on Colden and the De Lanceys, but it was as well an attack on the Livingstons and the handful of other great families. This became quite clear when the first broadside was followed by a second which demanded that the colony's "aristocrats" (the word was the broadside writer's) absent themselves from a public meeting called to consider moves against the Colden-De Lancey deal.

The change wrought by McDougall's broadside was quite remarkable. Within four years New York was on the verge of independence, a circumstance for which, at the local level at least, McDougall was in large measure responsible. During that four years New Yorkers along with Americans in the other Thirteen Colonies discovered each in their separate ways that the kind of changes McDougall and his counterparts at Boston, Philadelphia, Williamsburg, or Charleston were demanding could be realized only under a system of government which was entirely separate from the British model. Radicals such as McDougall did not deliberately conspire to foment rebellion—despite what loyalists might later think to the contrary—but neither did they stumble blindly from event to event, from idea to idea. McDougall and men like him provided radicals with a program for change and a purpose.

Significantly the radicals were helped by the ineptitude or complacency of the very elite of which they were so critical. In New York the rapid decline of De Lancey and Livingston influence after 1770 was especially noteworthy. From being initiators of action or policy, the De Lanceys and Livingstons increasingly found themselves mere spectators on the sidelines, often excluded from the most crucial decision-making. The formal instruments of government remained in the hands of the De Lanceys, but after 1770 the role of the governor, lieutenant governor, and Assembly declined steadily in importance. There was no better indication of this than the prolonged fight to seat a representative for Livingston Manor. For about four years both the De Lanceys and the Livingstons poured enormous amounts of energy into this fundamentally trivial issue. Both valiantly tried to attach to it the graver significance of the imperial quarrel, but with indifferent success. Meanwhile the radicals were making a revolution.

As the form of the new republic emerged slowly in the hectic months between September 1774 and July 1776 New York's patriots and loyalists struggled to define their final positions. The choice for the loyalists was the more difficult to make. In an age dominated as few in history have been by political ideology and experimentation the revolutionaries were seen and certainly saw themselves as fulfilling not only the hope of the Enlightenment but also the messianic dreams of the Anglo-American founders of the New World. The loyalists thus appeared to be standing against the tide of history.

As with so many questions of great historical importance—questions that involve a society's view of itself, or its "world view"—the question of loyalism in the final analysis was a moral question, and the choices facing individual loyalists were moral ones. It came down to this: Was it right to rebel? Loyalists agonized over an answer. They equivocated. They said, like the New York City loyalists who in July 1775 published their own "Association" in answer to "the main or principal Association": "we would not countenance rebellion . . . but at the same time . . . shall never consent to taxation without being fully represented with our consent." Or, like William Smith, whose conversion to loyalism shows how the issue of independence could shatter a man's comfortable assumptions about life and oblige him to redefine his beliefs in ways that were often unfamiliar and unexpected, they agreed, "I was the Friend of both Countries and wished for Peace for the Sake of both and that I thought we wanted more Light than Heat." Loyalists postponed answers. William Smith drew on his undoubted knowledge of history and government to try to find some "mode" or accomodation, dreaming up loyalist remonstrances the Continental Congress might care to send to London. Peter Van Schaack shut himself in his study to pore over his copy of John Locke in a vain effort to find peace with himself and his country. But in the end, the loyalist answer was no. No, it was not right to rebel; no, the colonies were not justified in declaring the independence of the United States.[20]

In this last crisis of the old Anglo-American empire, one name was missing from the ranks of the New York loyalists: Captain James De Lancey. De Lancey had departed for England in the closing days of the last Assembly in March 1775. He never returned to New York, and died at Bath, England, in 1800. Though De Lancey attempted in England to work for imperial reconciliation, attempted, in other words, to do in England what he could not do in America, it is significant that he left the scene of his greatest political triumphs and failures before he was personally confronted with the choice of rebellion or loyalism. De Lancey never fitted easily into either the loyalist or the rebel mold. For all his superb mastery of local politics and his extraordinarily well-developed family connections, De Lancey's views on broad imperial questions appear to have been somewhat limited. He described himself as a Rockingham Whig, though it is doubtful that he really understood what Rockingham stood for. The truth was that James De Lancey, like his father, was a brilliant colonial politician, the preeminent New York colonial of his day. But De Lancey was a colonial, and as New York ceased to be a colony, his place in the scheme of things simply disappeared.

If the accidents of political fortune led the De Lanceys to loyalism, so the same accidental working of events led to the Livingston triumph. For 20 years from the middle of the 1750s the Livingstons had lived in the shadow of the De Lancey family. They responded to the De Lanceys ascendancy in two fundamentally contradictory ways. On the one hand, they befriended the governor, and, on the other hand, they developed a radical antiauthoritarian ideology. In the first tendency lay the seeds of loyalism; in the second lay the seeds of revolution. Here was the difference between William Smith and William Livingston. Had the De Lancey-Sears alliance held, the Livingstons might well have remained, as Smith wished, the governor's friends, but as it was the Livingstons adhered to the idealism of the Triumvirate and followed the course of action that idealism implied.

The Livingston-De Lancey rivalry thus symbolized fundamental tensions within New York and more generally in colonial American society, and within the old colonial empire as a whole. Their rivalry was a vital factor in the making of the revolution in New York. The Livingstons contributed mightily to the evolution of America revolutionary ideology and the egalitarianism of the new republic. The De Lanceys opposed independence to fight a rearguard action for the old colonial order that in the end proved futile. But the De Lanceys' role was not wholly negative. In fighting a losing battle, they added a not insignificant chapter to the continuing American tradition of political dissent. In the final analysis, however, the De Lanceys embodied much of what America had been, the Livingstons much of what America would become. In the rivalry of these two great families was dramatized America's past and its future.

NOTES

1. Maier, *From Resistance to Revolution*, p. xv.
2. Stanley N. Katz, "Between Scylla and Charybdis: James De Lancey and Anglo-American Politics in Early Eighteenth-Century New York," *Anglo-American Political Relations 1675-1775*, Alison O. Olson and Richard M. Brown, eds. (New Brunswick, N.J., 1970), pp. 92-108.
3. Carl E. Prince, *William Livingston: New Jersey's First Governor. New Jersey's Revolutionary Experience*, vol. 21 (Trenton, N.J., 1975), p. 15.
4. Jones, *History of New York*, I, p. 143.
5. L.F.S. Upton, *The Loyal Whig: William Smith of New York and Quebec*, (Toronto, 1969), pp. 161-217.
6. William A. Benton, *Whig-Loyalism: An Aspect of Political Ideology in the American Revolutionary Era* (Rutherford, N.J., 1969).
7. Sung Bok Kim, *Landlord and Tenant in Colonial New York: Manorial Society, 1664-1775* (Chapel Hill, N.C., 1978).
8. De Lancey to Rockingham, undated early 1771, in Lucy S. Sutherland, ed., *The Correspondence of Edmund Burke*, II, p. 215 note.
9. Clinton to Colden, February 9, 1750, *Letters and Papers of Cadwallader Colden*, IV, pp. 189-190.
10. Chandler, *A Friendly Address to all Reasonable Americans* (New York, 1774).

11. Seabury, *The Congress Canvassed* (New York, 1774). Seabury's career as a loyalist writer is discussed in detail in L.S. Launitz-Schurer, "A Loyalist Clergyman's Response to the Imperial Crisis in the American Colonies: A Note on Samuel Seabury's *Letters of a Westchester Farmer,*" *Historical Magazine of the Protestant Episcopal Church,* XLIV (June, 1975), pp. 107-119.

12. Seabury, *Free Thoughts on the Proceedings of the Continental Congress* (New York, 1774).

13. Chandler, *The American Querist* (New York, 1774).

14. Jones, *History of New York,* I, p. 6.

15. Ibid., pp. 44-45.

16. Smith, *Historical Memoirs,* I, pp. 271-277; Robert M. Calhoon, ed., "William Smith, Jr.'s Alternative to the American Revolution," *William and Mary Quarterly,* 3rd series, XXII (January, 1965), pp. 105-118.

17. Seabury, *The Congress Canvassed.*

18. Bernard Friedman, "The Shaping of the Radical Consciousness in Provincial New York," *Journal of American History,* LVI (March, 1970), pp. 781-801.

19. Maier, "Popular Uprisings and Civil Authority in Eighteenth-Century America," *William and Mary Quarterly,* 3rd series, XXVII (January, 1970), pp. 3-35.

20. Ibid., III, pp. 594-595; Smith, *Historical Memoirs,* I, p. 226; L.S. Launitz-Schurer, Jr., "Whig-Loyalists: The De Lanceys of New York," *New York Historical Society Quarterly,* LVI (July, 1972), pp. 179-198. The loyalist dilemma is perceptively analyzed in Carl Becker, "John Jay and Peter Van Schaack," *New York History,* I, (October, 1919), pp. 1-12; Mary Beth Morton, "The Loyalist Critique of the Revolution," *The Development of a Revolutionary Mentality,* Library of Congress (Washington, D.C., 1972), pp. 127-148; William A. Benton, "Peter Van Schaack—The Conscience of a Loyalist," *The Loyalist Americans: A Focus on Greater New York,* Robert A. East and Jacob Judd, eds. (Tarrytown N.Y., 1975), pp. 44-55; "Frederick Philipse III of Westchester County: A Reluctant Loyalist," ibid., pp. 25-43; Michael Kammen, "The American Revolution as a *Crise de Conscience:* The Case of New York," *Society, Freedom, and Conscience: The Coming of the Revolution in Virginia, Massachusetts, and New York,* Richard M. Jellison, ed. (New York, 1976), pp. 125-189.

Alexander McDougall's *To the Betrayed Inhabitants of the City and Colony of New York*, December 16, 1769

My dear fellow-citizens and countrymen.

In a day when the minions of tyranny and despotism in the mother country and the colonies, are indefatigable in laying every snare that their malevolent and corrupt hearts can suggest, to enslave a free people, when this unfortunate country has been striving under many disadvantages for three years past, to preserve their freedom; which to an Englishman is as dear as his life,—when the merchants of this city and the capital towns on the continent, have nobly and cheerfully sacrificed their private interest to the public good, rather than to promote the designs of the enemies of our happy constitution: It might justly be expected, that in this day of constitutional light, the representatives of this colony would not be so hardy, nor be so lost to all sense of duty to their constituents, (especially after the laudable example of the colonies of Massachusetts Bay and South Carolina before them) as to betray the trust committed to them. This they have done in passing the vote to give the troops a thousand pounds out of any monies that may be in the treasury, and another thousand out of the money that may be issued, to be put out on loan, which the colony will be obliged to make good, whether the bill for that purpose does or does not obtain the royal assent; and that they have betrayed the liberties of the people, will appear from the following consideration, to wit: That the ministry are waiting to see whether the colonies, under their distressed circumstances, will divide on any of the grand points which they are united in, and contending for, with the mother country; by which they may carry their designs against the colonies, and keep in administration.—For if this should not take place, the acts must be repealed; which will be a reflection on their conduct, and will bring the reproach and clamour of the nation on them, for the loss of trade to the empire, which their malconduct has occasioned.

Our granting money to the troops, is implicitly acknowledging the authority that enacted the revenue acts, and their being obligatory on us, as these acts were enacted for the express purpose of taking money out of our pockets without our consent; and to provide for the defending and support of government in America; which revenue we say by our grant of money, is not sufficient for the purpose aforesaid; therefore we supply the deficiency.

This was the point of view in which these acts were considered, by the Massachusetts and South Carolina Assemblies, and to prevent that dangerous construction, refuted it. On this important point we have differed with these spirited colonies, and do implicitly approve of all the tyrannical conduct of the ministry to the Bostonians, and by implication censure their laudable and patriotic denial. For if they did right (which every sensible American thinks they did) in refusing to pay the billeting money, surely we have done wrong, very wrong, in giving it. But our Assembly says, that they do their duty in granting money to the troops: Consequently the Massachusetts Assembly did not do theirs, in not obeying the ministerial mandate. If this is not a division in this grand point, I know not what is: And I doubt not but the ministry will let us know it is to our cost; for it will furnish them with arguments and fresh courage. Is this a grateful retaliation to that brave and sensible people, for the spirited and early notice they took of the suspending act? No, it is base ingratitude, and betraying the common cause of liberty.

To what other influence than the deserting the American cause, can the ministry attribute so pusillanimous a conduct, as this is of the Assembly; so repugnant and subversive of all the means we have used, and opposition that has been made by this and the other colonies, to the tyrannical conduct of the British Parliament! to no other. Can there be a more ridiculous farce to impose on the people than for the Assembly to vote their thanks to be given to the merchants for entering into an agreement not to import goods from Britain, until the revenue acts should be repealed, while they at the same time counteract it by countenancing British acts, and complying with ministerial requisitions, incompatible with our freedom? Surely they cannot.

And what makes the Assembly's granting this money the more grievous, is, that it goes to the support of troops kept here not to protect but to enslave us. Has not the truth of this remark been lately exemplified in the audacious, domineering and inhuman Major Pullaine, who ordered a guard to protect a sordid miscreant, that transgressed the laudable non-importation agreement of the merchants, in order to break that, which is the only means left them, under God to baffle the designs of their enemies to enslave this continent? This consideration alone ought to be sufficient to induce a free people, not to grant the troops any supply whatsoever, if we had no dispute with the mother country, that made it necessary not to concede anything that might destroy our freedom; reasons of economy and good policy suggest that we ought not to grant the troops money.

Whoever is the least acquainted with the English history, must know that grants frequently made to the crown, is not to be refused, but with some degree of danger of disturbing the repose of the Kingdom or Colony. This evinces the expediency of our stopping these grants now, while we are embroiled with the mother country, that so we may not, after the grand controversy is settled, have a new bone of contention about the billeting money; which must be the case if we do not put an end to it at this time: for the colony, in its impoverished state, cannot support a charge which amounts to near as much per annum, as all the other expenses of the government besides.

Hence it follows that the assembly have not been attentive to the liberties of the continent, nor to the property of the good people of this colony in particular, we must therefore attribute this sacrifice of the public interest, to some corrupt source. This is very manifest in the guilt and confusion that covered the faces of the perfidious abettors of this measure, when the house was in debate on the subject. Mr. Colden knows from the nature of things that he cannot have the least prospect to be in administration again; and therefore, that he may make hay while the sun shines, and get a full salary from the Assembly, flatters the ignorant members of it, with the consideration of the success of a bill to emit a paper currency; when he and his artful coadjutors must know, that it is only a snare to impose on the simple, for it will not obtain the royal assent. But while he is solicitous to obtain his salary, he must attend to his posterity, and as some of his children hold offices under the government, if he did not procure an obedience to his requisition, or do his duty in case the Assembly refused the billeting money, by dissolving them, his children might be in danger of losing their offices. If he dissolved the assembly they would not give him his salary.

The De Lancey family knowing the ascendancy they have in the present house of Assembly, and how useful that influence will be to their ambitious designs, to manage a new Governor, have left no stone unturned to prevent a dissolution. The Assembly, conscious to themselves, of having trampled on the liberties of the people, and fearing their just resentments on such an event, are equally careful to preserve their seats, expecting that if they can do it at this critical juncture, as it is imagined the grand controversy will be settled this winter, they will serve for seven years, in which time they hope the people will forget the present injuries done to them. To secure these several objects, the De Lancey family, like true politicians, although they were to all appearance at mortal odds with Mr. Colden, and represented him in all companies as an enemy to his country, yet a coalition is now formed in order to secure to them the sovereign lordship of this colony. The effect of which has given birth to the abominable vote, by which the liberties of the people are betrayed. In short, they have brought matters to such a pass, that all the checks resulting from the form of our happy constitution are destroyed. The Assembly might as well invite the council to save the trouble of formalities, to take their seats in the house of Assembly, and place the Lieut. Governor in the Speaker's chair, and then there would be no waste of time in going from house to house, and his honour would have the pleasure to see how zealous his former enemies are in promoting his interest to serve themselves. Is this a state to be rested in, when our all is at a stake? No, my countrymen, rouse! Imitate the noble example of the friends of liberty in England, who rather than be enslaved, contend for their right with k--g, lords and commons. And will you suffer your liberties to be torn from you, by your representatives? Tell it not in Boston; publish it not in the streets of Charles-Town! You have means yet left to preserve a unanimity with the brave Bostonians and Carolinians; and to prevent the accomplishment of the designs of tyrants. The house was so nearly divided, on the subject of granting the money in the way the vote passed, that one would have prevented it; you have, therefore, a respectable minority. What I would advise to be done is, to assemble in the fields, on Monday next, where your sense ought to be taken on this important point; notwithstanding the impudence of Mr. Jauncey, in his declaring in the house that he had consulted his constituents, and that they were for giving money. After this is done, go in a body to your members, and insist on their joining with the minority, to oppose the bill; if they dare refuse your just requisition, appoint a committee to draw up a state of the whole matter, and send it to the speakers of the several houses of assembly on the continent, and to the friends of our cause in England, and publish it in the newspapers, that the whole world may know your sentiments on this matter, in the only way your circumstance will admit. And I am confident it will spirit the friends of our cause and chargin our enemies. Let the notification to call the people be so expressed, that whoever absents himself, will be considered as agreeing to what may be done by such as shall meet;—and that you may succeed, is the unfeigned desire of

A SON OF LIBERTY

Bibliography

PRIMARY SOURCES

Unpublished manuscript collections, New York Historical Society, New York City

John Alsop Papers
Goldsbrow Banyar Papers
Nicholas Bayard Papers
Cadwallader Colden, Jr. Day Book, 1767-1768
Henry and John Cruger Letter Book, June 1766-August 1767
James De Lancey, Jr. Papers
William Duer Papers
Daniel Horsmanden Papers
John Jay Papers
David Jones Papers
Samuel Jones Papers
John Tabor Kemp Papers
John Lamb Papers
Livingston Family Papers
Judge Robert R. Livingston Papers
Chancellor Robert R. Livingston Papers
Alexander McDougall Papers
Joseph Reed Papers
Rutherfurd Collection

Schuyler Family Papers
John Morin Scott Papers
William Smith, Jr. Papers
William Tryon Papers
Van Schaack Family Papers
Jacob Walton Family Papers
Warren-De Lancey Papers, one reel of microfilm
Watts Family Papers

New York Public Library, New York City

Samuel Adams Papers
American Loyalists: Transcript of the Manuscript Books and Papers of the Commission of Enquiry into the Losses and Services of the American Loyalists held under Acts of Parliament of 23, 25, 26, 28 and 29 of George III, preserved amongst the Audit Office Records in the Public Record Office of England, 1783-1790.
Bancroft Transcripts:
 England and America 1761-1775
 Colonial Documents 1761-1774
 American Series 1765-1775
 Letters of Samuel Cooper to Pownell and Franklin
 Letters of Thomas Pownell to Samuel Cooper, 1769-1774
 Correspondence of Samuel and William Cooper, 1737-1789
 Livingston Family Papers, transcripts and originals
George Chalmers Papers relating to New York
James Duane Papers
Emmet Collection
John Jay Papers
Livingston Family Papers
Gilbert Livingston Papers
William Livingston Papers
William Smith, Jr. Papers
Letters to Ezra Stiles, 1761-1776
Van Cortlandt Wills and Miscellaneous Papers
Abraham Yates, Jr. Papers

New York State Library, Albany, New York
Goldsbrow Banyar Papers
Council Minutes 1668-1783
Diary of George Folliott, New York Merchant 1765-1766, (microfilm of the original in the Public Library, Wigan, England)
Manuscripts of the Colony and State of New York in the Revolutionary War, 1775-1800
Proceedings of the Albany Committee of Correspondence
Philip Schuyler Papers

Museum of the City of New York, New York City
De Lancey Family Papers
Jones Family Papers
Livingston Family Papers

The Butler Library of Columbia University, New York City
John Jay Papers
Samuel Johnson Papers
King's College Papers
Gouverneur Morris Papers

The Franklin Delano Roosevelt Library, Hyde Park, New York
Livingston-Redmond Papers, available on microfilm at the New York Historical Society

The Sterling Memorial Library of Yale University, New Haven, Connecticut
William Livingston-Noah Welles Correspondence, Johnson Family Papers

NEWSPAPERS AND PERIODICALS

New York Gazette, 1759-1767
New York Gazette, and Weekly Mercury, 1768-1783
New York Gazette, or Weekly Post-Boy, 1747-1773
New York Gazetteer, or, the Connecticut, Hudson's River, New Jersey, and Quebec Weekly, 1773-1775

New York Journal, 1766-1776
New York Mercury, 1752-1768
Pennsylvania Journal 1763-1777
Annual Register
The Gentleman's Magazine

NEW YORK PUBLIC DOCUMENTS

Annals of Albany, 10 vols., Joel Munsell, ed. Albany, N.Y., 1850-1859

Burghers of New Amsterdam and the Freemen of New York 1675-1866. Collections of the New York Historical Society, XVIII. New York, 1886

"Calendar of Council Minutes 1668-1883," *New York State Library Bulletin,* VIII. Albany, N.Y., 1902.

Calendar of Historical Manuscripts in the Office of the Secretary of State, Albany, N.Y., 2 vols., Edmund B. O'Callaghan, ed., Albany, N.Y., 1865-1866.

Calendar of Historical Manuscripts Relating to the War of the Revolution in the Office of the Secretary of State, Albany, N.Y., 2 vols. Albany, N.Y., 1868.

Calendar of New York Colonial Manuscripts Endorsed Land Papers in the Office of the Secretary of State of New York 1643-1803. Albany, N.Y., 1864.

Collections on the History of Albany, from its Discovery to the Present Time, 4 vols. Albany, N.Y., 1850-1859.

Colonial Laws of New York from the Year 1664 to the Revolution, 5 vols. Albany, N.Y., 1894-1896.

Colonial Records of the New York Chamber of Commerce, 1768-1784, with Historical and Biographical Sketches. John A. Stevens, ed. New York, 1867.

Documentary History of the State of New York, 4 vols., Edmund B. O'Callaghan, ed. Albany, N.Y., 1851.

Documents Relative to the Colonial History of the State of New York Procured in Holland, England, and France, 15 vols., Edmund B. O'Callaghan and Berthold Fernow, eds. Albany, N.Y., 1856-1887.

Journal of the Legislative Council of the Colony of New York, 1691-1775, 2 vols. Albany, N.Y., 1861.

Journal of the Votes and Proceedings of the General Assembly of the Colonial of New York, 2 vols. New York, 1764-1766.

Journals of the Provincial Congress, Provincial Convention, Committee of Safety of the State of New York, 2 vols. Albany, N.Y., 1842.

Minutes of the Common Council of the City of New York, 1675-1776, 8 vols. New York, 1905.

Records of the States of the United States of America. A Microfilm Compilation, reel III, New York, 1760-1775, William S. Jenkins, comp. Washington, D.C., 1949.

MISCELLANEOUS PUBLIC DOCUMENTS

American Archives, 4th and 5th series, 9 vols., Peter Force, comp., Washington, D.C., 1837-1853.

American Bibliography: A Chronological Dictionary of all Books, Pamphlets, and Periodical Publications Printed in the United States of America [1639-1820], 14 vols., Charles Evans, comp. Chicago, 1903-1959.

Ecclesiastical Records of the State of New York, 7 vols., Edward T. Corwin, ed. Albany, N.Y., 1901-1905.

Journals of the Continental Congress, 34 vols., W.C. Ford and Gaillard Hunt, eds. Washington, D.C., 1904-1937.

Prologue to Revolution: Sources and Documents on the Stamp Act Crisis, 1764-1766, Edmund S. Morgan, ed. Chapel Hill, N.C., 1959.

CORRESPONDENCE, MEMOIRS, JOURNALS

Adams Papers: Diary and Autobiography of John Adams, 4 vols., L.H. Butterfield and others, eds. New York, 1964.

Aspinwall Papers, 2 vols. Collections of the Massachusetts Historical Society, 4th series, IX-X. Boston, 1871.

Beekman Mercantile Papers 1746-1799, 3 vols., Philip L. White, ed. New York, 1956.

Colden, Cadwallader. *The Colden Letter Books 1760-1775*, 2 vols. Collections of the New York Historical Society, IX-X. New York, 1877-1878.

————. "The Colden Letters on Smith's History," *Collections of the New York Historical Society*, I-II. New York, 1868-1870.

————. *Letters and Papers of Cadwallader Colden*, 9 vols. Collections of the New York Historical Society, L-LVI, LXVII-LXVIII. New York, 1918-1934.

————. *History of the Five Indian Nations Depending on the Province of New York in America*. Ithaca, N.Y., 1958.

"Duane Letters," *Publications of the Southern Historical Association*, VII, VIII, X. 1903-1906.

Grant, Anne. *Memoirs of an American Lady*. Albany, N.Y., 1876.

Hamilton, Alexander. *The Papers of Alexander Hamilton*, 21 vols. to date, Harold C. Syrett and others, eds. New York, 1961–

Honyman, Robert. *Colonial Panorama 1775: Dr. Robert Honyman's Journal for March and April 1775*, Philip Padelford, ed. San Marino, Cal., 1939.

Historical Manuscripts Commission. *Fourteenth Report, Appendix, Part X. Manuscripts of the Earl of Dartmouth, American Papers*. London, 1895.

————. *Report on the Manuscripts of Mrs. Stopford-Sackville, of Drayton House, Northamptonshire*, 2 vols. London, 1904-1910.

Jay, John. *John Jay: The Making of a Revolutionary. Unpublished Papers, 1745-1780*, Richard B. Morris, ed. New York, 1975.

————. *Correspondence and Public Papers of John Jay*, 4 vols., Henry P. Johnston, ed. New York, 1890-1893.

Johnson, William. *The Papers of Sir William Johnson*, 14 vols., John Sullivan and others, eds. Albany, N.Y., 1931-1965.

Jones, Thomas. *History of New York During the Revolutionary War and of the Leading Events in the Other Colonies at that Period*, 2 vols., Edward F. De Lancey, ed. Reprint, New York, 1968.

Letters of the Members of the Continental Congress, 7 vols., Edmund C. Burnett, ed. Washington, D.C., 1921-1934.

"Livingston-Beekman Letters," *Year Book: Dutchess County Historical Society*. Poughkeepsie, N.Y., 1921.

Livingston, Robert R. *Revolution Letters of Importance: The Unpublished Correspondence of Robert R. Livingston, First Chancel-*

lor of New York, American Art Association Catalogue of a Sale, January 18, 1918. New York, 1918.

McAnear, Beverly, ed. "The Albany Stamp Act Riots," *William and Mary Quarterly,* 3d series, IV, October, 1947, pp. 486-498.

Mason, Bernard, ed. "Robert R. Livingston and the Non Exportation Policy: Notes for a Speech in the Continental Congress, October 27, 1775," *The New York Historical Society Quarterly,* XLIV, July, 1960, pp. 296-307.

Montresor, John. *Journals of Captain John Montresor.* Collections of the New York Historical Society, XIV. New York, 1882.

Morris, Gouverneur. *Diary and Letters of Gouverneur Morris,* 2 vols., Anne C. Morris, ed. New York, 1888.

Osgood, Herbert L., ed. "The Society of Dissenters founded at New York in 1769," *American Historical Review,* VI, April, 1901, pp. 498-507.

Smith, William. *History of the Province of New York,* 2 vols., Michael Kammen, ed. Cambridge, Mass. 1972.

———. *Historical Memoirs from 16 March 1763 to 25 July 1778 of William Smith,* 2 vols., William H.W. Sabine, ed. Reprint, New York, 1969.

Van Schaack, Henry C. *The Life of Peter Van Schaack.* New York, 1842.

Watts, John. *Letter Book of John Watts: Merchant and Councillor of New York.* Collections of the New York Historical Society, LXI. New York, 1928.

Zeichner, Oscar, ed. "William Smith's 'Observations on America,'" *New York History,* XXIII, July, 1942, pp. 328-340.

PAMPHLETS

An Authentic Account of a Late Military Massacre at Boston, or the Consequences of Quartering Troops in a Populous Town. March 12, 1770. New York, 1770.

Chandler, Thomas Bradbury. *An Appeal to the Public in Behalf of the Church of England in America.* London, 1769.

———. *A Free Examination of the Critical Commentary on Archbishop Secker's Letter to Mr. Walpole.* New York, 1774.

———. *A Friendly Address to all Reasonable Americans, on the*

Subject of our Political Confusions; in which the Necessary Consequences of Violently opposing the King's Troops, and of a General Non-Importation are Fairly Stated. New York, 1774.

———. *The American Querist: or, Some Questions Proposed Relative to the Present Disputes between Great Britain and her American Colonies.* Boston, 1774.

———. *What Think Ye of the Congress Now?* New York, 1775.

Colden, Cadwallader, *The Conduct of Cadwallader Colden, Esquire, Late Lieutenant-Governor of New York: Relating to the Judges Commissions, Appeal to the King, and the Stamp-Duty.* New York, 1767.

Inglis, Charles. *A Vindication of the Bishop of Landaff's Sermon from the Gross Misrepresentation and Abusive Reflections contained in Mr. William Livingston's Letter to his Lordship.* New York, 1768.

———. *The True Interest of America Impartially Stated.* Philadelphia, 1776.

Kennedy, Archibald. *Observations on the Importance of the Northern Colonies under Proper Regulations.* New York, 1750.

———. *The Importance of Gaining and Preserving the Friendship of the Indians to the British Interest. Considered.* New York, 1751.

———. *An Essay on the Government of the Northern Colonies.* New York, 1752.

———. *Serious Considerations on the Present State of the Northern Colonies.* New York, 1754.

Livingston, William. *A Review of the Military Operations in North America from the Commencement of the French Hostilities on the Frontiers of Virginia in 1753, to the Surrender of Oswego, on the 14th of August, 1756; in a Letter to a Nobleman.* New York, 1770.

———. William Smith, and John Morin Scott. *The Independent Reflector or Weekly Essays on Sundry Important Subjects More Particularly adapted to the Province of New York,* ed. Milton M. Klein. Cambridge, Mass., 1963.

———. *Letter to the Right Reverend Father in God, John, Bishop of Landaff; occasioned by some Passages in his Lordship's Sermon, on the 20th of February, 1767, in which the American Colonies are loaded with great and undeserved Reproach.* New York, 1768.

Seabury Samuel, *Letters of a Westchester Farmer 1774-1775*, Clarence H. Vance, ed., New York, 1970.

SECONDARY SOURCES

Books

Adams, Randolph G. *Political Ideas of the American Revolution: Britannic-American Contributions to the Problem of Imperial Organization 1765-1775*. Reprint, New York, 1961.

Alexander, Edward P. *A Revolutionary Conservative: James Duane of New York*. New York, 1938.

Ammerman, David. *In the Common Cause: American Response to the Coercive Acts of 1774*. New York, 1975.

Bailyn, Bernard. *The Ideological Origins of the American Revolution*. Cambridge, Mass., 1967.

————. *The Origins of American Politics*. New York, 1968.

Barrow, Thomas C. *Trade and Empire: The British Customs Service in Colonial America 1662-1775*. Cambridge, Mass., 1967.

Becker, Carl L. *The History of Political Parties in the Province of New York, 1760-1776*. Reprint, Madison, Wis., 1960.

Benton, William A. *Whig-Loyalism: An Aspect of Political Ideology in the American Revolutionary Era*. Rutherford, N.J., 1969.

Bliven, Bruce. *Under the Guns: New York, 1775-1776*. New York, 1972.

Bonomi, Patricia U. *A Factious People: Politics and Society in Colonial New York*. New York, 1971.

Bridenbaugh, Carl. *Cities in Revolt: Urban Life in America 1743-1776*. New York, 1964.

————. *Mitre and Sceptre: Transatlantic Faiths, Ideas, Personalities, and Politics 1689-1775*. New York, 1962.

Burnett, Edmund C. *The Continental Congress*. New York, 1964.

Calhoun, Robert M. *The Loyalists in Revolutionary America 1760-1781*. New York, 1973.

Champagne, Roger J. *Alexander McDougall and the American Revolution in New York*. Schenectady, N.Y., 1975.

Colbourn, Trevor H. *The Lamp of Experience: Whig History and the Origins of the American Revolution*. Chapel Hill, N.C., 1965.

Cross, Arthur L. *The Anglican Episcopate and the American Colonies.* New York, 1902.

Dangerfield, George. *Chancellor Robert R. Livingston of New York, 1746-1813.* New York, 1960.

Davidson, Philip. *Propaganda and the American Revolution, 1763-1783.* Chapel Hill, N.C., 1941.

Dickerson, Oliver M. *The Navigation Acts and the American Revolution.* Philadelphia, 1951.

Dillon, Dorothy R. *The New York Triumvirate: A Study of Legal and Political Careers of William Livingston, John Morin Scott, and William Smith, Jr.* New York, 1949.

Donoghue, Bernard. *British Politics and the American Revolution: The Path to War, 1773-1775.* London, 1964.

East, Robert A. and Jacob Judd, eds. *The Loyalist Americans: A Focus on Greater New York.* Tarrytown, N.Y., 1975.

Edwards, George W. *New York as an Eighteenth Century Municipality, 1731-1776.* New York, 1917.

Ernst, Joseph A. *Money and Politics in America 1755-1775: A Study in the Currency Act of 1764 and the Political Economy of Revolution.* Chapel Hill, N.C., 1973.

Flick, Alexander C., ed. *History of the State of New York,* 10 vols. New York, 1933-1937.

————. *Loyalism in New York During the American Revolution.* New York, 1901.

Gerlach, Don R. *Philip Schuyler and the American Revolution in New York, 1733-1777.* Lincoln, Neb., 1964.

Gordon, William. *The History of the Rise, Progress and Establishment, of the United States of America: including an Account of the Late War; and of the Thirteen Colonies, from their Origin to that Period,* 4 vols. London, 1788.

Greene, Jack P., Richard L. Bushman, and Michael Kammen. *Society, Freedom, and Conscience: The Coming of the Revolution in Virginia, Massachusetts, and New York,* Richard M. Jellison, ed. New York, 1976.

Gwyn, Julian. *The Enterprising Admiral: The Personal Fortune of Admiral Sir Peter Warren.* Montreal, 1974.

Hamelin, Paul M. *Legal Education in Colonial New York.* New York, 1939.

Harrington, Virginia D. *The New York Merchant on the Eve of the American Revolution.* New York, 1935.

Hoffman, Ross J.S. *Edmund Burke, New York Agent, with his Letters to the New York Assembly and Intimate Correspondence with Charles O'Hara 1761-1776.* Philadelphia, 1956.

Ironside, Charles E. *The Family in Colonial New York: A Sociological Study.* New York, 1942.

Jensen, Merrill. *The Founding of a Nation: A History of the American Revolution, 1763-1776.* New York, 1968.

Judd, Jacob and Irwin H. Polishook, eds. *Aspects of Early New York Society and Politics.* Tarrytown, N.Y., 1974.

Kammen, Michael. *Colonial New York: A History.* New York, 1975.

Katz, Stanley N. *Newcastle's New York: Anglo-American Politics, 1732-1753.* Cambridge, Mass., 1968.

Kenney, Alice P. *The Gansevoorts of Albany: Dutch Patricians in the Upper Hudson Valley.* Syracuse, N.Y., 1969.

Keys, Alice M. *Cadwallader Colden: A Representative Eighteenth Century Official.* New York, 1906.

Kim, Sung Bok. *Landlord and Tenant in Colonial New York: Manorial Society, 1664-1775.* Chapel Hill, N.C., 1978.

Klein, Milton M. *Politics of Diversity: Essays in the History of Colonial New York.* Port Washington, N.Y., 1974.

Kurtz, Stephen G. and James H. Hutson, eds., *Essays on the American Revolution.* Chapel Hill, N.C., 1973.

Labaree, Benjamin W. *The Boston Tea Party.* New York, 1964.

Leake, Isaac Q. *Memoir of the Life and Times of General John Lamb.* Albany, N.Y., 1857.

Leder, Lawrence H., ed. *The Colonial Legacy,* 2 vols. New York, 1971.

———. *Robert Livingston 1654-1728 and the Politics of Colonial New York.* Chapel Hill, N.C., 1961.

Levy, Leonard W. *Freedom of Speech and Press in Early America: Legacy of Suppression.* New York, 1963.

Maier, Pauline. *From Resistance to Revolution: Colonial Radicals and the Development of American Opposition to Britain, 1765-1776.* New York, 1972.

Mark, Irving. *Agrarian Conflicts in Colonial New York, 1711-1775.* New York, 1940.

Martin, James K. *Men in Rebellion: Higher Governmental Leaders and the Coming of the American Revolution.* New Brunswick, N.J., 1973.

Mason, Bernard. *The Road to Independence: The Revolutionary Movement in New York 1773-1777.* Lexington, Ky., 1966.

Meaney, Neville K., ed. *Studies on the American Revolution.* Melbourne, 1977.

Morgan, Edmund S. and Helen M. Morgan. *The Stamp Act Congress: Prologue to Revolution.* Revised ed., New York, 1963.

Nelson, William. *The American Tory.* Boston, 1964.

Neuenschwander, John A. *The Middle Colonies and the Coming of the American Revolution.* Port Washington, N.Y., 1973.

Norton, Thomas E. *The Fur Trade in Colonial New York 1686-1776.* Madison, Wis., 1974.

Olson, Alison G. and Richard M. Brown, eds. *Anglo-American Political Relations of 1675-1775.* New Brunswick, N.J., 1970.

Sedgwick, Theodore. *A Memoir of the Life of William Livingston.* New York, 1833.

Singleton, Esther. *Social New York Under the Georges, 1714-1776.* New York, 1902.

Steiner, Bruce E. *Samuel Seabury, 1729-1796: A Study in the High Church Tradition.* Athens, Ohio. 1971.

Stokes, Isaac N.P. *The Iconography of Manhattan Island,* 7 vols. New York, 1915-1928.

Story, D.A. *The De Lanceys: A Romance of a Great Family.* Toronto, 1931.

Sutherland, Lucy S. *The East India Company in Eighteenth Century Politics.* Oxford, 1952.

Thomas, P.D.G. *British Politics and the Stamp Act Crisis: The First Phase of the American Revolution, 1763-1767.* Oxford, 1975.

Upton, L.F.S. *The Loyal Whig: William Smith of New York and Quebec.* Toronto, 1969.

Articles

Becker, Carl L. "John Jay and Peter Van Schaack," *New York History,* I, October, 1919, pp. 1-12.

Bonomi, Patricia U. "Political Patterns in Colonial New York City:

The General Assembly Election of 1768." *Political Science Quarterly*, LXXXI, September, 1966, pp. 432-447.

Boyer, Lee R. "Lobster Backs, Liberty Boys, and Laborers in the Streets: New York's Golden Hill and Nassau Street Riots," *New York Historical Society Quarterly*, LVII, October, 1973, pp. 281-308.

Champagne, Roger. "Family Politics versus Constitutional Principals: The New York Assembly Elections of 1768 and 1769," *William and Mary Quarterly*, 3rd series, XX, January, 1963, pp. 57-79.

———. "Liberty Boys and Mechanics of New York City, 1764-1774," *Labor History*, VIII, April, 1967, pp. 115-135.

———. "New York and the Intolerable Acts," *New York Historical Society Quarterly*, XLV, April, 1961, pp. 195-207.

———. "New York Politics and Independence, 1776," *New York Historical Society Quarterly*, XLVI, July, 1962, pp. 281-303.

———. "New York's Radicals and the Coming of Independence," *Journal of American History*, LI, June, 1964, pp. 21-40.

———. "The Military Association of the Sons of Liberty," *New York Historical Society Quarterly*, XLI, July, 1957, pp. 338-350.

D'Innocenzo, Michael and John L. Turner. "The Role of New York Newspapers in the Stamp Act Crisis, 1764-1766," *New York Historical Society Quarterly*, LI, July, October, 1967, pp. 215-231, 345-365.

Friedman, Bernard. "The New York Assembly Elections of 1768 and 1769: The Disruption of Family Politics," *New York History*, XLVI, January, 1965, pp. 3-24.

———. "The Shaping of the Radical Consciousness in Provincial New York," *Journal of American History*, LVI, March, 1970, pp. 781-801.

Kim, Sung Bok. "A New Look at the Great Landlords of Eighteenth-Century New York," *William and Mary Quarterly*, 3d series, XXVII, October, 1970, pp. 581-614.

Klein, Milton M. "New York Lawyers and the Coming of the American Revolution," *New York History*, LV, October, 1974, pp. 383-407.

Launitz-Schurer, Leopold S. "A Loyalist Clergyman's Response to the Imperial Crisis in the American Colonies: A Note on Samuel Seabury's *Letters of a Westchester Farmer,*" *Historical Magazine of the Protestant Episcopal Church,* XLIV, June, 1975, pp. 107-119.

————. "Whig-Loyalists. The De Lanceys of New York," *New York Historical Society Quarterly,* LVI, July, 1972, pp. 179-198.

Leder, Lawrence H. "The New York Assembly Elections of 1769: An Assault on Privilege," *Mississippi Valley Historical Review,* XLIX, March, 1963, pp. 675-682.

Lemisch, Jesse. "New York's Petitions and Resolves of December 1765: Liberals vs. Radicals," *New York Historical Society Quarterly,* XLIX, October, 1965, pp. 313-326.

————. "Jack Tar in the Streets: Merchant Seaman in the Politics of Revolutionary America," *William and Mary Quarterly,* 3d series, XXV, July, 1968, pp. 371-407.

Lynd, Staughton. "The Mechanics in New York Politics, 1774-1788," *Labor History,* V, Fall, 1964, pp. 225-246.

Maier, Pauline. "Popular Uprisings and Civil Authority in Eighteenth-Century America," *William and Mary Quarterly,* 3d series, XXVII, January, 1970, pp. 3-35.

Mason, Bernard. "The Heritage of Carl Becker: The Historiography of the Revolution in New York," *New York Historical Society Quarterly,* LIII, April, 1969, pp. 127-147.

Olm, Lee E. "The Mutiny Act for America: New York's Noncompliance," *New York Historical Society Quarterly,* LVIII, July, 1974, pp. 188-214.

Olson, James S. "The New York Assembly, the Politics of Religion, and the Origins of the American Revolution, 1768-1771," *Historical Magazine of the Protestant Episcopal Church,* XLIII, March, 1974, pp. 21-28.

Shammas, Carole. "Cadwallader Colden and the Role of the King's Prerogative," *New York Historical Society Quarterly,* LIII, April, 1969, pp. 103-126.

Teeter, Dwight L. " 'King's Sears, the Mob, and Freedom of the Press in New York, 1765-1776," *Journalism Quarterly,* XLI, Autumn, 1964, pp. 539-544.

Vail, R.W.G. "The Loyalist Declaration of Dependence of November 28, 1776," *New York Historical Society Quarterly*, XXXI, January, 1947, pp. 68-71.

Varga, Nicholas. "Election Procedures and Practices in Colonial New York," *New York History*, XLI, July, 1960, pp. 249-277.

———. "The New York Restraining Act: Its Passage and Some Effects, 1766-1768," *New York History*, XXXVII, July, 1956, pp. 233-258.

UNPUBLISHED DOCTORAL DISSERTATIONS

Champagne, Roger. "The Sons of Liberty and the Aristocracy in New York Politics, 1765-1790." University of Wisconsin, 1960.

Klein, Milton M. "The American Whig: William Livingston of New York." Columbia University, 1954.

McAnear, Beverly. "Politics in Provincial New York 1689-1761." Stanford University, 1935.

Varga, Nicholas. "New York Government and Politics During the Mid-Eighteenth Century." Fordham University, 1960.

Index

221